evaluation practice reconsidered

Studies in the
Postmodern Theory of Education

Joe L. Kincheloe and Shirley R. Steinberg
General Editors

Vol. 211

PETER LANG
New York • Washington, D.C./Baltimore • Bern
Frankfurt am Main • Berlin • Brussels • Vienna • Oxford

Thomas A. Schwandt

evaluation practice reconsidered

PETER LANG
New York • Washington, D.C./Baltimore • Bern
Frankfurt am Main • Berlin • Brussels • Vienna • Oxford

Library of Congress Cataloging-in-Publication Data

Schwandt, Thomas A.
Evaluation practice reconsidered / Thomas A. Schwandt.
p. cm. — (Counterpoints; vol. 211)
Includes bibliographical references and index.
1. Evaluation research (Social action programs).
I. Title. II. Counterpoints (New York, N. Y.); vol. 211.
H61 .S4436   361'.0068—dc21   2001042728
ISBN 0-8204-5705-1
ISSN 1058-1634

Die Deutsche Bibliothek-CIP-Einheitsaufnahme

Schwandt, Thomas A.:
Evaluation practice reconsidered / Thomas A. Schwandt.
–New York; Washington, D.C./Baltimore; Bern;
Frankfurt am Main; Berlin; Brussels; Vienna; Oxford: Lang.
(Counterpoints; Vol. 211)
ISBN 0-8204-5705-1

Cover design by Joni Holst

The paper in this book meets the guidelines for permanence and durability
of the Committee on Production Guidelines for Book Longevity
of the Council of Library Resources.

Printed in the United States of America

For W. F. C. S.

Contents

Acknowledgments

I am indebted to many colleagues and students for their questions, advice, patience, criticism, encouragement, and often lively discussion as I first developed the ideas expressed here in lectures and conference papers. I have particularly benefited from conversations with Tineke Abma, Wilfred Carr, Jeffrey Davis, Norman Denzin, David Flinders, Deborah Fournier, Davydd Greenwood, Jennifer Greene, Ernest House, Ove Karlsson, Colleen Larson, Morten Levin, Judith Lysaker, Melvin Mark, Michael Patton, Robert Stake, Johans Sandvin, Christina Segerholm, and Nick Smith. I doubt that the revisions that I have undertaken in light of the good advice offered by these colleagues and friends will do justice to the collective wisdom they shared with me. Two anonymous reviewers read an earlier draft of the entire manuscript and offered very useful suggestions. The University of Illinois at Urbana-Champaign provides an environment conducive to thoughtful scholarship and the lively exchange of ideas, and I am fortunate to be a faculty member there.

Some of these chapters or portions of these chapters are based on essays that appeared previously in somewhat different form. I thank the publishers for permission to draw from the following:

"Better living through evaluation? Images of progress shaping evaluation practice," *Evaluation Practice*, 1992, 13(2): 135–44. Used with permission from Elsevier Science.

"Evaluation as practical hermeneutics," *Evaluation*, 1997, 3(1): 69–83. Used with permission from Sage Publications, Inc.

"On understanding understanding," *Qualitative Inquiry*, 1999, 5(4): 451–64. Used with permission from Sage Publications, Inc.

"Farewell to criteriology," *Qualitative Inquiry*, 1996, 2(1): 59–73. Used with permission from Sage Publications, Inc.

"The landscape of values in evaluation: Charted terrain and unexplored territory," in D. J. Rog and D. Fournier, eds., *Progress and future directions in evaluation: Perspectives on theory, practice, and methods* (New Directions for Evaluation no. 76 San Francisco: Jossey-Bass, 1997, 25–39). Used with permission from Jossey-Bass Publishers, Inc. a subsidiary of John Wiley & Sons.

"Whose interests are being served?: Evaluation as a conceptual practice of power," in L. Mabry, ed., *Evaluation and the post-modern dilemma* (Greenwich, CT: JAI Press, 1997, 89–104). Used with permission from JAI Press, Inc. Greenwich, CT and London, England.

"Reading 'The problem of evaluation' in social inquiry," *Qualitative Inquiry*, 1997, 3(1): 4–25. Used with permission from Sage Publications, Inc.

Preface

Evaluation is the activity of judging the merit, worth, or significance of some human action like a policy, program, or project. This book is meant to encourage a different way of thinking about that activity. However, it is not a book about another model, procedure, or methodology for evaluation. Taken collectively, the ideas explored here suggest a way of thinking about and engaging in evaluation that is not bound either to the characterization of evaluation as an applied social science or to efforts to foster the development of evaluation as a professional practice of experts. Rather, the aim is to explore evaluation as a particular kind of pedagogy. My general thesis is that when properly conceived as an activity of teaching and learning resulting in an action-oriented self-understanding, evaluation becomes more continuous with the ways we are as human beings in our everyday lives.

Two very significant consequences follow from this reunion of evaluation and everyday life. First, we recover a sense of evaluation as a practical-moral undertaking rather than a modern scientific task. Hence, we come to see that evaluation requires a kind of knowledge other than the technical knowledge of the scientific expert. Second, the idea that disengagement is the key to sound evaluative judgment is overturned. Current evaluation practice proceeds on the assumption that it can eliminate or at least offer a substantial correction to the wrongheaded, frequently well intentioned but misguided thinking of practitioners who are not in possession of the kind of knowledge generated through objective and systematic scientific evaluation methods. That practice is based on the belief that only by careful and thoughtful infusion of knowledge generated by scientific means can the realm of daily evaluation practice in education, social services, health care, and so on be demythologized, demystified, and made more scientifically rational. In other words, disengagement from practice is thought to be essential to judging value. However, if evaluation is viewed as continuous with our ordinary ways of being engaged in the world, then we are led to consider more carefully the particular moral obligation and responsibility that we shoulder when we evaluate our own and others' actions. As this awareness develops, evaluation becomes less like the practice of skilled technical experts rendering judgments of the merit, worth, or significance of human activities and more like one of the important, but fairly commonplace, situated moral-political practices necessary for navigating and interpreting social life. The essays in this book take up ways of reconsidering evaluation practice that may make it possible for us to realize this new understanding and obligation.

Introduction

What kind of science is it that presents itself more as a cultivation of a natural gift and as theoretically heightened awareness of it?... [I]nquiry into the history of science indicates that the notion of method, fundamental to modern science, brought into dissolution a notion of science that was open precisely in the direction of such a natural human capacity.

—Gadamer, 1981, p. 114

The activities that comprise evaluation of social and educational programs constitute a discourse-practice (Cherryholmes, 1988). The meaning of evaluation flows back and forth between what is said and written and what is done. What is said, written, and done in the name of evaluation is constituted by connected sets of norms, traditions, values, and interests that organize the discourse-practice and give it coherence and meaning. Traditions, interests, and norms informing the purpose of evaluation and its methodologies have their origins in the social science disciplines and related fields of study—for example, social psychology, applied sociology, educational research, organizational development. The intellectual and practical resources for the development of evaluation practice as a modern methodology and professional practice that wields a special kind of cultural authority have been drawn from and shaped by these ways of doing and thinking.

To think about evaluation in a different way, we not only need to submit this discourse to critical scrutiny but also to imagine what it might be like to speak about evaluation differently. The discourse that is drawn upon in this book does not originate in the social scientific language of method, validity, knowledge utilization, professionalism, and the like but in the language of the humanities with its concern for the human condition and the way we are in relation to each other and to the world.

I doubt that we can do without a social scientific conception of evaluation practice that aims to deliver a special kind of expert knowledge about the value of social policies, programs, and projects. That way of thinking about evaluation seems to be an ineradicable feature of modern social institutions' demand for expert information. However, I believe we might be able to do something more with a conception of evaluation practice that is foregrounded in the natural human capacities to deliberate, to reach agreement in language, and to persuade others of our point of view. This latter view of evaluation might well be better suited to helping us improve the very practices of teaching, counseling, managing, and so forth out of which policies, projects, and programs arise.

The essays presented here explore a wide territory, but they share a central preoccupation with several issues. First, they reflect a bid to restore Aristotelian notions of *praxis* and practical competence (*phronesis*) to the center of our way of thinking about evaluation. Practical competence or practical wisdom is the kind of knowledge required for personal and social action, especially in its ethical and political aspects. It is distinguishable from the kind of knowledge found in the mastery of technique and skill for the production of prespecified results. In these essays the focus on *praxis* or socially embedded action and ways of being is specifically intended to decenter the primary discourse of method in evaluation practice.

The language and action of evaluation practice is dominated by concerns with a multiplicity of methods: methods for defining evaluation, for doing evaluation, for generating and analyzing data, for warranting evaluative claims, for linking evaluation to political decision making, for presenting evaluation reports, for using evaluation results, for behaving responsibly as an evaluator, and so on. Throughout these essays I suggest a way we might talk about evaluation practice without this preoccupation with method. That way of talking—which is referred to as an alternative discourse, framework, and language—takes its cue from the tradition of philosophical hermeneutics, and specifically from the efforts of Hans-Georg Gadamer and Charles Taylor, who argue that properly understood, this kind of hermeneutics is a way of doing practical philosophy. I am particularly concerned with supplementing the tendency to frame the practice of evaluation exclusively in terms of conceptual warrants (argument, logic, and method) with a way of thinking that grounds evaluation in perception and attention to concrete particulars. The latter resonates with our ordinary efforts to make sense of lived experience and to persuade one another of what it is right to do and good to be (Schwandt, 2001b).

Second, and in a related way, the essays explore what is lost by insisting on the posture of disengagement that lies at the heart of contemporary evaluation practice. The more that teachers, counselors, administrators, social workers, and other kinds of practitioners look to outside experts to tell them what has value, the more these practitioners become alienated from the evaluative aspects of their practices. Disengagement is a particular view of human agency, or a kind of philosophical anthropology (Taylor, 1985). It is analogous to what Pendlebury (1995, p. 53) describes as a view of human action characterized "by rational deliberation undertaken from the vantage point of situational distance and guided by principles that are general in form and universal in application." In evaluation practice, this agency posture is most evident in the defense of objectivist evaluation. The principal concern of objectivist evaluation is bias control. This is achieved by taking steps to ensure that the evaluator has a critical distance from that which is being evaluated. Steps include using third-party, external evaluators; employing objective measurement procedures; relying on a formal logic for making evaluative claims, and so on. The kind of knowledge that this disengaged perspective yields is what Bauman (1992, p. 116) calls "legislative reason": knowledge that transcends the common understanding composed of mere belief and opinion. Bauman adds that the *raison d'être* of legislative reason is the possibility of a method, a procedure that all but guarantees "the validity of the result by the sheer fact that it has been scrupulously followed; and the principle that the findings at the end of the methodical procedure carry superior validity no nonmethodical effort can claim" (p. 129). The essays explore what evaluation might be if the logic of disengagement, method, and procedural knowledge were replaced by a focus on dialogue, understanding, and practical wisdom.

Third, the essays share a concern with understanding what Taylor (1991a) calls the ethical space in which humans are situated. Taylor (1989) argues that it is a non-contingent fact of human identity that a person is a being for whom things matter. N. H. Smith (1997) explains this ontological condition as follows:

> As a person is a being for whom things matter, so a particular person's identity is what particularly matters for that person, and in both senses of 'particularly.' In the first sense, I am specifically this person rather than that ... because I take this kind of life to be fulfilling and that kind of life to be empty, or because I interpret this course of action as right and that action as wrong, or because I find this species of motivation admirable but that species contemptible. In the second sense, what I find fulfilling or empty, right or wrong, admirable or contemptible, is no small matter, but is of particular *fundamental* significance to me as a person. In answering the question of identity, I am forced to take a stand. (p. 39)

As self-interpreting beings, we are embedded in some moral reality, some particular relational space. My concern is the ethical space and the identity that evaluators (and, more generally, social scientists) define for themselves.

Examining this ethical space does not mean simply paying special attention to the ethical obligations and responsibilities of evaluators as professionals, although these, in part, flow from the more broadly conceived notion of ethical space. It means attending to a classical understanding of the symbiotic relationship between ethics and politics: We cannot rightly understand professional ethics (habits, obligations, and modes of thought that shape and define 'good' evaluation practice) without thinking through our political commitments and responsibilities, and the kinds of human community that form the necessary conditions for the good life (Benhabib, 1986; R. J. Bernstein, 1991). Thus, what is at stake is evaluators' sense of who they are as "defined partly by some identification of what are truly important issues, or standards, or goods, or demands; and correlative to this by some sense of where they stand relative to these or where they measure up on them or both" (Taylor, 1991a, p. 306). There is a long tradition in social science supporting the notion that the most important standard or demand for the work of the social scientist is disinterest, contemplation at a distance, or disengagement. I question whether it is necessary to conceive of the evaluator's identity in terms of such goods as disengagement, a preoccupation with method, and monological consciousness.

Fourth, more indirectly, and perhaps even as subtext, I call into question the assumption that the continued development of a professional practice of evaluation experts and all the trappings of certification, credentialling, and institution building are unqualified goods. I have no illusions that such a practice can be undone. Even so, I invite readers to speculate on the gain in wisdom and the improvements in action that might be acquired by all kinds of practitioners in education, nursing, social service agencies, and the like if they were able to make sense of evaluation as a kind of undertaking more continuous with the everydayness of their own practices.

Fifth, another notion addressed only indirectly, but nonetheless one which forms the backdrop for much of my thinking, is the lack of wisdom forthcoming from casting many of the central issues in evaluation in terms of the so-called qualitative-quantitative methods debate. What I address here has little, if anything, to do with that debate. Rather, readers are presented with a set of ideas stemming from the tradition of practical hermeneutics that might help them transcend the methods debate.

Finally, this is a book that suggests that there is another possible narrative for understanding evaluation practice, another story in which we might seek to make sense of what it means to evaluate (McEwan, 1995). The past thirty years or so of evaluation philosophy and methodology can be characterized as an essentialist project that aims to identify those features, definitions, methods, and so forth that distinguish evaluation from nonevaluation. It is a project that is concerned with setting out the necessary and sufficient conditions for some activity to be called evaluation. We might be better served by thinking of evaluation practice in terms of a narrative that evaluators have been telling themselves about who they are, what they do, and why that is important. The language of the narrative is not simply about the practice, but is part of the practice it constitutes. My aim is not to explain yet another theory of evaluation practice that defines its essential features. Rather, I offer the possibility of another narrative by presenting a series of readings of the practice that offer an interpretation of what it is and suggest what it might become.

These issues are elaborated in the essays that follow. Part I takes up the question of how evaluation practice is currently viewed as a professional undertaking of applied social scientists and how it might be reconceived if the practice looked to resources in the humanities, particularly the tradition of philosophical hermeneutics, for its self-understanding. This means realigning evaluation with everyday life and recasting evaluation practice as moral-political *praxis* rather than technical performance.

Contemporary evaluation assumes that its task is to produce particular kinds of knowledge claims (i.e., value claims) about the objects (policies, programs, projects) it studies. Hence, it is preoccupied with determining the right methods for producing those claims, the right methods for warranting or judging their objectivity and validity, and the right methods for applying or translating those claims to the world of the practitioner. These tasks are undertaken by a monological subject—one who stands over and against the object he or she aims to analyze and know. Philosophical hermeneutics challenges the view that these conceptions of knowledge and of the knower are central to moral-political life. It holds that *praxis* requires a different kind of knowledge, variously spoken of as understanding or wise judgment. This kind of knowledge arises in a dialogue with others. The essays in Part II aim to elaborate the meaning and nature of understanding as dialogue, how understanding is accomplished, how understanding is represented, and how the quality of understanding is judged.

In practical hermeneutics, dialogue is not simply (or even) a procedure but an ethic. It refers to an ontology of relation—a way of understanding the self, a way we are as human beings in the world, or our ethical or moral orientation as human beings. One of the strongest and most articulate defenses of this idea can be found in the work of Taylor (1989; 1991a; 1991b) who argues for the fundamentally dialogical character of human life and is strongly critical of what he calls the disengaged first-person-singular (or monological) self. An important issue at stake in this discussion of dialogue as a way of being concerns the question of identity. To say that human life is fundamentally dialogical in character is to say that our identities as individuals are "formed in dialogue with others, in agreement or struggle with their recognition of us…. My discovering my identity doesn't mean that I work it out in isolation but that I negotiate it through dialogue, partly overt, partly internalized, with others" (Taylor, 1991b, pp. 45–46, 47).

This issue has implications for thinking about the professional practice of evaluation. For example, it calls traditional sociological conceptions of professional role into question. Evaluation practice is traditionally defined in terms of the roles and responsibilities of evaluator, clients, stakeholders, beneficiaries, participants, and so on in stating evaluation 'problems,' defining those problems, gathering information to address those problems, and reaching agreement on how to solve those problems. In other words, the entire practice is about problem solving in which each party to the practice plays a particular role and carries out some particular set of responsibilities. The literature on evaluation is replete with extended discussions of what the right roles and responsibilities are for each party.

However, to begin to think about evaluation practice in terms of identity and dialogue is to suggest that as evaluators and participants come together to discuss what it is right to do in a given situation (say, for example, the design and operation of after-school programs, or choosing the best mix of social services for a client) what is at stake is not simply the adoption and implementation of various roles and tasks in problemsolving but the formation of a sense of self (an identity) as a person of a particular kind. Studies of this notion can lead to a way of reconceiving of the aims and purpose of evaluation practice itself as a kind of teaching. Moreover, notions of dialogue as constitutive of being challenge the dominant Kantian conception of ethics (as developed most notably by Rawls and Habermas) that exists in a symbiotic relation with theories of liberal democracy (Jodalen and Vetlesen, 1997). This ethical-political framework is assumed in virtually all current discussions of the ethical aims of evaluation practice [e.g., House and Howe's (1999) view of the relationship between evaluation and deliberative democracy] and in discussion of professional ethics in evaluation. The essays in Part III take up these matters of ethical identity, moral orientation, and political responsibility in evaluation.

The broad issues addressed in Parts I, II, and III—redefining evaluation as *praxis* as opposed to a technical undertaking; understanding and criticizing objectivist and modernist assumptions underlying current evaluation practice; recovering the centrality of notions of being and ethics for our self-understanding; and aligning evaluation practice with everyday life—are necessarily interrelated. Thus, the essays are perhaps best viewed as a series of readings or interpretations of these matters all aimed at understanding a new discourse-practice of evaluation.

Part I

Rethinking the Enterprise
of Evaluation

1

Understandings of Evaluation Practice

Practitioners of any social practice, whether it is law, teaching, or in the present case, evaluation, operate with a more or less self-conscious understanding of that practice. That understanding comprises a view of what one is up to in performing the practice: what purposes, goals, norms, and means define the practice and how they are manifest in the actual work of the practitioner. The understanding in question might be thought of as a self-understanding or personal awareness. However, by self-understanding here I do not mean something that is purely subjective or simply a matter of individual consciousness. An understanding is a shared, *intersubjective* orientation grounded in a tradition of practice and a discourse of what it means to be a practitioner of one sort or another. That discourse comes long before the individual practitioner's personal awareness of her or his practice, and stretches far beyond it.

In this chapter I sketch two different understandings of the practice of program evaluation: the more commonly understood modernist/naturalistic orientation with its attention to procedural rationality and the methodical production of knowledge about objects, and the less commonly understood hermeneutic and humanistic self-understanding that focuses attention on lived practices. The label *naturalistic* reflects the view, as commonly discussed in philosophy of social science, that human phenomena can be known in the same way and via the same means as natural phenomena (e.g., the naturalistic interpretation of the social sciences). *Humanistic* refers to the kind of understanding of our selves forthcoming from the study of the humanities as opposed to the natural sciences. (I am not using the term to refer to the

nse of humanism—i.e., that humans are defined pri-
...ily by virtue of their individual self-consciousness and freedom—that is criticized by Nietzsche, Heidegger, Deleuze, Derrida, and others.) Each understanding or orientation comprises
many aspects. I discuss only the following: what one considers the
proper object of evaluation study; the subject's attitude toward the
world; how evaluation relates to educational experience; what
evaluation knowledge consists of; what notion of dialogue is most
important; and, the basis of evaluator authority or expertise. A
summary of how the two self-understandings in question address
these aspects is presented in table 1.

Table 1: Two Understandings of Evaluation Practice

	Modernist/Naturalistic	Humanistic/Hermeneutic
"Object" of evaluation	"Evaluand"—an entity such as a project, program, policy	Lived human practice
Attitude toward the world	Subject is disengaged and 'in control' and aims to reduce uncertainty and eliminate ambiguity	Subject is always engaged and embraces the inherent ambiguity of life
Nature of educational experience	Acquire knowledge to manage, improve, control self and society	Action-oriented self-understanding
Nature of knowledge	Knowledge is power; a means to an end; technical and instrumental	Knowledge is self-transformative; moral-political; knowledge of means and ends
Conception of dialogue	A procedure for resolving differences, reaching agreement, or consensus	An educative encounter; aims at mutual understanding
Basis of authority or expertise	Superior "scientific" (compared to the ordinary folk) grasp of means-end knowledge and procedural rationality	Skills of interpretation and skills of teaching about the acquisition of practical wisdom

The Modernist Understanding

It is commonplace to hear program evaluation discussed as the activity of an expert consultant in a fashion similar to the definition of professional consultancy practices characteristic of contemporary modern societies. Evaluation consultants possess a special set of tools and competencies that enable them to deliver a particular kind of service to a client. That service comes in a variety of forms, but at base it reflects some kind of assessment of the value (merit, worth, or significance) of human action conceived in terms of an object-like entity. In other words, what the professional evaluator examines is an evaluand—a "thing" such as an educational or social program, project, or policy. That thing-like entity has properties or features, all of which, at least in principle, are observable and measurable.

A common, although largely unquestioned, assumption of this view of evaluation is that the evaluator best serves society by aiming to redeem evaluation decision making from the partisan, partial, allegedly often unreasonable and unreasoned world of everyday life. This is to be accomplished by reducing, if not altogether eliminating, the contingency, ambiguity, and situated particularity of evaluation decision making by making it more rational. Making it more rational means importing into everyday life some procedure for evaluating human action that will not permit judgments of value to be tainted by personal preferences, mere tastes, old habits, or subjective wants and desires. The rationale here is distinctly modernist reflecting at least implicit acceptance of the aim to tame and domesticate disorder and ambiguity in society by means of molding citizens and society to reflect a rational social design. Evaluators, along with other social scientists, play a key role in modern, scientifically guided societies (Lindbloom, 1990) as the providers of the expert knowledge necessary to shape and control the natural and social environments.

It seems beyond dispute that this self-understanding of evaluation practice is intimately related to modernist definitions of educational experience. The kind of education assumed here is largely utilitarian and instrumentalist; it is an education in learning to solve problems. Education is about acquiring power so that one can manage and control environment, society, and self. To be educated is to be capable of solving problems in those domains. Moreover, education is cast in terms of the ability of the individual—either as individual mind or as political individual working with others in social groups—to demonstrate and exercise conscious and complete control over self, nature, and society (Gallagher, 1992). Accordingly, acquiring and disseminating evaluation knowledge is thought to be a useful educational activity because it is a means by which the instrumental action of social problem solving—most notably making society ordered, less messy, more rational and reasonable—can be carried out. The history of evaluation is largely a story of how to construct and deliver evaluation knowledge in ways that will make that knowledge eminently usable for the purpose of taming an unruly social order.

The history of modern evaluation reveals that evaluators have learned much about their abilities and obligations to serve society in this instrumental way. A few evaluators still insist on suspending the world and its messiness as the correct road to clarity and control. However, most are skeptical that this is possible and argue that it is naïve to assume that social practices will become more rational if evaluators simply hand over the right scientific information in the right form to the right people. Thus, for example, there is broad awareness of the need for strategies to generate and provide nonpartisan evaluation in a partisan world (Datta, 2000).

It is also generally recognized that professional evaluation practice will be more useful in helping manage the blooming, buzzing confusion of everyday life if it attends more carefully to ethical and political aspects of the very conduct of the evaluation. In other words, the more democratic and inclusive the evaluation process, the more likely it will be an effective tool for changing social circumstances (an appeal evident in both utilization based, participatory, and empowerment approaches to evaluation).[1] Evaluators committed to this way of thinking use terms such as *dialogue, participation,* and *empowerment* to signal the opening up of all or parts of an evaluation process to more extensive or more significant involvement by those with a stake in that which is being evaluated, particularly those stakeholders not often heard from or those who are routinely disenfranchised in moral-political decision making. Inclusion and wider participation not only meet ethical and political goals of equity and fairness, but they are means to reduce the contentious nature of evaluation in everyday life, reach agreement, and thereby enhance the probability that evaluation will be used as an effective social steering mechanism.

Of even more recent vintage is yet another instrumental approach to enhancing use and to improving the rationality of everyday evaluation practice. This approach is based on the notion that the activity of the evaluator requires at base something like a "good reasons" approach to making an evaluative judgment. In other words, what evaluators should be doing in offering their professional service is not simply summing up empirical evidence and delivering a report of their "findings" as it were. Rather, they should be engaging in a process of deliberation—using reasons, evidence, and principles of valid argumentation to combine statements of fact and value to reach a judgment (House and Howe, 1999). This approach to enhancing the use of evaluation to society shares some of the same interests in equity and fairness as noted above. Even so, it differs in the particular way it conceives of dialogue.

In what has been called the deliberative democratic view of evaluation, it is assumed that the confusion that accompanies conflicting values and interests will be reduced, and the use of evaluation subsequently will be enhanced, once evaluators come to understand dialogue as a particular form of argument suitable for evaluation in democratic societies.[2] Such societies seek to reach informed, well-reasoned decisions about what kinds of changes ought to be made in social life in a way that it is neither autocratic nor authoritarian. To avoid this danger, evaluators and stakeholders are encouraged to deliberate the merit, worth, or significance of some human action. By "working toward unbiased statements through the procedures of the evaluation discipline, observing the cannons of proper argument and methodology, maintaining a healthy skepticism, and being vigilant to eradicate sources of bias," the parties to an evaluation will together reach an objective, supportable evaluative conclusion (House and Howe, 1999, p. 9) in a reasonable and rational way. In this way of thinking, dialogue and deliberation are procedures or means (ideal forms of procedural rationality); in fact they are regarded as the best means to enhance the use of evaluation.

The professional practice of evaluation in modern society has traditionally sought to establish its cultural authority on the grounds that evaluators are scientific experts who, by virtue of their special knowledge of scientific method, can stand above the fray and deliver objective information about the value of our everyday efforts to improve society. Recent thought seeks to shift the basis of the authority of the evaluation consultant away from this image of the disengaged scientist and toward a picture of the evaluator as an expert in the skills of processing or facilitating an evaluative decision. In this newer conception of evaluator expertise, special methodological skills for solving the disorder and ambiguity of everyday life are not necessarily renounced. Rather, they are enhanced or complemented—methodological prowess in generating and weighing up evidence of facts and values is now accompanied by being especially adept in facilitating discussion to reach consensus and agreement. In other words, evaluator authority is currently being reestablished on grounds of expert knowledge of a particularly efficacious *process* of evaluation. Regardless of the basis, either justification for authority rests on two assumptions: (a) the inherent messiness of the lived reality of everyday evaluative decision making must be brought under control, and (b) the evaluator can effectively assist in enacting this kind of cleanup (improving the rationality of everyday evaluative decision making) by providing a special knowledge of fact or procedure.

In a very small nutshell, this is a picture of the fairly commonplace understanding of evaluation practice. The guiding theme of this understanding is that evaluation is a professional practice that serves as an instrument for improving society. The practice is dedicated to providing a special kind of expert consulting, and that service ought to be an improvement over our ordinary ways of making evaluative judgments. In a phrase, the aim of the practice is better living through evaluation. Just *how* to make evaluation useful in reducing the confusion and ambiguity that marks everyday life, thereby making ordinary evaluative activity more reasonable and rational, continues to be widely disputed among defenders of, for example, objectivist, participatory, empowerment, and utilization-focused approaches to evaluation. However, these are more or less disputes over the proper skill set for evaluators and the basis of their professional authority. There is virtually no dispute among these approaches over the notion that taming the unruly character of everyday evaluative decision making and thereby improving our social circumstances is in fact the proper aim of the expert service of evaluation. Professional evaluation has been built on faith in its ability to contribute to the solution of society's problems. Its intellectual work is regarded as redemptive. That is, through its activities it can smooth the rough ground of everyday life, facilitate the evaporation of diversity and difference, and make possible agreement and consensus about which policies, programs, and so on should be valued in society.

A Humanistic Understanding of Evaluation Practice

In what follows I invite consideration of a different way of thinking about evaluation. I am not suggesting another evaluation model or approach, nor is this a contribution to the long-standing quarrel over defining what evaluation "really" is. Rather, I suggest we explore evaluation as another way we are in the world and bring our notions of evaluating and evaluation practice closer to the realities of thinking and doing in everyday life.

Let us begin with the observation that all evaluation is fundamentally local. By local I mean engaged, native, concrete, indigenous, lived, or performed as opposed to abstract, transcendent, disengaged, or somehow removed from the erratic, contentious, uncertain, ambiguous, and generally untidy character of life itself. All judgments of the merit, worth, or significance of human action are undertaken within specific jurisdictions and circumstances where these judgments both reflect and depend upon the thinking (including socioeconomic, political, and moral values) and doing of the specific parties involved at the distinct time and place in question. There may indeed be broader or more global societal values (such as equity, justice, fairness, and so on) but these are interpreted and adjudicated in particular ways in particular circumstances where some group of people is attempting to decide whether they are doing the right thing and doing it well. Moreover, within each of these particular local situations, these values are contested, never certain, forever subject to reinterpretation.

This is the case whether it is a matter of the program officers and directors of the World Bank coming together to decide if the socioeconomic and educational interventions that they fund are the right ones, or whether it is a group of parents, teachers, and administrators in some local high school arguing over whether they ought to have an accelerated curriculum in mathematics and science for students wishing to go to college.

So conceived, evaluation is fundamentally a matter of specific people in distinct settings at particular times struggling to reach an understanding (an interpretation) of the value of their actions (taken or about to be taken) in circumstances that are always characterized by disagreement. But not simply disagreement: Efforts to reach an understanding are also marked by ambiguity, uncertainty, situational specificity, contingency, a good deal of (some might say, endless) criticism, and often something like radical diversity of views about what is the right thing to do or whether one has done the right thing well. These conditions, in part, reflect differing bases for knowing and doing. For example, in a situation where administrators, parents, teachers, and school board members are deciding whether or not to add a required course in adolescent sexual behavior to the curriculum, each party to the understanding acts from its own sense of responsibility and obligation. These responsibilities and obligations are always contestable and often conflict. People also act in light of their substantive understandings of what it means to be the right kind of person in the situation at hand and to do the right kind of thing. People assign value to various ways of thinking about being a person of a particular kind. Thus, parents act on their conceptions of what it is good to be as a parent; administrators on a sense of their duties as, for example, leaders, stewards, or caretakers; and so on for other parties involved in reaching an evaluative judgment in the situation at hand.

Understood in this way, the very reality of evaluation—its significance as a human undertaking—is grasped not in the distanced, abstract contemplation of the properties and performance of some "evaluand," some object-like entity such as a program or an intervention, but in its very enactment, or lived reality, if you will, as a moral-political practice. In other words, evaluation is a performative activity; what it means unfolds in its very doing or actualization. This doing is invariably marked by ambiguity, contingency, circumstantiality, and always contested ways of what it means to do the right thing.

The idea that evaluation is principally a means to bring about a desired end of a more rational and ordered society is predicated on the assumption that this lived reality of diverse, contested, messy evaluative decision making must be brought under control and made more rational. My primary concern here is with what gain in self-understanding evaluators of all kinds might realize if they welcomed and profoundly respected social differences, local traditions, diversity, disorder, ambiguity, and uncertainty instead of working so hard to overcome, eradicate, or control these facets of everyday life. At issue here is not simply the liberal *tolerance of,* or deference toward diverse points of view, but the idea of *embracing* the very idea of difference.

Our conception of the nature and purpose of dialogue figures prominently in this concern. Dialogue in evaluation, as so ably articulated by House and Howe, is aimed at unity, convergence, and the resolution of difference. House and Howe's conception of dialogue grounded in the liberalist democratic tradition assumes that the fair and equal treatment of parties holding differing views is best assured by regulating the *process* whereby social decisions are made, and that a fair process requires deliberation based on relevant information about facts and values (Bull, Fruehling, and Chattergy, 1992). A deliberative, democratic dialogue is thus a particular kind of procedural rationality aimed at achieving order and agreement. To resolve moral-political differences in a rational and reasonable way, one follows this dialogic procedure.

Of course, this way of thinking about the role of dialogue in evaluation seems eminently sensible. All the more so because many postmodern scholars encourage us to believe that this kind of convergent dialogue, one directed toward conformity and agreement, is chimerical. They argue that this view of dialogue naïvely assumes that conflicts can be resolved, when in fact a dialogue is always running up against issues of power and deep linguistic, cultural, and conceptual incommensurabilties. They claim that these deep differences can never be eradicated or overcome, and what passes for reasonable, rational exchange is nothing more than an imposition of one group's views on the other(s).

Thus, we are confronted with an either-or choice with respect to how we are to cope with the inevitable and inescapable facts of the ambiguity, contentiousness, and diversity that characterize evaluation in everyday life: *Either* these circumstances can be overcome by means of a dialogue whereby reasonable and rational people reach agreement and consensus, *or* the very idea of a so-called dialogue is testimony to irreconcilable and incommensurable differences. House and Howe pose this distinction as the choice between smoothing disagreements and reaching consensus across differences via a procedure of rational deliberation or endorsing the indefinite play of difference and hyperpluralism.

However, this either-or choice makes sense only if our conception of dialogue is limited to a matter of rational procedure, logical demonstration, and argumentation. Suppose that dialogue was not primarily a matter of how to argue but concerned with understanding and education. Suppose we looked to dialogue not as a means of converging on agreement and consensus but as nonconvergent and aimed at understanding and respect across difference (Burbules and Rice, 1991). This alternative conception of the aim of dialogue is premised on valuing difference and embracing diversity rather than on seeking consensus and intersubjectivity. Thus, the situation wherein one confronts another who holds a different view is not so much an occasion for debate and deliberation but an opportunity for opening oneself up to a kind of conversation that promises transformation of the self (Buker, 1992). Dialogue of this kind proceeds pedagogically and has the aim of understanding self and other, rather than unfolding technically as a method for resolving difference. Dialogue of this kind does not aim to escape the messiness of human life, the lived reality of difference and diversity, by always seeking consensus. Hence, as explained by Burbules and Rice (1991, p. 409), the outcome of these kinds of dialogue might include: (a) not agreement, but a common understanding in which parties do not agree but establish common meanings in which to discuss their differences; (b) not a common understanding, but an understanding of differences in which the parties do not entirely bridge these differences, but through analogies of experience or other indirect translations can understand, at least in part, one another's position; (c) little understanding, but a respect across differences, in which parties do not fully understand one another, but by each seeing that the other has a thoughtful, conscientious position, they can come to appreciate and respect even positions with which they disagree. This idea of an evaluation "dialogue across differences" (Burbules and Rice, 1991) embraces difference, diversity, and the messiness of human life rather than seeking to resolve it.

All of this suggests that evaluation practice can be conceived of as an educative experience in a sense that is quite different from the modernist notion of education as a means to the end of managing and controlling self and society. Efforts to reach an evaluative understanding can be useful simply because they help people to come to a clearer understanding of who they (and others) are, to a clearer picture of the meaning of their practices and the extent of their moral responsibility for their actions, all as a "step in becoming different sorts of people with different sorts of social arrangements" (Fay, 1987, p. 89). This kind of education is premised on making people morally answerable rather than technically accountable for their actions.

This distinction can be elaborated in the following way: When evaluation and education are conjointly conceived instrumentally, all the problems we face in deciding about how to deal with one another's views (which is the central problem of providing the "right" educational and social services) are regarded as technical problems to be solved. Solutions to these problems are thought to be forthcoming from acquiring either a special knowledge that we lack or a special method or procedure of which we are unaware. Once we are in possession of this knowledge and/or procedure, the fundamental messiness, ambiguity, and contingency of everyday evaluative decision making can be eliminated. The assumption is that there is no *inherent* fundamental ambiguity, diversity, or uncertainty in life—we believe that our control of life (self, society, environment) can be complete.

However, the lived reality of evaluation does not so much present us with problems to be solved as with mysteries to be faced. This distinction was explained by the French philosopher Gabriel Marcel and elaborated by Hans-Georg Gadamer. Gallagher (1992) explains this view as follows:

> A problem is something that can be totally objectified and resolved in

objective terms because the person confronting the problem can completely detach himself [sic] from it and view it externally. For example,
my car breaks down. I can hire a mechanic or I can attempt to fix it myself by examining, cleaning, dismantling, and rebuilding the carburetor
or pump, and so forth. This is a problem to which there is an objective
solution. Things are relatively clear-cut. A mystery, on the other hand, is
somewhat different. A mystery is something that involves the person in
such a way that the person cannot step outside of it in order to see it in
an objective [i.e., detached] manner. She is caught within the situation
with no possibility of escape, and no possibility of clear-cut solutions.
Indeed, ambiguity is the rule within a mystery. My car is a problem, but
my existence is a mystery, not because I understand my car and I do not
understand my existence, rather because I can junk my car or send it to
the shop, but I am inextricably immersed in my existence. (p. 152)

Treating the evaluative decisions that we face as teachers,
nurses, social workers, and so on as problems to be solved rather
than as mysteries to be faced creates an illusory self-
understanding that leads to our mistaking technical proficiency
for our responsibility to be morally accountable for the evaluative
decisions we make. Thus, for example, the evaluation enterprise
seeks to equip a classroom teacher with a kind of knowledge of
fact or procedure in such a way that every problem she faces, from
class size, to a decision about inclusion, to deciding the best curriculum for reading, is a technical problem to be solved. If this effort succeeds, we have made a technically adept teacher. However, equipping the teacher with our best science and decision
rules will do little to help her grasp the fact that in making
evaluation decisions she is morally accountable. In other words,
she is obliged to defend as appropriate and right the decision she
makes in arguing for reducing her class size this semester, for ex-
cluding Billy who has cerebral palsy from her classroom, and for
deciding that Mary's ability in reading will best be enhanced by
teaching her phonics. In sum, efforts to enhance the teacher's ability to manage and control her practice, over time, alienate the
teacher from the responsibility that inevitably befalls her for the
moral-political decisions she makes as a teacher. She need no
longer think about what it means to be educated and how her interpretations of that aim in the circumstances at hand are moral-
political evaluations of the right way to be as a teacher and thus
shape her very self-understanding *as* a teacher. Rather she is en-

couraged by evaluation consultants (and a variety of others) simply to become more technically proficient in knowing how to
control and manage the situations she faces.

The same state of affairs remains as we move beyond the case
of an individual teacher's evaluative deliberations to the case of
teachers, parents, and administrators thinking and doing in con-
cert. Encouraged to view dialogue as a procedure for resolving
their evaluative disagreements, the parties to the decision are simultaneously taught that they need not personally grapple with
the inherent ambiguity, the diversity of opinion, and the contingencies that characterize their everyday lives as they attempt to
make the right evaluation decision at this time, in this place, under these circumstances, facing these particular students. They are
not chiefly encouraged to embrace and dwell in the divergence of
views as an opportunity for self-transformation and new understanding, but to reach for knowledge and procedures that will assist them in eliminating the disorder and diversity that characterize the situation.

In emphasizing that we neglect the lived reality of evaluation
as a moral-political undertaking for which we are morally accountable, I am *not* claiming that parties to evaluative decisions do
not need valid and reliable information about facts and procedures. Rather, my claim is that when both evaluation and education are cast in exclusively instrumentalist terms, then individuals
are encouraged to frame the evaluative decisions they face as
technical problems to be solved, rather than to accept responsibility for their decisions in the face of the inherent ambiguity of
moral-political life.

The traditional scenario linking evaluation, dialogue, and education all within a frame of technologically oriented instrumental
control of our human activities is not the only frame available to
us. Evaluation, dialogue, and education can also be equally well-
conceived as practical (moral-political) activities—open, reflective,
indeterminate, contested, and complex forms of human action that
cannot be regulated, controlled, or "redeemed" by the provision
of expert knowledge (whether of product/fact or procedure). The
lived reality of evaluation (the struggle to determine the merit,
worth, or significance of our human actions) reveals it to be an
ethical and, hence, a self-constitutive activity. To paraphrase Gal-

lagher (1992), it is less a deliberative human enterprise concerned with power and control, and more like a process that happens to the human enterprise, something in which we must learn to participate. This process itself achieves our sense of ourselves as individuals (and a society) of a particular kind. As R. S. Peters once said of education, we are "put in the way" of evaluation experiences. We always already find ourselves in a process of valuing, of deciding whether we are doing the right thing and doing it well.

If the lived reality of evaluation decision making is *irreducibly* messy, ambiguous, and contested, thus requiring a kind of moral-political knowledge, and if there is no possibility of "redeeming" this reality by either scientific knowledge or procedural rationality, then the traditional basis of evaluator authority as scientist and/or process consultant is threatened. Just perhaps, if we attend more carefully to evaluation, education, and dialogue in the context of embracing the uncertainty, ambiguity, and contested nature of our efforts to do the right thing, then evaluators may set a new course for themselves as interpreters and teachers. They would interpret existing evaluative practices in some specific set of circumstances and they would teach others how to engage in an analysis of their own practices so that they might reach new self-understandings. As Carr (1995) explains it, the aim of such teaching would be to help practitioners in education, human services, and so on to see that their respective practices involve moral purposes and intentions, but that these are not to be construed as ends to which a practice is a technical means, but as commitments that can only be realized in and through the lived reality of practice.

There might be some important gains in evaluators' self-understanding (and in practitioners' own self-understanding of their evaluative decision-making) if they were to reconsider the activity of evaluation to be less like an applied science [or, in Scriven's (1991) view, a trans-disciplinary skill set] and more like a moral science. This reconsideration requires that we begin our thinking about evaluation by first turning to the inherently ambiguous lived reality of evaluative decision making in everyday life. There we might come to consider the kind of practical-moral knowledge that is demanded in life. And we might come to understand dialogue as a particular kind of pedagogically communicative relation essential to effecting a change in and by participants in the dialogue (Burbules, 1993). We might then be led to re-examine what role evaluators who claim special knowledge of evaluation might play in helping us with the struggle to understand one another and to do the right thing.

Notes

1   Regardless of their motive, the end-in-view of these different evaluation practices that aim for inclusion or wider participation is the "improved use" of evaluation. Motives for inclusion may be pragmatic—enhances the probability of evaluation utilization; ethical/moral—it is the right thing to do because it is the democratic (i.e., fair, just) way to proceed; or political—it is required to correct an imbalance of power brought about by the exclusion of program beneficiaries from the process of evaluation.

2   Dialogue here is defined as a *persuasion dialogue* (as distinct from dialogue as quarrel, debate, negotiation, information-seeking, educational) (Walton, 1989). This kind of dialogue arises from a difference of opinion or an issue to be resolved that has (at least) two sides. The basic goal is to prove a thesis (in this case a claim about the value of some human activity) in order to resolve a dispute or issue over whether the action in question has value (merit, worth, or significance). As Walton (1989) explains, the primary obligation in such a dialogue is a burden of proof. And this burden of proof typically falls to each party in an evaluative dialogue, because each is likely to be trying to convince the other of the merits of its view (versus the view of the other). In other words, it is rare that in an evaluation argument one party is not advancing a thesis about the value (or lack thereof) of some action and only has the burden of raising questions about the other party's claim. These kinds of dialogues have a number of both positive and negative rules (or prohibitions). For example, parties to the dialogue ought to abide by, for example, (a) rules of relevance (do not wander too far off the point), (b) cooperativeness (answer questions that have been asked; accept characterizations of one's position if they are accurate), and (c) informativeness (tailor one's presentation to what other parties to the dialogue know or don't know), and so on. Prohibitions necessary to a successful persuasion dialogue include not shifting the agenda at issue; not failing to make a serious effort to defend a

commitment when challenged; not failing to reply appropriately to questions; not failing to clarify, define, or justify the meaning or definition of some significant term, and so on (Walton, 1989).

2

Better Living Through Evaluation?

The last decade was a time of optimism about the growth of evaluation as a professional service. In 1991 the theme of the annual conference of the American Evaluation Association was "New Horizons for Evaluation," in 1995 "Evaluation for a New Century," in 1996 "A Decade of Progress," in 1998 "Transforming Society through Evaluation," in 1999 "The Territory Ahead: Foundations and Frontiers," and in 2000 "Mainstreaming Evaluation." These conference themes embody the myth of the American frontier—a vision of new horizons awaiting exploration by intrepid explorers. They reflect the growing interest in framing the practice of evaluation in the language of economics—a bid to find new markets and clients for buying and selling evaluation services. They repeat that uniquely American shibboleth, progress—extending the belief in the desirability and inevitability of evaluation as a tool for technological and economic development. Evaluators standing on the brink of the new technological frontier of the twenty-first century were confident that their practice would help realize the promise of steady improvement in social and material conditions. Echoing the phrases of an earlier era "Better living through chemistry" and "Progress is our most important product," evaluators claim "Better living through evaluation." The ideology of progress and its relationship to evaluation theory and practice is the topic of this chapter; although the significance for evaluation of images of the new frontier and the marketplace bear closer scrutiny as well.

Although we recognize as naïve the belief that social science can supply technocratic solutions to social problems, we nonetheless embrace an ideology of social progress grounded in the accomplishments of the social sciences. Ideology here refers to a set of integrated values and interests that are sedimented in a particular vision of what constitutes a practice (R. J. Bernstein, 1976). These beliefs and values function in the production, consumption, and representation of social scientists' and evaluators' ideas and behaviors. To the extent that the ethos of evaluation practice is shaped by the epistemological, methodological, and political concerns of social science, evaluation discourse reflects this ideology as well. What makes the extant ideology of social progress problematic is not the focus on progress per se, but the belief in social science as the engine of progress. In their service to society, evaluators promote the idea of better living through social science, or better living through evaluation as social science, and this notion effectively prohibits evaluators (and their clients) from engaging in a kind of evaluative inquiry principally concerned with moral and ethical reflection on proximal questions about what constitutes good practice and ultimate questions about what comprises the good society. Not only is this particularly ironic for a social practice that calls itself evaluation, but it is worrisome as well. This impairment in the willingness (and perhaps the ability) to probe questions of the good points to the limited utility of evaluation practice for addressing pressing problems of our shared life in institutions.

This chapter is written against the backdrop of the interpretive turn in the social sciences (Hiley, Bohman, and Shusterman, 1991; Rabinow and Sullivan, 1979, 1987). This new horizon concerns efforts of historians, anthropologists, sociologists, historians of religion, philosophers, and others to redescribe the human sciences and reconceptualize the enterprise of social investigation. A central theme is the turn away from a tradition of discourse (roughly, logical empiricism) that promoted a particular view of the nature and purpose of the social scientific undertaking: that "inquiry into the social world and the value of the understanding that results is to be determined by methodology"; that normative judgment must be clinically severed from cognitive analysis; and that human inquiries can be divorced from their historical, moral-practical, and political locations (Rabinow and Sullivan, 1987, pp. 20–21).

The interpretive turn is a widespread critique of this discourse, and it embraces not simply the many familiar criticisms of traditional social scientific methodology, but also the commentaries expressing alarm about the contemporary state of society and self brought about by unquestioned faith in technical-instrumental reason (e.g., Bauman, 1992; Lasch, 1991; Lindbloom, 1990; MacIntyre, 1984.) This essay is informed by this intellectual climate, and, more importantly, it aims to infuse thinking about evaluation with some of these contemporary criticisms.

The Ideology of Social Scientific Progress

In her history of the origins of the American social sciences, Ross (1991) argued that the ideology of social scientific progress was forged in the blend of Enlightenment thinking and English liberalism. That ideology embraced a theory of material progress in human affairs driven by the advancement of reason and knowledge, specifically, scientific rationality or reason, the most advanced, powerful form of knowledge. The social sciences, as one producer of such knowledge, were to serve as one of the principal agents of improvement. Despite a variety of criticisms of this ideology almost from its inception, this solidly positivist, scientistic vision of the social sciences as the venue through which we hope to establish some ability to predict and control the social world persists.[1] Bernstein (1976) argues that this vision is part of the generalized picture of social and political inquiry promoted by mainstream social scientists and held by the culture as a whole:

> The ideal has long been cherished that the advancement of science, and of scientific knowledge of social and political phenomena, must bring progress toward ideals and social goals accepted by reasonable human beings. We have learned how much more difficult it is to achieve and utilize such knowledge than was anticipated by some of our Enlightenment forefathers, but this goal—this regulative ideal—is still advocated by social scientists. (p. 52)

What Bernstein identifies here as a substantial part of the total intellectual orientation of the social sciences, Lindbloom (1990) criticizes as the vision of a scientifically guided society. According to Lindbloom, this vision or prescriptive model of how societies can best use knowledge for social problem solving:

puts science, including social science, at center stage. In that model, social problem solving, social betterment, or guided social change (regarded as roughly synonymous) calls above all for scientific observation of human behavior such that ideally humankind discovers the requisites of good people in a good society and, short of the ideal, uses the results of scientific observation to move in the right direction. (p. 214)

Because, with few exceptions, theories of evaluation practice are a special application or extension of the social sciences, they embody this vision, orientation, and ideology.[2] The majority of evaluation approaches promote instrumental rationality and endorse the view that there is or can be progress in human affairs through the solution of social problems by means of scientific reasoning. These approaches assume that social problems have scientific solutions, albeit not simple ones, and that evaluation is one important source of the scientific information useful in designing and implementing ameliorative strategies, i.e., new types of social programming.

Of course, the path to gathering and applying this information is an extremely complicated one. We know, for example, that evaluation is not equivalent to scientific appraisal (Cronbach and Associates, 1980); that evaluation cannot be neatly coupled with a rational problem-solving model (Cook and Shadish, 1986); that politics and science are ineluctably intertwined in evaluation practice; that there is always the possibility of managerialist bias in evaluation (Scriven, 1983); that evaluation is often more a matter of enlightenment than instrumental change, and so forth.[3] Yet, the core assumption is that the kind of scientific knowledge generated by program evaluation, as Rossi and Freeman (1989, p. 13) claim, helps "better the lot of humankind by improving social conditions and community life." That assumption holds regardless of whether evaluation knowledge is to be used incrementally in modifying social programs at the margins, or more dramatically, in designing and testing manipulable social interventions or solutions (i.e., demonstration projects) (Cook and Shadish, 1986).

Ironically, although adherents to this ideology of social scientific progress might claim that it is an amoral or value-neutral view, it is, in fact, a moral posture. Social betterment or progress in human affairs through the collection and application of social scientific information is promoted as a human good. The systematic and disciplined collection of social scientific information is thought to have a particular purchase in dealing with human affairs, and, hence, this is a normative stance. Morality is an evaluative undertaking concerned with human purpose and relationships—with answering Socrates' question, what shall we do and how shall we live? The ideology of social scientific progress—in this case, better living through evaluation—both constructs and promotes a particular answer to that evaluative question, namely, "we shall live better by shaping our social practices by means of sound scientific evidence." This answer also implicates other values (e.g., instrumentalism and utilitarianism) that shape the language within which we understand the sociohistorical world (Ross, 1991).

The problem is that the moral purchase of this answer to the evaluative question, how shall we live, is limited because it effectively excludes any kind of probing into aspirations, commitments, ideologies, values, and the like that shape our conceptions of the social good. When evaluation focuses exclusively on the provision of scientific evidence as the best means to improve social practice, it seals off moral inquiry. By moral inquiry, I mean what Moody-Adams (1997, p. 225) describes as "that critical (sometimes unsystematic) reflection on the kind of life worth living that human experience consistently renders unavoidable." In sum, our ability to fully evaluate social practices is impaired because moral inquiry is not part of the purview of the practice that calls itself evaluation.

Evidence for this limited moral vision in evaluation comes from scholars in both the social sciences and evaluation. For example, Lindbloom (1990) argues that insofar as social scientists help citizens,

> they do so less effectively for their standing volitions, the most severely impaired, than for action volitions. That is to say, they help citizens more on tax policy, current issues on space exploration, or toxic waste disposal than on persisting issues in perception of society, social philosophy, and ideology, issues that are both important in themselves and to improved formation of action volitions. (p. 181)

Cook and Shadish (1986) discuss three strategies for social problem solving in program evaluation: incrementalism, the use of demonstration projects, and a third strategy that "involves changes in basic social structures and beliefs that touch on such fundamental matters as the nature and locus of political authority, the form of the economy, and the distribution of income and wealth" (p. 200). Clearly, this third strategy requires a probing of moral commitments and normative patterns of relationships. However, Cook and Shadish do not include this kind of inquiry in social problem solving within the scope of evaluators' interests and responsibilities. They argue that "such changes are not part of the routine government [or, more generally, bureaucratic or administrative] functioning that evaluators aspire to improve and so are more properly the purview of historians, sociologists, and political scientists" (p. 200).

However, if evaluation practice for a good society requires challenging the practices of social institutions (Bellah, Madsen, Sullivan, Swidler, and Tipton, 1991), then, arguably, without engaging in Cook and Shadish's third strategy, evaluators are unlikely to question the central values that shape institutions and programs. If evaluators' assessments of programs are made only on instrumental grounds, then evaluators at least implicitly endorse the view that technical fine-tuning will solve problems of program effectiveness. Effectiveness itself, though, raises a value question: Effective for what and for whom? These questions can only be addressed by examining whether a program lives up to the moral purposes claimed for it and by inspecting and debating the basic value assumptions that shaped the program to begin with.

It will be objected here that program evaluation, as often practiced, does involve moral probing. The stakeholder concept, for example, signals the importance of surfacing various affected parties' values underlying program design and implementation. However, even setting aside criticisms of the misuse of that innovation (e.g., House, 1991; Stake, 1986), at best the stakeholder notion is but an endorsement of a pluralist conception of the value bases for programs, a means for constructing an inventory or description of various value stances of stakeholders and audiences. No assessment of reasons for value stances, no moral inquiry or critique is required.

Because we have good reason to believe that ways of seeing are ways of not seeing, that how we talk eventually comes to be how we represent what we talk about (Bruner, 1986), an unexamined, and anything but self-critical endorsement of this ideology of better living through evaluation is impairing. It is impairing because it promotes a view of problem solving in which attention to moral probing of core principles, values, commitments, and the like is at best outside the evaluator's sphere of concern. Furthermore, program evaluation devoid of moral probing and critique is impairing to clients and citizens more generally because it fosters the mistaken notion that we simply need better scientific information for improved decision making.

Toward a Morally Engaged Evaluation Practice

I do not wish to dispute the idea of human betterment or progress in human affairs. Nor am I arguing that scientifically informed means-to-social-end thinking characteristic of most evaluation has no purchase on our ability to shape a better social life. Rather, I am interested in our understanding and acceptance of the notion that we achieve progress through evaluation, and our willingness to view progress as tied almost exclusively to the provision and use of social scientific evidence. Because of its identification with social science, the practice of evaluation is seemingly blind to a longstanding discussion about the nature of the good life and the means to attain it, to a view of progress as enlightened understanding grounded in moral reflection (Bellah et al., 1991). Lindbloom (1990, pp. 136 ff.) makes a strong case against the indispensability of social scientific knowledge. He quotes MacIntyre's observation that "what we have to learn from the social sciences as they now exist is how little understanding the social sciences can give us beyond the everyday understanding of social life that we have anyway" (p. 156). Even granting that Lindbloom may have overstated the case, the fact remains that evaluators should not accept without question the image of achieving social progress through science. There is great irony in a practice that labels itself *evaluation* yet refuses to deal with this fundamentally evaluative concern. The professional imperative to evaluate includes evaluating the very ideology of progress itself.

If there truly is a sense of better living through evaluation, then evaluation practice must be morally (and not simply scientifically) engaged. It should address the core principles and values of individuals and institutions, one of which is the idea of "better living through evaluation." All of this reflects a call for evaluation as a kind of public philosophy—public in the sense that it openly engages its public (clients and other stakeholders) in a dialogue about the moral meaning of practices; philosophical in the sense that it takes a more synoptic view of the meaning of evaluands, a view that is at once scientific, historical, sociological, and political (Bellah, Madsen, Sullivan, Swidler, and Tipton, 1975). The remainder of this chapter sketches three requirements of such a social practice. By no means are these three sufficient, but they are minimally necessary.

First, a morally engaged practice of evaluation requires a special form of normative attention, receptivity, or mindfulness to both individuals and institutions as a prerequisite to awareness of meanings and to the cultivation of human possibilities and purposes (Bellah, Madsen, Sullivan, Swidler, and Tipton 1991; Noddings, 1984).

Second, this kind of moral engagement does not preclude converting what is being attended to into a problem that must be probed or solved. However, that problem is always concrete rather than abstract, grounded in a particular case or dilemma. As Noddings (1984) points out, we must "keep our objective thinking tied to a relational stake at the heart of caring. When we fail to do this, we can climb into clouds of abstraction, moving rapidly away from the caring situation into a domain of objective and impersonal problems where we are free to impose structure as we will" (p. 36). Thus, an evaluation practice that is attentive in a normative sense requires a socio-anthropological, as opposed to a scientific-technical, lens for viewing human activity. Stake (1991, p. 76) emphasizes that this approach does not mean seeing through the various theoretical frameworks of anthropological interpretation. Rather, it refers to a kind of "anthropological sensitivity"—an ability to pay careful attention to the texture and concrete details of people's experience, their activities over time, their physical and social surroundings.

This way of seeing can be contrasted to a scientific way of viewing social and educational programs. Noddings (1984), drawing on Aristotle's notion of ethical reasoning, claims that in our traditional way of seeing, our first move is to abstraction "where thinking can take place clearly and logically in isolation from the complicating factors of particular persons, places, and circumstances" (p. 37). In this way, a social problem becomes an intellectual problem to be solved by abstract reasoning. In contrast, the first move in socio-anthropological viewing is toward "concretization," where one's feeling of the situation "can be modified by the introduction of facts, the feelings of others, and personal histories" (Noddings, 1984, p. 37). In this view, social problems are seen as "concrete human problems to be lived and to be solved in living" (p. 96). Lindbloom's (1990) argument for a self-guided (in contrast to a scientifically guided) society also places this kind of viewing at center stage:

> That the origin of problems lies in sensitivities, feeling, or affect continues to be an embarrassment to the model of scientifically guided society, for such a model aspires to more objective indicators of the existence of problems that can be stripped of sentiments, feelings, or emotions. The self-guiding model takes for granted that no escape from feeling can be found. (p. 218)

Third, this kind of evaluation practice requires social criticism predicated on the immediacy of ordinary life and everyday understandings (Walzer, 1987, 1988). It is aimed, as Eisner (1991) following Dewey suggests, at the reeducation of perception. The critic, according to Eisner, describes, interprets, evaluates, and points to enduring qualities or aspects of a phenomenon so that readers can see it anew. This criticism makes use of language in an expressive way, because it is neither empirical nor logical; it presents a coherent picture without "proving" anything (Noddings, 1984). Drawing on the work of MacIntyre, Stout (1988) suggests that our criticism be stereoscopic—that we simultaneously bring into view the goods (aims, purposes, values) of particular social practices (e.g., teaching, social work, administration, medical care) and the structures and circumstances of institutions that support them. In this kind of criticism we would examine the concrete lived experiences of practitioners, seeking to understand and portray the virtues or the internal goods sought by a practice, while also looking at how external goods (prestige, money, status, and so forth) support or subvert the attainment of those virtues. This ap-

proach will help us envision the configuration of practices and institutions we should strive for.

This third requirement embraces a different understanding of
the evaluator role. The evaluator neither adopts the dominant
value perspectives of the client, nor promotes some higher moral
ground, acting as a philosopher king. The notion of a scientific (or
moral) expert gives way to social commentator or critic exploring
the moral and political meaning of programs with stakeholders.
The evaluator seeks to foster the posture of a reflective practitioner among stakeholders and is far more concerned with probing
than with proving.

Postscript on New Horizons

No part of this call for a morally engaged evaluation practice
should be interpreted to mean that we must choose between a
technical means-end examination of programs and a moral examination. There is no good reason why reflective probing cannot involve both means and ends (Lindbloom, 1990). However, we must
ask whether the preoccupation with improving means to collect
and interpret data, to report evaluation findings, and so on really
will lead to new insights into the moral contours of social life.
Does a portfolio approach to individual achievement claiming
more authentic measurement or a program theory constructed
from a causal model make all that much difference in the way
program administrators, teachers, students, and parents evaluate
the reality of schooling? Shouldn't evaluators have something to
say about the way we live? There seems to be little else to do with
current approaches to evaluation but to increase their technical
sophistication and sell them in new markets. If this must be the
case, then new horizons for evaluation are simply new venues in
which to display the evaluator's wares.

However, new horizons can also mean looking in different
places for sources of ideas about evaluation practice. It can mean
attending far more carefully and publicly to the legacy of the humanities and the tradition of practical philosophy and what they
might contribute to understanding evaluation as a normative undertaking. There is a special urgency in recognizing the potential
for new horizons of this kind. That need is occasioned by the

growing dissatisfaction with our institutions of education and government, the dismal state of public discourse, the increasing insularity of our academic language, and the declining quality of contemporary life for all but a privileged few. Perhaps for many evaluators, this urgency to examine new sources of ideas for evaluation practice is as deeply felt as was the urgency of an earlier generation to adopt social scientific techniques and concepts that ushered in the practice of evaluation as we now know it.

Notes

1   It is not my purpose here to explain why this vision is a cultural force. Ross's work defends the thesis that this vision persists because the social sciences have been successful in denying their own history.

2   Scriven's (1991) theory of evaluation is an exception to the view that evaluation is a kind of social science. He argues that evaluation is a transdiscipline whose *intellectual* origins predate all of social science while its main *methodological* roots lie in the social sciences. We may hypothesize that it is this confusion of intellectual origins with methodological procedures that explains, in part, the failure of much evaluation theory to incorporate moral concerns. A similar situation is evident in postwar political science: The science of policy making and administration is dominated by economic and political science methodologies effectively displacing a judgmental, evaluative disposition of politics that predates the intrusion of these scientific methodologies (see, e.g., Berlin, 1996; Lowi, 1991).

3   Evaluation use is often spoken of as *enlightenment* (Weiss, 1977) of decision makers or as an effort to *demystify* understandings of social programs (Berk and Rossi, 1977). These terms are not without irony as metaphors for the ideology of social scientific progress. MacIntyre (1984) reminds us that the moderns heralded the triumph of the union of empirical-analytic thinking with instrumentalist and utilitarian principles by naming themselves the Enlightenment and casting the medieval, mystical, unreasoning, and barbarous past as the Dark Ages.

3

Recapturing Moral Discourse in Evaluation—Revisited

Beginning with its formal expansion as a specialty in the late 1960s, and continuing throughout efforts to develop and professionalize the practice in succeeding decades, evaluation has been intimately tied to the social sciences. The characteristic concerns of the social sciences have set the terms of evaluation discourse involving issues of method and methodology, purpose and use of evaluation research, validity of scientific claims, and the identity and ethical obligations of the researcher qua evaluator. Debates about these important issues in evaluation practice have generally followed the same trajectory of those debates in the disciplines of sociology, anthropology, and political science.

Of course, over the past three decades, numerous criticisms have been made of this link between evaluation and social science. Consider, for example, Scriven's (1980, 1991) repeated deconstruction of the value-free doctrine of social science as incompatible, at best, with the very definition of "evaluation." However, the social science legacy is durable. It continues to provide the terms in which theorists and everyday practitioners conceive of the meaning, value, purpose, and methods of evaluation.

My purpose here is not to explore why that legacy has such drawing power. Rather, I want to focus on the constitutive features of an alternative to social scientific discourse. Wrestling with understanding what this different way of acting and speaking entails is worthwhile because this alternative is often dimly or wrongly perceived. Thus, its import for reconceptualizing the meaning and purpose of evaluation practice is not fully understood or appreciated. This chapter begins by naming this alternative and explaining how it has arisen as a central preoccupation in my thinking about evaluation. Subsequent sections of the chapter compare the features of this discourse to the allegedly primary way of thinking about and doing evaluation and point to what a reconceptualized evaluation practice might look like if this new discourse were adopted.

Origins of an Idea

At the 1988 annual meeting of the American Evaluation Association (AEA) in a paper entitled, "Recapturing Moral Discourse in Evaluation" I argued for the restoration of moral concerns to the center of our way of thinking about evaluation practice (Schwandt, 1989). Having practiced evaluation for several years in different settings, I had grown increasingly uncomfortable with the fact that evaluation theory and practice seemed preoccupied with an excessively narrow set of technical and methodological concerns having to do with the best ways of making claims about evaluation objects and the best ways of delivering that information to clients. These concerns per se were (and are) not unimportant, but they seemed to severely overshadow other equally important issues in evaluation. Only minimal attention was being paid to implicit assumptions about the expertise and authority of the evaluator in society, the relationship of matters of fact to matters of value, the belief in social scientifically informed and managed social change, and the near exclusive reliance on technical-instrumental reason in evaluation.

At the time I argued, and I still believe this to be true, that evaluation practice effectively sealed off examining these questions because it was based on a politics of meaning-making that relegated such issues to the anteroom of evaluation theory and practice. That politics grew out of a largely unquestioned, collective set of beliefs that comprise a philosophical anthropology of disengaged human agency that, in turn, sustained evaluation as a neutral, objectifying science of human life and action (Taylor, 1995).

In that paper, I used the phrase "moral discourse" to connote a different way of thinking about ourselves and our practices of research and evaluation. Of course, as noted in the previous chap-

ter, conventional social science is itself a moral discourse. The institutions of social science mediate our relations to the social
world. They promote and sustain particular patterns of moral expectations for the way we ought to be in the world. Hence, it is
more correct to say that my concern is with recapturing a form of
moral discourse that is an alternative to the moral discourse of
traditional social science.

Michael Patton prompted me to this latest reconsideration
and to the necessity of better explaining the features of the alternative view. In the third edition of *Utilization-Focused Evaluation*
(Patton, 1997), he claimed that my viewpoint on the importance
of moral discourse in evaluation is a kind of philosophical imperialism—substituting a focus on moral inquiry for methodological
inquiry. Patton (1997) argued that he parts company from me "in
the superior position" that I assign to the moral questions that I
raise. He stated that:

> Issues of morality do not shine brighter in the heavens than more mun-
> dane issues of effectiveness. [Schwandt] attacks methodological ortho-
> doxy and narrowness, which deserve attack, but makes himself vulner-
> able to the counterattack that he is substituting his superior moral in-
> quiry for others' superior methodological inquiry. He derides the techni-
> cal expertise evaluators strive for and the arrogance attached to such
> expertise, yet he can be accused of merely offering another form of exper-
> tise and arrogance, this time in the trappings of moral discourse and
> those who know what questions are *really* important. (p. 367)

Philosophical reflection in general is not always more important than empirical study nor is it the case that normative inquiry
necessarily takes precedence over efforts to describe and explain.
However, there is an important way of thinking about ourselves as
evaluators (and as citizens more generally) and our relations to
others and the world that is in fact more oriented toward practical, moral-political concerns than toward technical and methodological matters. This way of thinking about ourselves *is* primary; it
is the way we "first" are in the world. Moreover, there does seem
to be a great deal of evidence today suggesting that society generally is shaped by expert-intensive techniques and an unquestioned
acceptance of the merits of technical-instrumental reason. Bauman
(1992), for example, notes "the modern state [has] presided over

an unprecedented growth of 'experts'—this thoroughly modern phenomenon, transforming on a massive scale esoteric, minority knowledge into bureaucratic power.... Among the expert-intensive techniques, one spots immediately those central to panoptic control, like surveillance, 'correction,' welfare supervision, 'medicalization,' or 'psychiatrization,' as well as the servicing of the general legal/penal system...." (p. 15). To this list we might add "expert" evaluation that, particularly via the current focus on performance assessment and auditing, shapes much of everyday life in institutions (Hanson, 1993; Power, 1997; Strathern, 2000).

Contrary to what Patton thinks I am up to, making everyone a moral philosopher will not redress this situation. We need to counterbalance the technicism (overreliance on technical reason) and deference to expertise that characterizes much of the current public discussion about issues and practices in education, health care, and the like. This goal can be accomplished by attending to the ways we think of ourselves being in the world and the consequences of those ways of thinking for the kinds of research and evaluation practices we enact. To engage in this kind of study requires reflection on the conditions of knowing, understanding, and speaking that characterize everyday life with others. This kind of reflection, in turn, can lead to a self-understanding with moral and practical implications; thus, the genesis of the phrase "recapturing moral discourse."

The possibilities of such a discourse originate with Aristotle and are resurrected in early twentieth-century continental philosophy and its varied criticisms of scientism, technicism, and instrumental rationality. A general phenomenological insight shared by Husserl, Heidegger, Sartre, and others was that science, or the scientific worldview, offers a secondary or derivative account of the world. They argued that human existence is first and foremost intentional or semantic and that our fundamental relationship to the world which we engage is through structures of meaning or significance. (Cooper, 1996). They concluded that we have neglected these structures of meaning and objectified the world (including both self and society), hence alienating ourselves from it.

The Allegedly Primary Discourse of Disengagement

Before considering an alternative way of conceiving of self-world relations that takes shape in the traditions of phenomenology and hermeneutics, it is necessary to sketch first the kind of discourse that is accepted as primary or definitive of our way of thinking, acting, and speaking about our relation to the world. This discourse centers on the perspective of disengaged human agency. By human agency I mean how we see ourselves in relation to self, other, world. Consider first the following perspective on human agency:

> As human beings we give ourselves to—or find ourselves in—projects through which we shape our environments and our relationships with each other. In the history of this projecting, particularly since the rise of modern science in the seventeenth century, we have moved more and more into a position where, as 'subjects,' we confront a world which is ours to objectify and control. And, increasingly, the substance of our human lives has become part of this objectified world over which we exercise mastery. Our lives are resolved into a series of projects—all our "wanting and doing," our "making, producing and constructing"—occur within this overall project or 'frame' of mastery itself. It is this frame which defines the scope of our ambitions and the meaning of success; our attitudes, our modes of thought, the very questions which are our problems arise already within this framework or else are smoothly, and inexorably, assimilated to it. (Dunne, 1993, p. 366)

This picture of human agency as fundamentally disengaged from the world is inextricably part of what might be called a *methodological frame* for knowing and being. In this frame, we organize our relation to the world on the basis of the assumption that as subjects (knowers) we confront a world (objects) that is ours to objectify and ultimately control (Dunne, 1993). In this frame, subjects are preoccupied with finding the best methods to produce genuine knowledge of the world, the best ways to manage bias in the process of knowing, and the best criteria for judging knowledge claims that result from the application of method. This frame is made possible by a philosophy of disengagement and is sustained by a preoccupation with continuous refinement of method.

Disengagement means a stance of objectification, best captured in the German word *Gegenstand*. It means that an object is that which stands over and against the subject (knower) who experiences or encounters it. Thus, to objectify that which one seeks to understand is to treat things that do not stand over and against the knower as if they did. In the methodological frame, self, other, and society are objectified. The knower is conceived as one who is capable of standing independently of objects of knowledge. Acquiring knowledge is a matter of correctly representing those objects. Knowledge is something that results from the faculty or capacity to reason in a way free from one's standpoint, that is, independent of historical context, prejudices, tradition, and so on. This is precisely how we conceive of most evaluation practice, regardless of preference for quantitative or qualitative methods. Third-party external evaluators and well-insulated internal evaluators stand apart from the programs and policies they evaluate. Through the application of various methods, evaluators develop objective evaluative claims *about* these objects (e.g., policies, programs).

The correct exercise of method or procedure in this act of knowing is absolutely necessary. This is so because method or procedure is a device to screen out engagement with the world and thus prevent reason from being corrupted by prejudice, tradition, and so forth. Following the rules of method permits the distancing of the object of study from the observer, thereby making objectivity possible. The ideal here is something like perfect procedural epistemology (Elgin, 1996). Without an appeal to method, it is difficult, if not impossible, to validate a claim to know. Hence, evaluation practice is preoccupied with finding the right method for producing knowledge claims in evaluation, whether it is Scriven's four-step logic, Patton's utilization-focused methods, the causal-comparative methods of Cook and Shadish, mixed-methods, or some set of so-called qualitative methods. (That some evaluators defend multiple methods as legitimate is not evidence of escaping this preoccupation; mixed-methods remains an argument about the centrality of methods to the act of knowing.)

Equally important in this view is a near exclusive preoccupation with the *epistemological* role of experience. The concern with validated knowledge leads to a standardization of experience, and to a preoccupation with methods that "attempt to guarantee, through the objectivity of their approach, that these basic experiences can be repeated by anyone" (Gadamer, 1989, p. 311). In the methodological frame, knowledge and experience are distinguished. Experience itself is objectified as we take a third-person perspective toward our experience. In this way, experience becomes the world 'out there' that serves as the tribunal for testing and validating knowledge claims. In a similar way, the acts of understanding (knowing) and applying knowledge are separated. Knowledge is a product that the knower comes to possess about experience. In a separate step, this knowledge can then, if one chooses, be applied.

This notion that knowledge of a state of affairs and the application of that knowledge are distinguishable steps in a process is manifest in the extensive discussion of the nature, causes, and consequences of evaluation use and misuse. Some knowledge product produced by an evaluator must in turn be applied or put to use by clients. Hence, the concern in the evaluation literature with a meta-analytic approach to assessing the relative weight of various factors that predict use, as well as the need to identify what comprises legitimate and illegitimate use of an evaluation (Cousins and Leithwood, 1986; Shulha and Cousins, 1997).

The methodological frame and the belief in disengaged human agency support practices of social problem solving—program evaluation, testing and assessment, applied social science, and educational research—that define the researcher/evaluator acting on the world as a maker or craftsman. This is a mode of activity that Aristotle called productive (*poiesis*), and it has to do with making or fabrication. *Poiesis* requires a distinct type of practical knowledge (*techne*). This knowledge can be learned and forgotten, or taken up and set aside at will. For example, when I need to perform some statistical test, I take up the knowledge of how the choice of an appropriate statistical test is related to different ways in which variables are measured, or when I face the task of designing and administering a questionnaire, I take up the requisite knowledge of questionnaire design and sampling. Once either task is completed, I am able to set the required knowledge aside. I have no need for that knowledge again until the next time the task arises.

Having this kind of technical knowledge is not, however, simply a matter of choosing and applying the right tools to define problems and develop solutions that make mastery of the world possible. *Techne* is more than a skill set: it constitutes a particular view of rationality. Productive activity *(poiesis)* requires a reasoned state or capacity to make—that is, a particular kind of cognitive capacity that makers have at their disposal. When skilled researchers and evaluators possess this capacity, they have acquired a kind of habitual ability of makers who can reliably produce and reproduce useful solutions (Dunne, 1993). This capacity consists of the following: (a) an understanding of the principles underlying the production of a state of affairs (e.g., being literate, being healthy, a well-managed organization, what constitutes a good evaluation); (b) the material (factors, forces, dimensions, causes, beliefs, attitudes, policies, programs), which gives them something to work on; (c) skill in the use of means or tools to produce a product (or solution); (d) a grasp of the end or purpose of the products (or solutions) that they make.

Evaluation expertise is comprised of this particular habitual ability to produce a product, i.e., an evaluation. Furthermore, in laying claim to this particular capacity (with its special knowledge of evaluation methods), evaluators imply (if not actually state) that laypersons lack this ability or are incapable of this kind of rationality. In other words, program participants, developers, and others involved in a program lack an understanding of the principles underlying the production of a good evaluation, skill in the use of methods, and so on.

In sum, in the disengaged methodological frame, a subject (knower) stands over and against a world of objects to which that subject has two basic relations: representation and action. The type of knowledge and rationality associated with this frame is cognitive-instrumental: A subject acquires knowledge of self and world and is capable of putting it to effective use.

It makes little sense to speak of escaping this frame or being liberated from it for it *is* part of our way of being in the world. The aspiration to disengage from those features of our knowing that distort genuine understanding is an indispensable condition for pursuing knowledge of the material world. The real problem is to undo what Taylor (1995, p. 66) refers to as "the fateful move" of ontologizing the disengaged perspective; that means "reading it into the constitution of the mind itself." This frame has become our commonsense view, and stands, Taylor claims, as "the default position: Powerful philosophical arguments have to be marshaled to convince people to think differently about these matters, to shake them out of what seems obvious. But in the absence of such a challenge, the model itself seems to need no defense" (p. 68).

An Alternative Discourse of Engagement

It is possible to resist this fateful move and simultaneously to mount a challenge to the model of disengaged human agency. This can be done by drawing attention to a different frame that takes up aspects of human existence that do not appear in the disengaged frame (Dunne, 1993). In so doing, the outlines of a different science of evaluation practice might become apparent. This new science of evaluation would allow us to rehabilitate and cultivate several natural human capacities and thereby allow evaluation to be more continuous with the way we live in the world (Gadamer, 1981).

The phrase "recapturing moral discourse" is a shorthand way of referencing this different discourse. It points to the kind of work required in reorienting the self-understanding of evaluation practice in terms of practical philosophy. This kind of work simply is not possible within a frame that is essentially inimical to engagement with the world.

What is required is a new beginning point, a new language, for language makes possible different purposes: Language is "a pattern of activity by which we express and realize a certain way of being in the world" (Taylor, 1995, p. 97). The reorientation of the human science of evaluation and the recovery of a different language for its practice is made possible by the work of Heidegger, Husserl, Habermas, Gadamer, Ricoeur, Taylor, and others. In what follows I draw on these sources and others, often with a great deal of liberty, to fashion an image of evaluation as practical hermeneutics.

Practical hermeneutics is concerned with the mode of activity called the practical (*praxis*). Its subject matter is how an individual conducts her or his life and affairs as a member of society. The goal of practical philosophy is to raise to the level of reflective awareness the exercise of distinctly human traits or basic human capacities involved in this kind of moral-political action in the world. These capacities include practical deliberation, producing agreement through persuasive speech, and achieving understanding through language. These are all forms of acting (being) in the world that take shape in the constantly changing situations in which we find ourselves. As Gadamer (1981) explains, the kind of knowledge necessary for these ways of being/acting is always called for

> by concrete situations in which we are to choose the thing to be done; and no learned and mastered technique can spare us the task of deliberation and decisions. As a result, the practical science directed toward this practical knowledge is neither theoretical science in the style of mathematics nor expert know-how in the sense of a knowledgeable mastery of operational procedures (*poiesis*) but a unique sort of science. It must arise from practice itself and ... be related back to practice. (p. 92)

The notions of *praxis* and *practical knowledge* have a special meaning here. Previously, I pointed out that the practical activity of making (*poiesis*) requires a kind of practical knowledge called *techne* or a reasoned capacity to make. That kind of knowledge fits within a means-end framework: Within this capacity, the maker's materials and tools are the means by which he/she creates an end product (i.e., a solution to some problem); and, the capacity itself, viewed as an overall process, is a means to the achievement of the final product (Dunne, 1993).

In contrast, *praxis* is concerned with a different kind of practical activity and hence a different kind of knowledge or rational power. *Praxis*, in the tradition of philosophical and critical hermeneutics, is

> a type of human engagement that is embedded within a tradition of communally shared understandings and values, that remains vitally connected to people's life-experience, that finds expression in their ordinary linguistic usage, and that, rather than being a means through which they achieve outcomes separate from themselves, is a kind of enactment through which they constitute themselves as persons in a historical community. (Dunne, 1993, p. 176)

Teaching, managing, nursing, governing, policing, parenting, and so on are examples. *Praxis* has three essential characteristics

(Pendlebury, 1995): First, it is mutable—it changes over time, not only from situation to situation but on a larger scale within institutions that support and shape it. Second, it is indeterminate, because questions of how to act and to live well arise within particular contexts, and appropriate action is thus contextually relative. Third, it is characterized by particularity; it unfolds in the fine-grained particulars of specific situations.

Praxis also assumes a quite different understanding of experience than what is found in *techne* associated with the disengaged frame. Experience is not a repository of sense data or a tribunal against which one tests a knowledge claim, nor is it something that is perfected and replaced by knowledge. Rather experience has a processional, historical character; it is anticipatory and open. Gadamer (1989) explores these different senses of experience using the two German words for the notion: *Erlebnis* denotes experience as something one has, an event or adventure connected with a subject; it permits a plural "experiences." *Erfahrung* refers to experience as something one undergoes so that subjectivity is drawn into an "event" of meaning; experience so understood is integrative and hence singular.

These characteristics of *praxis* point to the necessity of a particular kind of practical knowledge (a kind that is inaccessible to method, as discussed below). *Praxis* does not require knowledge of how to make something, but knowledge of how to be a particular kind of person; it is "action-oriented self-understanding" (Habermas, 1988, p. 162). *Praxis* is always related to our being and becoming a particular kind of person and requires a mode of knowledge called practical wisdom (*phronesis*) (Gadamer, 1977). Habermas (1988) identifies several important characteristics of this kind of knowledge:

1) It has a reflexive form; it is also self-knowledge. Hence, "we experience errors in areas of practical knowledge personally. False opinions have the habitual form of false consciousness. Lack of insight has the objective force of blindness." (p. 163)

2) It is internalized: "It has the power to determine drives and to shape passions. Technical knowledge in contrast remains external. We forget technical rules as soon as we are out of practice." (p. 163)

3) It is global: "It does not refer to particular goals that can be determined independently of the means of their realization." (p. 163)

4)   It orients one to the 'rules' of interaction: "These traditional rules
     are acquired through training, but the historically changing condi-
     tions of application require an application that, in turn, further de-
     velops the rules through interpretation." (p. 164)

Dimensions of a science of practical philosophy

Discussions of the social science of evaluation revolve around
a vocabulary of validity, method, objectivity, and the like. In contrast, the alternative discourse under discussion here employs a
different language in which the terms *ethics, deliberative excellence,
poetics,* and *rhetoric* occupy center stage.

Ethics. A science of practical philosophy is first an *ethics* of
judgment or a moral science. It is a theory of good judgment relevant to every instance of human judgment. Practical knowledge is
not exercised in making some kind of product (or solving some
kind of problem) separate from oneself. Rather it is acquired and
deployed in one's actions with one's fellow human beings. Practical knowledge is not a cognitive capacity that one can use at one's
choosing, but a way of knowing bound up with the kind of person
that one is. It is expressly concerned with questions of the good,
for the actions one takes as a result of exercising practical wisdom
are not merely effective but appropriate.

Deliberative excellence. The kind of practical knowledge (*phronesis*) in question here is variously characterized as wisdom, wise
practice, deliberative excellence, or good judgment. It has also
been referred to as "ethical know-how" (R. J. Bernstein, 1983, p.
147). Even so, it does not simply mean knowledge of ethical behavior. It points to a union of ethics and politics. It is a kind of
knowledge that is embedded in *praxis* and distinguishable from
technical knowledge guaranteed by method. Deliberation means
choosing a course of action and defending one's choice by means
of a practical argument that is concrete, temporal, and refers to
actual events.
    Deliberative excellence thus entails a different relation between
means and ends than that found in technical knowledge. In practical deliberation, "there can be no prior knowledge of the right

means by which we realize the end in a particular situation. For the end itself is only concretely specified in deliberating about the means appropriate to a particular situation" (R. J. Bernstein, 1983, p. 147). Furthermore, in practical knowledge or *phronesis*, understanding is always application. To have such knowledge is bound up with one's being and becoming. Good judgment or deliberative excellence is not detached from the person who has such knowledge, rather that knowledge becomes constitutive of her or his *praxis* (R. J. Bernstein, 1983).

Deliberation is not a monological act in which a solitary knower exercises her rational powers to achieve transparent self-knowledge of an object. Rather to deliberate is to engage a situation dialogically or with a conversational attitude. One does not recreate the meaning or understanding of a situation within oneself (monologically) but enters into a dialogue with that situation. For it is only in this interplay that one comes to understand the situation at all. As Dunne explains, "The whole point of conversation is that I allow some play to my own thinking and, in doing so, expose it to the counterweight of the other's contribution, which may confirm me in it or force me to amend or abandon it"(1993, p. 117).

In this dialogical engagement with a situation (or with a person), deliberation also requires an ability to mediate between particulars and principles in a dialectical fashion. A concrete situation, in all its richness of detail and particularity, presents itself to us demanding interpretation and judgment. Interpretation is always context-bound, but this does not mean that it simply takes place in a specific situation. Rather, contextuality is formative. That is, the specific situation determines the form and direction of the deliberation or judgment. In this way the particular situation is always the primary consideration.

However, *praxis* is embedded within a tradition of communally shared understandings, values, commitments, and principles vitally connected to one's life experience. To deliberate well thus requires simultaneously avoiding two extreme ways of reaching a judgment and choosing a course of action (Pendlebury, 1995). One extreme is to become totally immersed in and fascinated with the particulars of the situation. This is attentiveness or interpretation without deliberation. It remains closed to the contributions that tradition, prior knowledge, principles, standing commitments, and so on make to our understanding of wise practice and excellence in deliberation.

The other extreme is to remove oneself from the particulars of the situation and endeavor to apply principles, values, commitments, and the like to the situation at hand in a deductive fashion. Here, the contingency and changeability of situations is ignored because experience is brought under the rule of principles and theory, and thus experience cannot contribute to the refinement, clarification, or revision of principles. This might be characterized as deliberation without interpretation.

In a dialectical approach, experience (particulars of situations) and principles (theories, standing commitments, and so forth) are brought into simultaneous relief. Models for this kind of deliberation or practical judgment are found in case law, ethics, and clinical medicine. Consider, for example, the case of the clinician faced with the task of making a diagnosis of a particular patient's condition. As Toulmin (1988) explains, the clinician's deliberation here is *informed* by biomedical theory and standards of what constitute good medical practice, but her practice is not *entailed* by these principles and standing commitments: "The patient is not merely an individual who happens to instantiate a universal law. His clinical state is local, timely, and particular, and universal theories at best only throw partial light on it" (p. 354).

Diagnosis requires a kind of perception, and the diagnostic conclusion is a refutable presumption, not a necessary entailment of logical premises. The inference from evidence to conclusion is not timelessly valid, but thoroughly circumstantial, tentative, and open to reconsideration (Jonsen and Toulmin, 1988). Whether in healing, teaching, or managing, *wise* practice, Pendlebury (1995) claims, requires a "subtle interplay between several binary oppositions: reason and imagination, experience and innocence, cleanness of argument and richness of story, respect for principles and attunement to particulars" (p. 50). The wise practitioner, she argues, adopts an engaged agency posture of "perceptive equilibrium" that is characterized by "deliberation undertaken from a vantage point of situational immersion and guided by imaginative discernment of the salient particulars of the situation" (p. 53).

Poetics. As explained above, the ability to deliberate well rests on the habit of attentiveness or interpretive perspicuity by which one recognizes what is at stake in a particular situation. This is a kind of insight, an awareness of the morally relevant features of a situation. This ability might be spoken of as the *poetics* of practical reason, for it invokes images of a creative, inventive, imaginative mind; one with an ability to decipher a situation. The use of the term *poetics* here is intended to signal a sharp contrast with epistemology. It indicates that practical reasoning is more art than science. As Miller (1996) explains, art is the more appropriate notion because the kind of knowing that *praxis* demands "is not easily formalized into a technique that admits of systematized training. Powers of discrimination and interpretation are unsystematic and, in part, idiosyncratic depending on our individual talents of apprehension" (p. 227).

However, that this ability to discriminate and apprehend is unsystematic does not mean that it is arbitrary and unlearnable. Kant argued that while there could be no theory of human judgment, it is nonetheless necessary and desirable to educate or train human perception. This can be accomplished through the study of cases. Miller also is careful to point out that 'art' does not denote bad or imperfect science. Rather, practical reasoning is an art "because its subject matter (the contingency of experience) does not admit of any fixed, unchanging formulations" (Miller, 1996, p. 227).

Rhetoric. Dialectical rationality or deliberation is a faculty we exercise in making a practical argument, the conclusion of which is adopting a proper course of action in some particular situation. When the activity of deliberation is coupled with the activity of convincing others of the rightness of one's action and inspiring them to act accordingly, it follows that we are interested in the *rhetoric* of practical reasoning. Rhetoric refers to the art of persuasion, the ability to move an audience to action. Miller (1996) argues that rhetoric and practical reasoning share several features: (1) they are deliberative arts, seeking to render judgments about issues of everyday life; (2) both establish their particular conclusions presumptively, not necessarily; (3) both produce local rather than universal knowledge, speaking to problems of the moment experienced by a particular person or group of people in a specific place and time; (4) neither rhetoric nor practical reasoning is disinterested, both the rhetor and the wise practitioner aim to persuade us of the rightness of an action and appeal to desires and passions, attitudes and feelings, memories, and cultural vocabularies in doing so; (5) in a related way, both are "embodied"; there is an important noncognitive dimension to these actions that is neither impersonal nor cerebral.

Clarifying New Directions

"Recapturing moral discourse" points to the possibility of developing a science of evaluation foregrounded in these features of hermeneutic practical philosophy. This effort, however, is not some way of resurrecting the dispute between so-called qualitative and quantitative methodologies. This is not an insignificant dispute by any means (although at times it has degenerated into silly quarrels about the merits of various methods), yet the entire dispute takes place within the disengaged frame. Both empiricists and interpretivists alike are primarily concerned with what constitutes adequate knowledge given the assumption of a disengaged subject standing over and against the object of her knowledge (Giddens, 1993; Habermas, 1988). Only with the advent of philosophical and critical hermeneutics do we begin to see the development of an alternative discourse not preoccupied with generating methodical knowledge.

Nor does "recapturing moral discourse" mean a renewed focus on the moral and ethical behavior of the evaluator and paying special attention to applied ethics in evaluation (Newman and Brown, 1996; Shadish, Newman, Scheirer, and Wye, 1995). Examining the ethical obligations and right conduct of the professional evaluator is, of course, salutary. However, as Miller (1996) explains, applied ethics most often

> is modeled on a geometrical, deductive account of practical reasoning. The general approach is to take an abstract principle and apply it to a problem in a 'top down' fashion, or to pick out features of a situation and ascertain whether they abide by a more general rule. Cases are resolved by subsuming them under principles that are crafted antecedent to experience. (p. 237)

Applied ethics, so conceived, is also a conversation that unfolds within the terms of the disengaged frame. Method and disengagement set the terms for what one ought to do as well as what one knows. Furthermore, applied ethics generally assumes a sharp distinction between the spheres of morality and politics. The discourse of practical philosophy, in contrast, signals a reunion of ethics and politics, and a relationship between practical reasoning and experience that is less deductive and unilateral and more dialectical and symbiotic (Miller, 1996).

Finally, "recapturing moral discourse" does not mean that evaluators must serve as arbiters or judges of the moral worth of programs. Delegating questions of values served and promoted in social and educational programs to third-party, detached, neutral, expert evaluators fosters the estrangement and alienation of social actors from their own judgments of and responsibilities for the value or worth of their practices. "Recapturing moral discourse" signals efforts to relocate decisions about the moral worth of human actions in the lived experience of the actors making those decisions.

Perhaps the idea of "recapturing moral discourse" most strongly signifies efforts to resist the assimilation of evaluation practice to technique. The language of this new science—practical reason, wise practice, poetics, and rhetoric—stands as an alternative to an evaluation science grounded in the discourse of epistemology (e.g., valid knowledge, method, knowledge transfer and utilization). To recapture moral discourse is to bring the natural human capacities of ethical and political deliberation and persuasion to self-reflective awareness. These are our ordinary ways of being in the world and what is already given in the world, "prior to our objectifications and prior to any understanding of ourselves as being capable, through our will, of shaping our affairs. These are the necessary conditions of human experience, which all our projects at mastery actually build on but which, despite our ambitions, we cannot supplant or co-opt" (Dunne, 1993, p. 366).

The inevitable question concerning this new science of evaluation is what would evaluators do differently?[1] Recovering an interest in practical philosophy for evaluation may be worthwhile if for no other reason than that it will help evaluators and clients clarify the centrality of the notions of practice, practical deliberation, and acting in evaluation. It will foster an understanding of both the essential nature and the fallibility of our capacity to interpret and make sense of a situation, to decipher experience individually and collectively, and to deliberate and adopt defensible courses of action. It might encourage evaluators to pay much more careful attention to the way in which *phronesis* or practical wisdom is always required in applying the results of evaluation or social scientific inquiries.

However, many may feel that the near wholesale assimilation of *praxis* to technique evident in contemporary nursing, teaching, social work, and other practices demands something more radical. Perhaps the situation calls for nothing short of resistance to the further development of a professional practice of evaluation. Thus the bid to "recapture moral discourse" can be read as an antidote to the rapid rise of the modern professional specialty of evaluation. It is a discourse of evaluation aimed at helping practitioners develop the capacity for wise practice, not a means contributing to the further development of a professional evaluation practice. It is a discourse that resists handing over judgments of what it is right to do in teaching, healing, administering, and the like to the ministrations of outside experts in evaluation.

To pursue this discourse requires a new identity and role for evaluators. They would no longer conceive of their work as that of a scientist or researcher (or the currently more fashionable "collaborator," "facilitator," or "empowerer") but rather, as more of a Socratic interlocutor and teacher. Hence, the evaluator's disposition would be more poetic than theoretical and analytic (Miller, 1996). The latter approach casts evaluation activity in terms of the selection and application of methods, problem setting and definition, investigation and testing of claims, strategies for implementing solutions, and so on. In contrast, a poetic approach to the practice views it as interpretive, topical, and eclectic, focusing on the particularities of cases that present themselves in the ongoing situations of a given practice.

In this alternative discourse, the practice of evaluation itself becomes more contiguous with the practices it aims to assist. Those who call themselves evaluators would be principally concerned with helping practitioners of various kinds (teachers, managers, social workers, and so forth) become better practitioners. It is not the case that, in seeking to realize this aim, evalu.... would not see the value of empirical inquiry into circumstances, beliefs, conditions, and so on. There is an important role for generating and interpreting data that bear on the practical deliberation in question both in terms of the particulars of the situation at hand and the general principles, standing commitments, theories, and the like that shape a given practice.

Even so, the principal focus of the evaluator's work (reconceived as practical philosophy) would be to help practitioners acquire the ability to deliberate well—to assist them in developing their own wise practice. In brief, it would mean helping them to cultivate and bring to the level of reflective awareness a sophisticated set of interpretive skills. This may be accomplished in part by teaching them about practical deliberation as a poetics and rhetoric of judgment. It may also mean assisting them in developing critical (versus operational) intelligence—a capacity to question and debate the value of various ends of a given practice.

There is strong evidence of an extensive encroachment of the methodological frame in the daily lives of practitioners. For example, in schools and universities alike, external mandates for performance-based measurement, uniform curriculum standards, and research-based practices of "what works," continue to transform the open texture of educational *praxis* into technical know-how. A similar situation obtains in the health care industry. Resistance to this transformation does not seem likely to come from the contemporary practice of evaluation that, for the most part, continues to unfold within the methodological frame.

Notes

1   In current evaluation practice, collaborative and participatory approaches may be related to notions of practical hermeneutics if the latter are largely pragmatic efforts to establish the types of communities in which the recovery of practical rationality and *praxis* can flourish. However, if collaboration and participation mean nothing more than efforts to open up

the methods of evaluation to wider stakeholder participation, then there is a profound tension between these evaluation approaches and a science of evaluation grounded in practical philosophy. Disengagement, objectification, and the primacy of method characteristic of the methodological frame do not disappear simply by virtue of decentering the authority of an outside evaluator through enabling more democratic, wider participation in the processes of planning, executing, and using an evaluation. If participation, however expanded to be more inclusive, remains focused on seeking methodological solutions to problems of practice or seeking productive knowledge, then it is at odds with the notion of developing the knowledge needed for *praxis*. Efforts to link evaluation to practical philosophy can also be found in the literature on action research (e.g., Carr, 1995; Elliott, 1991; Winter, 1987). For example, Gustavsen (1992), inspired in part by Toulmin's discussions of practical philosophy, has criticized the preeminence in social inquiry of monological consciousness and theoretical reasoning and offered a series of arguments for a neo-pragmatic, democratic, dialogical approach to evaluation.

4

Evaluation as Practical Hermeneutics

Here then [is] the prototypical declaration of the modern self, established as a fully separate, self-defining entity, for whom its own rational self-awareness was absolutely primary—doubting everything except itself, setting itself in opposition not only to traditional authorities but to the world, as subject against object, as a thinking, observing, measuring, manipulating being....

—Tarnas, 1991, p. 280

Life by its very nature is dialogic. To live means to participate in dialogue: to ask questions, to heed, to respond, to agree, and so forth. In this dialogue a person participates wholly and throughout his [sic] whole life; with his eyes, lips, hands, soul, spirit, with his whole body and deeds.

—Bakhtin, 1984, p. 293

Recently, much attention has been focused on defining the practice of evaluation in terms of the "general logic" of evaluation (Fournier, 1995) or more simply the "theory *of* evaluation" or "the logic of evaluation" (Scriven, 1994, 1995). This chapter challenges the notion that the general logic of evaluation is self-evidently true and foundational for understanding evaluation practice. It attempts to show that, on the contrary, the general logic is but a particular way of speaking of evaluation. Activities like reasoning in evaluation or justifying claims in evaluation acquire meaning from the fact that they are situated within or indexed to this particular way of speaking.

My aim is to sketch contrasting contexts in which evaluation practice can be defined as a particular kind of activity. One context, the one in which the notion of the general logic acquires meaning, assumes that evaluation activity is guided by central concepts from the philosophy of reflection—that is, knowledge of objects, self-consciousness, and individual awareness. A different context reconceptualizes evaluation, drawing on concepts from the philosophy of *praxis*—that is, action, practical wisdom, and self-generation. The purpose of this exercise is to show a different way in which evaluators can engage the world of objects they evaluate (particularly, although not exclusively, the world of so-cial programs). By "engagement" I mean how evaluators stand in relation to the objects they evaluate, how they conceive of those objects, and consequently how they define their responsibility for rendering value judgments about those objects. Here at the outset, this redirection can be characterized as "a shift from a focus upon how we understand objects to how we understand each other—a shift from an interest in epistemology to one in practical herme-neutics" (Shotter, 1993, p. 6).

The chapter unfolds as follows: First, I describe the influences at work in shaping the way of speaking that gives meaning to the general logic. This way of speaking is referred to as the modernist paradigm or modernist discourse. Second, I sketch the characteris-tics of an alternative way of speaking that does not wholly elimi-nate the former, but foregrounds a different set of presupposi-tions. This way of speaking is referred to as practical hermeneu-tics. Third, I suggest what this alternative way of speaking means for the practice of evaluation.

The central thesis of this chapter may appear strange and un-familiar, not simply because of my own inability to articulate it clearly here. To recast evaluation in terms of practical hermeneu-tics requires suspending belief in a way of thinking about what it means to be rational and reasonable in evaluation practice that is so commonplace as to be virtually transparent to us most of the time. I also want to anticipate one potential misunderstanding of the project undertaken here. Some readers may mistakenly inter-pret my aim as that of describing an alternative methodology for evaluation. However, this chapter is not about methodology. Rather, it is about the philosophical anthropology that is pre-sumed in our way of speaking about evaluation. It aims to explain two different ways we have of imagining how we think and act as human beings in the world—ways we have of conceiving of ourselves as agents.

Modernist Discourse: The General Logic and Its Context

By applying the tools of conceptual analysis to the concept "evaluation," theorists like Scriven and Fournier conclude that evaluation is best understood in terms of an underlying general logic.[1] The general logic is said to define the fundamental nature of the evaluative undertaking—the determination of the merit or worth of some evaluand. It is held that the general logic is a pattern or set of principles for reasoning shared among various approaches to doing evaluation and across different fields in which evaluation is practiced. In Fournier and Scriven's view, the general logic is principally concerned with the basic problem of how an evaluator can reason soundly from empirical premises to evaluative conclusions. The general logic or pattern of reasoning instantiating this aim, as defined by Scriven (1980, 1991) and elaborated by Fournier and Smith (Fournier, 1995; Fournier and Smith, 1993), is displayed in four formal steps: (1) establish criteria of merit, (2) construct standards, (3) measure performance and compare with standards, (4) synthesize and integrate data on performance into a judgment of merit or worth. As Fournier argues, this general logic is, in turn, practiced via several kinds of working logics—specific strategies for establishing the steps in the general logic.[2] Developments in informal logic provide a set of issues and tools for examining different working logics of evaluation.

This general logic is typically presented as self-evidently true. No claims are made for its creation *ex nihilo*, but it is said to arise from sound conceptual analysis of the term *evaluation* and other foundational concepts including *merit, worth, value,* and the terms employed in the four basic operations noted above (Scriven, 1995) buttressed by examination of relevant philosophical examinations of value theory. Even so, there is more to the creation of this logic than derivation of terms via conceptual analysis. A general insight we learn from Hegel's critique of Kant is that every formalism presupposes a context. In the present case, the formal reasoning procedure represented in the general logic is indexed to certain assumptions and presuppositions regarding issues of knowledge, self, and society. In other words, the general logic takes its meaning from a particular way of thinking and behaving.

Chief among these presuppositions is the Cartesian-Kantian subject-centered, self-assertive view of reason that has gone largely unquestioned in the evaluation literature. This is a view with great staying power as Thomas McCarthy (1987, p. viii) reminds us: "The strong conceptions of reason and of the autonomous rational subject developed from Descartes to Kant have, despite the constant pounding given them in the last one hundred and fifty years, continued to exercise a broad and deep—often subterranean—influence." This way of speaking about reasoning and rationality retains strong connections to a philosophical anthropology built on notions of an ideally disengaged subject free to treat the world instrumentally, construing society atomistically as constituted by individual purposes (Taylor, 1987). What it means to be reasonable and rational in this modernist view involves a concatenation of ideas about bias control, authority and expertise, individual calculation, effective technique, and instrumentalism. At the risk of developing a caricature of this view, in what follows I sketch what is entailed in this modernist paradigm of reason.

Consider, first, the ways in which we typically seek to make sense of the fluid world of lived experience by imposing a sense of order on that experience. Shotter (1993) explains this impulse as follows:

> As with the natural world, so with our social lives, we have felt motivated by a desire to be able, contemplatively, as an external observer of it, to survey a whole *order*. Indeed, associated with the modern way of theory is a strong (in fact) embodied compulsion to search for such a form of knowledge, for without it, without an inner mental picture, an orderly, mentally surveyable image of a "subject matter's" structure, we feel that our knowledge is of quite an inadequate kind.... Thus, in our studies we have attempted to treat sets of essentially historical, often still temporally developing events, retrospectively and reflectively—as if they are a set of "already made" events in which we are not involved—with the overarching aim of bringing them all under a unitary, orderly, conceptual scheme. Thus, in following the way of theory, the project of individual researchers becomes that of formulating, monologically, a single framework to function as a "structured container" for all such events, thus to create a stable, coherent and intelligible order amongst them, one that can

be intellectually grasped in a detached, uninvolved way, by individual readers of the theoretical (textual) formulations they write. (p. 57)

This desire to impose order on the messiness of human practices is readily evident in the field of evaluation in two notable ways: first, in the bid to make sense of the practice as a whole, and second, in the making of evaluative claims. There is a strong impulse to bring order to the field of evaluation and to distinguish what evaluation is from what it is not. This is clearly evident in Shadish, Cook, and Leviton's (1991) bid to identify the "foundations" of program evaluation and to systematize the five "knowledge bases" of good evaluation theory. Other examples include Scriven's (1993, 1995) efforts to unpack the logic *of* evaluation in contrast to theories *about* evaluation practice; Stufflebeam's (1994, 2001) defense of the principles of genuine, objectivist evaluation versus pseudoevaluation; Guba and Lincoln's (1989) chronicle of progressive generations of evaluation.

Not only are these attempts to survey what Shotter called a "whole order" and to develop knowledge of evaluation as a "unitary, orderly conceptual scheme," but the particular kind of order sought is hierarchical. Each of these efforts to make sense of evaluation practice produces a graded or ranked series of ideas: There is *a* theory of evaluation that should govern all theories of practice; there is a ranked order of illegitimate to legitimate forms of evaluation; there is progress and development from less sophisticated and informed constructions of evaluation in earlier generations of practice to more sophisticated and informed constructions in later generations.

Efforts to reduce the messiness of evaluation practice and to develop a hierarchical ordering are also evident when attention is shifted away from viewing the practice of evaluation as a whole and toward the making of evaluative claims about specific evaluands. The project of reasoning here again treats evaluands as "already made events"—"objects" if you will—about which the evaluator can and must formulate statements that, in turn, allow consumers of evaluations to grasp in a "detached, uninvolved way" knowledge of the value of those evaluands. Again, the claims made about an evaluand are ordered hierarchically from simple observation claims about performance of the object on a set of standards to more complex inferential, synthesized evaluative claims. In sum, whether the object of our understanding is the enterprise of evaluation itself or knowledge of individual evaluands, a compulsion to objectify and order is apparent. Objectification is necessary in order to discern and then re-present the inherent order in these objects. Bourdieu explains that objectification describes a relationship between investigator (subject) and the object of investigation. It is a "theoretical relation" in which the social world is "a spectacle offered to an observer who takes up a 'point of view' on the action and who … proceeds as if it were intended solely for knowledge"(1990, p. 52).

A second feature of this modernist paradigm of the knowledge of objects is its preoccupation with epistemological questions: How can we know? How can we be certain of what we know? How can we best represent or state what we know? Epistemology here presupposes a dualism of mind (the subject, knower, consciousness) and object (the thing, person, or event to be known; the object of consciousness). Cognitive autonomy is a privileged value here: Knowers can and should be self-sufficient, and objects of knowledge are independent and separate from them (Code, 1991). Accordingly, genuine, legitimate knowledge of an object is defined as methodically self-conscious knowledge. This knowledge, in turn, requires both disengagement and the correct application of method (Taylor, 1989). The subject adopts a stance of disengagement toward the object of her inquiry. To obtain a clear and distinct understanding of an object, the inquirer must disengage both from her own immediate experience, tastes, prejudices, and desires and from the errors associated with custom, tradition, and authority.

To attain a self-sufficient certainty requires assembling a picture of the object of knowledge on a firmer ground. Reassembly is made possible only by following rules of thought. In other words, rationality means thinking according to certain canons or rules. Reasoning is procedural; and excellence of reasoning "is defined in terms of a certain style, method, or procedure of thought" (Taylor, 1989, p. 86). Hence, right reasoning in evaluation is defined as following the steps in the general logic as noted above. In general, this way of being reasonable or rational assumes the following:

- true knowledge begins in doubt and distrust of 'everyday' understanding;
- engaging in the process of methodical doubting is a solitary, monological activity;
- proper knowledge is found by following rules and method (rules guide us toward clear knowing, permit the systematic extension of knowledge, and ensure that nothing will be admitted as knowledge unless it satisfies the requirements of specified rules);
- proper, i.e., scientifically respectable, knowledge depends upon justification or proof;
- knowledge is a possession, an individual knower is in an ownership relation to that knowledge;
- in justifying claims to knowledge there can be no appeal other than the appeal to reason itself (R. J. Bernstein, 1983, pp. 115–18; Shotter, 1993, p. 166).

Third, this model of the rational mastery of knowledge of objects foregrounds the intellectual virtue of *techne* (technique, technical know-how). Hence, the kind of knowledge that evaluation requires is principally knowledge of craft or skill, a knowing-how. The practice of evaluation is, accordingly, a kind of action that Aristotle called *poiesis*—that is, action directed at the specific end of making or creating a product. The end-in-view, or product of evaluation practice, can be specified in advance of the undertaking. That product is claims about the evaluand. The kind of reasoning that must be employed in the practice is technical reasoning—a careful consideration of the relative effectiveness of different means to making evaluative claims.

In brief, this modernist discursive practice about what it means to be reasonable and rational embodies, as Taylor (1989) explains, connections

> between disengagement and objectification, on the one hand, and a kind of power or control, on the other; between this and the ideal of a correct procedure, a proper way of assembling or constructing our thoughts, which defines rationality; and lastly between rationality and the attaining of knowledge. These connections have become so strong in certain departments of modern culture that they might seem to be the only possible construal. (p. 163)

An Alternative Discourse: Practical Hermeneutics

This is but one way to define evaluation practice and reasoning. However, that activity can be recast in the alternative discourse of practical hermeneutics. This discourse indexes the practice of evaluation to a neo-Aristotelian focus on practical judgment and a hermeneutic concern with particularities of concrete situations. Central to this view is a different understanding of human agency. In Bourdieu's (1990) terms, the important contrast is between the "theoretical relation" to the world with its attendant attitudes of objectification and mastery and a "practical relation" to the world. In the modernist rationalistic paradigm of reason, human subjectivity is characterized by its ability to have a purely contemplative, theoretical, rational, or intellectual grasp of self and world (Grondin, 1995). In practical hermeneutics, human Being is a situated, ethical ongoing discussion of what we should, could, must be. Understanding is the way of Being: "The living human being understands the world as he [sic] finds himself already in it, not as an anemic egological entity eruditely confronting an opposing objective entity. Interpretation is not something that I (the epistemological ego) *do*, but something that I am *involved in*" (Gallagher, 1992, p. 45, emphasis added). Because of this distinction in understanding how we are in the world, it can be argued that, taken in its entirety, the modernist discourse of the general logic is severely limited. It minimizes the ethical, moral, and political ambiguities, ambivalences, and dilemmas that characterize the ongoing lived reality of planning, implementing, and evaluating in social-political life.

Gadamer and other apologists for philosophical hermeneutics have shaped the contours of an alternative discourse. In Shotter's view, this way of speaking about ourselves and how we can know rests on a set of beliefs very much at odds with the Cartesian picture of the disengaged knower. The presuppositions of this alternative way of thinking include the following:

- That the social world is not simply out there waiting to be discovered but is "a continuous flux or flow of mental activity containing regions of self-producing order [and] that such activity can only be studied from a position of involvement 'within' it, instead of as an 'outsider'";

- That knowledge of that world is practical-moral knowledge and does not depend upon justification or proof for its practical efficacy;
- "That we are not in an 'ownership' relation to such knowledge, but we embody it as part of who and what we are" (Shotter, 1993, p. 166).

Practical hermeneutics begins from a radical critique of epistemology as definitive of our primary relations to the world. It rejects the modernist paradigm of subject-object thinking with its ideal of a determinate object, out there waiting to be known through a process of methodical self-awareness by a disengaged knower. It holds that conceiving of knowledge as the product of this kind of activity overlooks the ontological character of understanding, that is, that we are self-interpreting beings. As R. J. Bernstein (1983, pp. 128–29) explains: "In opposition to Descartes' *monological* notion of purely rational self-reflection, Gadamer tells us that it is only through the *dialogical* encounter with what is at once alien to us, makes a claim upon us, and has affinity with what we are that we can open ourselves to risking and testing our prejudices." A critical insight here is that the knower does not stand as a solitary, subjective spectator over and against a self-contained, self-enclosed object, rather there is a dynamic interaction or transaction between that which is to be known and the knower who participates in it. (Gadamer used the concept of "play" here as a way of grasping the educational experience, the participation, the to-and-fro movement that characterizes our encounter with that which we seek to understand.)

The interpretive encounter with that which we seek to understand (be it a social program, another person, a text, etc.) can be characterized as follows (Gallagher, 1992, pp. 188–92; 348–51):

1) Interpretation is both constrained and enabled by traditions and preconceptions. A tradition is not simply some conceptual "place" from which we come to interpret but it also is projected ahead of us in shaping our way of understanding. In the process of interpretation, this tradition itself undergoes rearrangement and transformation. In this sense, the act of learning about evaluation as a practice or learning about a particular evaluand is always "productive."

2) The act of interpretation is structured as questioning. Questioning opens both the self-understanding of the interpreter and the meaning of the program, policy or project to be interpreted to possibilities and restructuring.

3) Interpreting or understanding always involves application. However, "[a]pplication is meant not in the instrumental or external sense of practicality, but in the more fundamental sense of making something relevant to oneself" (p. 190). The kind of application at stake here is a particular kind of knowledge that has been identified as knowing from within or practical-moral knowledge that Gadamer explains is "clearly not objective knowledge—i.e., the knower is not standing over against a situation that he [sic] merely observes; he is directly affected by what he knows. It is something that he has to do" (cited in Gallagher, p. 153). It differs from technical know-how in that it requires not cleverness in application but understanding: "we discover that the person who is understanding does not know and judge as one who stands apart and unaffected but rather he [sic] thinks along with the other from the perspective of a specific bond of belonging, as if he too were affected" (Gallagher, 1992, p. 153).

4) The understanding that results from the encounter is fundamentally a self-understanding, for "[i]nterpretation consists of an interchange that involves not only a questioning of subject matter between interpreter and the interpreted, but a self-questioning. The questioning is not just unidirectional or monological; it is reflective or dialogical. All understanding is self-understanding. Interpretation is a questioning of ourselves not only with respect to the subject matter ... it is also a questioning of ourselves with respect to ourselves and our circumstance." (p. 157)[3]

The dialogic encounter is both an ontological condition and the hermeneutic mode of inquiry. To recognize ourselves as dialogical beings is to acknowledge, as Shotter (1993, p. 38) explains, a way of being-in-the-world that remains "rationally invisible" to us in the modernist worldview. We come to understand that the apparently orderly, accountable, self-evidently knowable and controllable characteristics of our selves and our social forms of life are constructed upon a set of disorderly, contested conversational forms of interaction. It is through a dialogical encounter that we develop knowledge of our selves and our practices. This kind of knowledge is neither a "knowing that" (theoretical knowledge expressed in descriptive and explanatory claims) or a "knowing how" (knowledge of craft or skill) but a kind of knowledge "one has from within a situation, a group, a social institution, or society; it is what we might call a 'knowing-from'" (Shotter, 1993, p. 19). It is *phronesis* (practical-moral knowledge) characterized by choice, deliberation, and ethical-political judgment.

Dialogue is both a practice that helps us achieve *phronesis* and a regulative ideal that points us toward the kind of tasks we must undertake. As a practice, it is not eristic but constitutes, as Burbules (1993) explains, a "particular kind of pedagogical communicative relation: a conversational interaction directed intentionally towards teaching and learning." That process has no outcome set in advance. It is not aimed at changing other people but at affecting a change in and by participants in the dialogue. Participation in the dialogue demands what Burbules calls specific communicative virtues: "tolerance, patience, and openness to give and receive criticism, the inclination to admit that one might be mistaken, the desire to reinterpret or translate one's own concerns, ... the self-imposition of restraint in order that others may have a turn to speak, and ... the willingness to listen thoughtfully and attentively" (p. 42). As a regulative ideal this same conception of dialogue and communicative virtues orients our practical and political lives (R. J. Bernstein, 1983).

In the practical-hermeneutic tradition both the practice of evaluation as well as the practices of teaching, administering, caring, and so forth served by evaluation are reframed as dialogical, interpretive encounters. Neither the evaluator nor the practitioner is thought to face a problem to be solved as much as a dilemma or mystery that requires interpretation and self-understanding (see chapter 1). Furthermore, to understand a mystery is to deal with actual, concrete events and people, in specific places and times, under particular circumstances. The kind of reasoning required here involves judgment, deliberation, and the assembly of a variety of empirical, ethical, and political considerations necessary to cope with or make sense of the situation. Gadamer (1981) explains that the understanding that comes from this kind of reasoning has a unique quality:

> understanding, like action, always remains a risk and never leaves room for the simple application of a general knowledge of rules to the statements or texts to be understood. Furthermore, where it is successful, un-

derstanding means a growth in inner awareness, which as a new experience enters into the texture of our own mental experience. Understanding
is an adventure, and like any other adventure is dangerous.... [I]t af-
fords unique opportunities as well. It is capable of contributing in a special way to the broadening of our human experiences, our self-
knowledge, and our horizon, for everything under-standing mediates is
mediated along with ourselves. (pp. 110–11)

Implications for Evaluation Practice

Critics of modernism and the epistemological project have
pointed out that our contemporary hermeneutic situation (i.e., the
traditions that shape our current understanding of socio-political
life) is characterized by a devaluation of the intellectual virtue of
phronesis and the deformation of *praxis*. Habermas, among others,
has noted that technical or cognitive-instrumental rationality and
its accompanying "pattern of cultural and societal rationalization" have achieved "a one-sided dominance not only in our
dealings with external nature, but also in our understanding of the
world and in the communicative practice of everyday life"(1984,
p. 66).

Evaluation practice indexed to the modernist discourse of the
general logic supports and promotes this cognitive-instrumental
frame of mind. Rationality as defined in the general logic is
monological and a matter of having the correct procedure for constructing descriptive, interpretive, and/or evaluative statements,
assertions, or claims about various kinds of objects that are
evaluated. This approach in turn is wedded to a model of strategic political action aimed at solving problems in social programming. Clients, policymakers, and the like use claims made by the
evaluator instrumentally. This use may, on rare occasion, mean a
direct and immediate application of evaluation findings. More
commonly, use is thought of as more or less a kind of enlightenment of policymakers—an insertion of evaluative claims into the
complex political process whereby decisions are made to revise
and redirect social programming. Taken in its entirety, this discourse of evaluation seeks to minimize the ethical, moral, and political ambiguities, ambivalences, and dilemmas that character-ize
planning, implementing, and evaluating in social-political life. It
aims to eliminate plurality and heterogeneous views (both in con-

ceptions of itself as a practice and in the apparent value of any evaluand).

If, in contrast, the meaning of evaluation practice is indexed to practical hermeneutics, we acknowledge and accept a less tidy scene. The compulsion to objectify and order our knowledge of the socio-political world is recognized to be just that, a compulsion, and not necessarily *the* way we ought to engage the "problems" of life in social organizations. What Bauman (1993) describes as the wisdom of postmodernity is more readily accepted:

> What the postmodern mind is aware of is that there are problems in hu-
> man and social life with no good solutions, twisted trajectories that can-
> not be straightened up, ambivalences that are more than linguistic blun-
> ders yelling to be corrected, doubts which cannot be legislated out of ex-
> istence, moral agonies which no reason-dictated recipes can soothe, let
> alone cure.... The postmodern mind is reconciled to the idea that the
> messiness of the human predicament is here to stay. (p. 245)

Evaluation reasoning takes on a different character in this dis-course. This difference is not one of simply acknowledging that all evaluators have to deal with their prior knowledge and commit-ments or that we must now reason dialogically rather than monologically about the objects of evaluation (see chapter 9). Rather, there is a more profound difference in the way in which the evaluator both envisions and engages the socio-political world of programs, clients, and stakeholders. It involves a turn away from the sole preoccupation with knowledge as the use of system-atic procedures and principles to make and justify descriptive and explanatory claims about objects and toward practical wis-dom. Evaluators become less like social scientific experts who, after having employed rigorous procedures, authoritatively an-nounce that such and such an evaluand has the following charac-teristics, or is perceived to be valued in the following ways, or is worthwhile or valuable given a specific set of criteria. Instead of acting like impartial judges, evaluators would seek to make their practice continuous with the work of clients and stakeholders by becoming partners in an ethically informed, reasoned conversation about essentially contested concepts like welfare, health care, edu-cation, justice, work life, and so forth.

One way to achieve this is to aim at cultivating what May (1992) calls critical intelligence in clients and other stakeholders. The general logic of evaluation is suited to generating operational intelligence in clients. This kind of intelligence is instruction on the status of means and means-end reasoning; it is directed at helping a client get to there from here. Critical intelligence, on the other hand, is the ability to question whether the there is worth getting to. It requires not simply knowledge of effects, strategies, procedures, and the like but the willingness and capacity to debate the value of various ends of a practice. It is fundamentally an exercise in practical-moral reasoning. There is important difference in these two aims. Evaluation aimed at teaching operational intelligence seeks to improve the rationality of practitioner and decision maker's practices by applying knowledge that evaluation has produced. Evaluation concerned with teaching critical intelligence seeks to improve the rationality of practices in the fields of health care, social welfare, education, and so forth by enabling practitioners in these fields to refine the practices for themselves.

Critical intelligence can be forthcoming from local socio-historiography as a method or model for evaluation. As Gallagher (1992) explains, such a method begins with the analysis of existing interpretational practices (projects, programs, policies, and so forth) at specific interpretational sites (communities, schools, corporations, and so forth). Description and explanation of existing practices can unfold through co-generative learning (Elden and Levin, 1991) or dialogic conferences (Gustavsen, 1992). In these approaches the evaluator does not intervene as a knowledge-expert who will utter a pronouncement about the merits of an evaluand. Rather, the evaluator works more as partner—enabling conversations, introducing new ideas, facilitating examination and critique. The prescriptive component of socio-historiography is illustrated in the work of Freire (1975) and is guided by the following questions: "In any particular interpretational site, existing historically and in a specific place, what are the most immediate, the most local power relations at work? How do they produce and constrain the existing interpretations, and conversely, how are the existing interpretations used to support or transform such power relations?"(Gallagher, 1992, p. 333).

This reorientation cannot come about if the claim persists that the only legitimate way to conceive of reasoning in evaluation is in terms of the logic of evaluation—a monological practice dedicated to constructing and employing methods of sound reasoning from empirical premises to evaluative conclusions. Nor will change be forthcoming from refinements in descriptive empirical research. For while descriptive approaches to evaluation (e.g., Shadish, 1994) eagerly pursue more and better ways to prepare accurate inventories of knowledge claims about evaluands that are indexed to different stakeholder values, they are loath to engage in a practical-moral dialogue about such values. This fear stems from both the cognitive-instrumental outlook adopted in this kind of work and from the erroneous assumption that because there is no purely objective standpoint from which to engage in normative and prescriptive critique we must therefore not undertake any such critique. We must look in other arenas of social inquiry for ideas about what it would mean to treat the programs we evaluate as contested forms of conversational interactions.

Notes

1   The general logic is not *all* there is to the practice of evaluation. Scriven
     (1995, pp. 50–51; 1993, pp. 41–43), for example, explains that there are
     both the logic of evaluation and evaluation practice or practical methodology. The important point for this chapter is that he regards the former as
     prescriptive for evaluation and concerned with defining basic concepts
     (e.g., merit, worth, description, inference) and their interrelationships and
     distinguishing these basic concepts from related notions (e.g., assessment,
     measurement, explanation). The latter is *descriptive* for evaluation practice and is concerned with how evaluation operates in specific sociocultural situations. It is critical to the argument developed in this chapter to
     recognize that the general logic is said to be *foundational* to understanding
     what it means to evaluate. In other words, mastery of the general logic is
     necessary for doing good evaluation; one need not have either a theory of
     the phenomenon being evaluated nor a theory of the context in which
     evaluation unfolds in order to evaluate.

2   The most significant theme in contemporary working logics of evaluation is
         informal logic. Examples here include Scriven's (1991) notion of probative
         inference, House's (1995) defense of "all-things-considered" synthesis
         judgments, and Fournier's discussion of the relevance of Toulmin's (1958)
         claim-evidence-warrant model of reasoning for evaluation. Informal logic,
         as Walton explains, is concerned with examining and analyzing kinds of
         argumentative dialogues "as they occur in natural language in the real
         marketplace of persuasion on controversial issues in politics, law, science,
         and all aspects of daily life" (1989, p. ix). In contrast, formal logic is the
         study of deductive and inductive relations among—and valid and invalid
         forms of arguments constructed from—sentences or propositions abstractly
         considered. Formal logic bears little relation to the study of practical rea-
         soning or argumentation in which a speaker seeks to defend her or his the-
         sis to an audience by a variety of evidentiary and rhetorical appeals.

3   This way of understanding of our selves assumes a different paradigm or
         specimen knowledge claim. Rather than knowledge of objects expressible in
         observational claims, it looks to knowing other people as candidates for
         understanding what it means to know. Code (1991, pp. 38–39) character-
         izes this kind of knowledge in several ways:

   - it "develops, operates, and is open to interpretation at dif-
     ferent levels, it admits of degree in ways [that a simple ob-
     servational claim about an object] does not";
   - "precisely because of the fluctuations and contradictions
     of subjectivity, [knowing other people] is an ongoing, com-
     municative, interpretive process";
   - the knower-known positions are not fixed in this kind of
     knowledge; it works from a conception of subject-object re-
     lations quite different from that implicit in empiricist para-
     digms;
   - "the process of knowing other people requires constant
     learning: how to be with them, respond to them, act toward
     them."

Shotter (1993, p. 41) adds that this kind of knowledge is concerned with the
construction and maintenance of "conversational reality" in terms of
which people influence each other not just in their ideas but also in their
being. Practical-moral knowledge aims to actually move people, not simply
to give them good ideas.

Part II

Approaches to Understanding

5

On Understanding Understanding

The ability to understand is a fundamental endowment of man [sic], one
that sustains his communal life with others and, above all, one that
takes place by way of language and the partnership of conversation.
—Gadamer (cited in Michelfelder and Palmer, 1989, p. 21)

What does it mean to say that we understand or have an
understanding of something? In this chapter, I am not
particularly interested in the history of the term "to understand" and the many ways it has been theorized in the interpretive tradition (but see Schwandt, 2000). Rather, I am concerned
with the phenomenology of understanding as drawn from Gadamer and Taylor and what some have characterized as the conser-
vative wing of Heideggerian hermeneutics, not from the more
radical wing as developed by Derrida and Foucault.

Gadamer (1989, p. 263) has repeatedly emphasized that the
work of hermeneutics "is not to develop a procedure of understanding but to clarify the conditions in which understanding
takes place ... these conditions are not of the nature of a 'procedure' or a method which the interpreter must of himself bring to
bear on the text." My aim is to clarify in a rather brief way four
such conditions of understanding:

1) as different than knowing,
2) as learning rather than reading,
3) as relational and hence requiring openness, dialogue,
   and listening, and
4) as entailing the possibility for misunderstanding.

Knowing and Understanding

Consider the following statements: "Do you understand what I mean?" "I just don't understand you." "They understood each other perfectly." "I hope to understand you better." "She felt that she was completely misunderstood." "They reached an understanding." Without putting too fine a point on it and without opening a very old argument about the differences, if any, between understanding and explanation, when we say that we understand what others are doing or saying we are stating something quite different than that we know. To understand is literally to stand under, to grasp, to hear, get, catch, or comprehend the meaning of something. To know is to signal that one has engaged in conscious deliberation and can demonstrate, show, or clearly prove or support a claim. In Anglo-American thought, knowing and knowledge are more often than not associated with intellectual achievement, cognitive performance, or a special kind of mastery of subject matter (Kerdeman, 1998)—"she really knows her stuff," we say. Understanding is a different phenomenon, perhaps more evident in the German language in words which derive from the word for understanding (*verstehen*): *Verständis* means comprehension, insight, appreciation; *Verstehen* thus also means to have an appreciation for something, to comprehend it—*für etwas Verständis haben*. This difference between knowing and understanding is well expressed in the questions *"Woher weißt du das?"* and *"Wie verstehen Sie das?"*—"How do you know that?" and "What do you make of that?"

In life in general we are always engaged in trying to make something of "that." We are always about the business of construing the meaning of something. You are reading this chapter, and you are trying to make something of it. You observe a teacher approach a seventh-grader in a crowded hallway and put his arm around her shoulder, and you ask, "What am I to make of that?" You see two friends walking side by side, and he reaches out and touches her cheek, and you ask yourself "What am I to make of that?" You are observing in what has been described to you by the teacher as a learner-centered classroom. You witness an exchange between a student and the teacher in which the teacher tells the student to put away his building blocks and get out his reading book and get to work. Again, you ask yourself, "What am I to make of that?" We are always trying to understand the meanings that actions and utterances have in the inhabited world, the world of everyday life, the world in which we go about living. This is the ground that lies before us, the quest for the meaning of our actions as situated beings.

We need to remind ourselves that empiricism is the quest to somehow get beneath this rough ground. Empiricist theory aims to trump our lived experience (our everyday understandings of actions and utterances) by getting to the bottom of things, providing the last word, discovering the real structure of human behavior and consciousness that is thought to somehow lie beneath the terms of everyday life (Taylor, 1988). The empiricist pursues a particular kind of interpretation "that can be reliably protected from whatever snares or obstacles might beset it and thus put on a sound objective footing" (Dunne, 1993, p. 125). Modernist evaluation is an empiricist practice. It seeks to deliver objective knowledge claims (claims about the value of some human activity) that are free of the contingencies and ambiguities that mark our everyday efforts at judging the value of our actions.

Reframing evaluation as practical hermeneutics restores a focus on our efforts to reach evaluative understanding in everyday life. It urges us to attend to the *lebenswelt*—to the practical and communal life of persons, to dialogue and language. The "conversation that we are," to borrow a phrase from Gadamer, is about the meaning of speech and action, and meanings are expressed in language. That language is not private but shared, and hence meaning is not subjective but intersubjective. Moreover, the significance of our language use does not reside solely in its capacity to designate, discover, refer, or depict actual states of affairs. Rather, language is used to carry out or perform actions and to disclose how things are present to us as we deal with them. This is the historical, cultural, and linguistic context of our practices and our shared being—it can never be fully objectified or grounded (Guignon, 1991). We both start and end our efforts to make sense of things in our best grasp, our best account, of ourselves as agents in the world.

Moreover, to formulate our best accounts as practical agents we depend upon the world around us. We are always in and of the world, and, as Guignon (1991) explains:

> There is no way to sever ourselves from our ties to the world without undercutting our ability to be human at all. In Heidegger's vocabulary, our being-in-the-world—our involvement in contexts of significance—is the bedrock of all theorizing. And to the extent that there is no external vantage point from which we can describe this all-pervasive background of everydayness, there is no way to make it explicit once and for all. But the fact that our quest for insight into our being as situated agents is open-ended does not imply that everything is up in the air, a matter of mere "play." This seems to be Wittgenstein's point when he says, "The difficult thing is not to dig down to the ground; no, it is to recognize the ground that lies before us as ground." (p. 99)

There is a truth to the matter about what we make of things as we traverse this rough ground. However, it is not the truth that is expressible in propositions that abstract from the meanings of actions and utterances in the everyday world and that take the form of an absolute account of reality (Smith, 1997). Nor is it the kind of truth that comes from standing over and against an object that must be broken down and mastered through acquiring knowledge of it. Nor is it the kind of truth that is the methodically achieved knowledge of the empirical scientist and whose theoretical guarantee is to be found in the modern conception of method itself (Dunne, 1993). Rather, it is the truth of the best account possible. It is the truth that is disclosed by the better—the more perspicuous, more coherent, or more insightful—of competing interpretations. Practical hermeneutics is concerned with refining our ordinary understanding of the practices of teaching, healing, managing, learning, and so forth, rather than with leaping out of the lived reality of those practices. The question of what it means to understand while we dwell in the life-world is the second concern I wish to address.

Understanding as Learning Rather Than Reading

We are in the grip of the text. Almost four centuries ago, Shakespeare opined that "All the world's a stage, and all the men and women merely players" (*As You like It*). Now, though, at the beginning of the twenty-first century, we seem to believe that all the world's a text and all the men and women merely readers. Denzin (1997) has characterized the problems, prospects, and forms of interpretive, qualitative, and ethnographic work in the sixth moment of its development as all having to do with the text. Geertz (1980) tells us that social institutions, social customs, and social changes are all in some sense "readable"; Ricoeur (1981) defends the view that social action can be read like a text; Taylor (1985) employs a textual paradigm in explaining the aim of the hermeneutical human sciences; Gadamer's philosophical hermeneutics appeals to a textual model, and of course, for Derrida and Rorty, *everything* is a text. In sum, the text is the primary model for the object of interpretation.

If all interpretation is modeled on textual interpretation then, as Gallagher (1992, p. 321) explains, "it follows that interpretation must be a kind of reading, since its object is always a kind of text." Gallagher argues that

> [t]he modern, Romantic emphasis on the interior subject, the mind as the theatre of interpretation (in contrast to the public theatre of the ancients), goes hand in hand with the focus on textual interpretation, where interpretation is reading and reading is an interior process. To the extent that modern hermeneutics takes its orientation from the text as its model object and makes interpretation a silent reading, and thus an interior understanding, it tends to exclude explication, pedagogical presentation, and educational experience from the interpretive process. (p. 325)

There are two problems with modeling understanding on the reading of a text. First, as Gallagher suggests, in such a model, understanding and interpretation become private, interior undertakings. To be sure, at least two current conceptions of reading—the interactive and the transactional or constructionist approaches (Straw and Sadowy, 1990)—define reading as a generative act involving both text and reader, yet that act remains largely internal. It is internal (or interior) in the sense that understanding and interpretation are under the control of a self-reflective, autonomous, rational subject. Reading is conceived of as a mental act, an activity of an individual conscious mind. Self-reflection and autobiography are primary starting points for this kind of reading. Second, when we model understanding on textual interpretation, on reading comprehension, we are inclined to conceive of the task of understanding as that of the interior, private reconstruction (or construction) of meaning (i.e., understanding) followed by the public representation of that meaning (i.e., interpretation).

Each of these problems are addressed, if, following Gallagher, we model understanding not on textual interpretation, reading, and the object of the text, but on an educational process, a process of learning. On this model, understanding and interpretation are not acts of an individual conscious mind but enactments, performances, or a kind of *praxis*. Moreover, the starting point for understanding and interpretation is not the autonomous individual self and her or his self-examination. Rather, the starting point is the tradition in which the interpreter stands. Gadamer (1989) explains:

> Self-reflection and autobiography ... are not primary and therefore not an adequate basis for the hermeneutical problem, because through them history is made private once more. In fact history does not belong to us; we belong to it. Long before we understand ourselves through the process of self-examination, we understand ourselves in a self-evident way in the family, society, and state in which we live. The focus of subjectivity is a distorting mirror. The self-awareness of the individual is only a flickering in the closed circuits of historical life. That is why the prejudices of the individual, far more than his judgments, constitute the historical reality of his being. (pp. 276–77)

Gadamer (1989) is arguing that understanding is not a private act of the individual subject as we commonly conceive of it. Rather, understanding is a kind of simultaneous interplay of the movement of tradition and the movement of the interpreter:

> The anticipation of meaning that governs our understanding is not an act of subjectivity, but proceeds from the commonality that binds us to the tradition. But this commonality is constantly being formed in our relation to tradition. Tradition is not simply a permanent precondition; rather we produce it ourselves inasmuch as we understand, participate in the evolution of tradition, and hence further determine it ourselves. (p. 293)

Understanding and interpretation are here concei
practical-moral activities that have less to do with g₁
content, a noetic meaning, and more to do with engag
dialogue (Grondin, 1994) with that which is to be   ...uer-
stood—that which makes a claim upon us. Gadamer used the concept of "play" here as a way of grasping the educational experience, the participation, or the to-and-fro movement that characterizes our encounter with that which we seek to understand.

Moreover, when we seek to understand what others are doing
and saying, we simultaneously publicly explicate that understanding. In fact, our efforts to present, to articulate, to pronounce,
or to say what we think we understand are inseparable from our
efforts to understand. To say it more simply, there isn't first a si-
lent act of comprehension followed by a public recitation; rather,
understanding and speaking meaning are intertwined.

When we seek to understand what others are doing and saying, we ask of them in a variety of ways the more general questions "What are you up to?" and "What do you mean?" Consider
the following example (based on an account of conversation as
interpretation found in Dunne, 1993, p. 84): My daughter and I
are talking about her current job and whether she wants to give it
up and look for something else more challenging or go to gradu-
ate school. She says to me in a voice with a hint of resignation,
"Well, Dad, they like me here, I got a raise, it's interesting
enough." I am listening and trying to understand what she means,
what she is telling me. In that process of learning, I do not speak
back her words to myself, I *speak back words of my own to her*. I
don't take what *she says* as the only kind of expression involved in
understanding here. If I did, then I would be engaged only in an
interior process of understanding (of reading) what she had in
mind when she spoke the words to me. Rather, I seek to express
what I hear by speaking back to her—in my own words. I say,
half-questioning, to her, "Well, I'm glad that they value you,
Sarah. But are you telling me that you are successful but not really
satisfied with what you are doing now?"

Thus, in understanding and in interpreting her, I do not
merely rehearse within myself my daughter's speech. Rather, my
interpreting is a speaking back. In trying to understand what my
daughter means, what she is up to, I am not attempting to get be-

hind her words to her real meaning. Rather, I am letting her words "sow their meaning in other words" (Dunne, 1993, p. 84) which are then spoken back to her. The interpretation that comes into being in this exchange is tentative and provisional. We each go on listening and speaking, and in so doing, we come to hear differently or better, and this is expressed in a new, amended understanding, a better account. The crucial point here, as Dunne explains is that "the language of the interpretation does not merely offer what is understood a means of presenting itself. Rather, the presenting *is* the understanding" (1993, p. 142 emphasis added). Gadamer reminds us that "language is the element in which we live, as fishes live in water. In linguistic interaction, we call it conversation. We search for words, and they come to us, and they either reach the other person or fail [her]. In the exchange of words, the thing meant becomes more and more present"(1997, p. 22). When we model understanding on learning, we think of the task of understanding as *conversation*, as the expression in language of what is understood.

Understanding as Relational

In a provocative essay written a number of years ago entitled "If Persons are Texts," Ken Gergen (1988, p. 47) argued that understanding is best grasped from a relational perspective: "[U]nderstanding is not contained within me, or within you, but in that which we generate together in our form of relatedness." As his later writings reveal, Gergen will not draw an ontological conclusion from this observation, but, following Gadamer, that is precisely what I believe is at stake in understanding. In philosophical hermeneutics, the act of understanding is existential, not merely, or even, exegetical. Where understanding is defined as an act of exegesis, we imagine it to be a kind of critical analysis or explanation of an action or text using the method of the hermeneutic circle. Kerdeman (1998, p. 251) explains that, in an exegetical methodology, the interpreter "plays the strange parts of a narrative [or some social action] off against the integrity of the narrative as a whole until its strange passages are worked out or accounted for. An interpreter's self-understanding neither affects nor is affected by the negotiation of understanding. Indeed, insofar as interpreters and linguistic objects are presumed to be distinct, self-understanding is believed to bias and distort successful interpretation." Kerdeman adds that on an exegetical account of understanding, the notions of familiarity and strangeness that characterize efforts to make sense of something are seen as evaluations that the interpreter assigns to various parts of the action or text that confronts him. More precisely, the kind of understanding that results from the process of tacking back and forth between the familiar and the strange has no real import for the way of being of the interpreter, other than perhaps experiencing the thrill of discovery.

However, when understanding is conceived as relational and existential, familiarity and strangeness are not simply cognitive or rational *assessments* of aspects of our experience, but ways in which we actually experience being in the world. The true locus of our being, says Gadamer (1989, p. 295), is this being "in-between" familiarity and strangeness. Kerdeman explains how it is that we inhabit the world in this way as interpretive beings:

> Defined as an existential event, the familiar is not a proximal object or something we have grasped before. The familiar is that which we live through as an experience of affirmation and comfort. Familiarity is a condition of belonging, of being at home in the world. Strangeness, no less than familiarity, is emblematic of human existence. That which is strange is not an objective problem we solve or finally transcend. Strangeness is an experience of disorientation, exile, or loss. We live through and are implicated in a situation in which we feel confused, unable to find our bearings. Pulled between familiarity and strangeness, we find ourselves in the middle of an ongoing liminal experience, not quite at home in the world, yet not entirely estranged from it. The existential tension between 'home' and 'exile' at once distinguishes our human situation and also is the very condition that makes understanding it possible. (p. 252)

When we genuinely seek to understand what others are doing and saying we are always standing in this in-between of familiarity and strangeness. Gadamer (1989, p. 268) argues that we are "pulled up short" when we encounter situations and people that challenge our expectations and assumptions, those situations wherein answers to the question "What should I make of this?"

are not easy to come by. Gadamer explains that we can make sense of these challenging encounters with others in three ways. The first is to try to discover the typical behavior of the other and to make predictions about others on the basis of experience. We thereby form what we call knowledge of human nature. Here we treat the other as an object in a free and uninvolved way, much as we would any other object in our experiential field. This is the methodological attitude of the social sciences, the idea of theoretical contemplation of an object of our understanding. In such a process, "no essential reference is made to the interpreter, to the individual who is engaged in the process of understanding and questioning" (R. J. Bernstein, 1983, p. 135).

In a second way of understanding the other, the interpreter acknowledges the other as a person, but this understanding is a form of self-relatedness. Here, the interpreter claims to know the other from the other's point of view and even to understand the other better than she understands herself. To be sure, the interpreter understands the immediacy of the other's claim, but it is co-opted from the standpoint of the interpreter. This can be understood as a form of sympathetic listening in which we interpret others in our own terms and refuse to risk our own prejudgments in the process. Gadamer notes that by claiming to know the other in this way, one robs her claims of their legitimacy, and he argues that charitable or welfare work operates in this way.

A third way of understanding begins from the full acknowledgment that as interpreters we are situated within a tradition. It is only from such a posture that an interpreter can experience the other truly as an other and not overlook her claim, but let her really say something to us. Gadamer states: "[W]ithout such openness to one another there is no genuine human bond. Belonging together always means being able to listen to one another" (1989, p. 361). Thus, it seems that it is only the person awake to this living in-between who can have new experiences and learn from them. Hence, understanding requires an openness to experience, a willingness to engage in a dialogue with that which challenges our self-understanding. To be in a dialogue requires that we listen to the other and simultaneously risk confusion and uncertainty both about ourselves and about the other person we seek to understand.

It is only in an engagement of this kind, in a genuine conversation, that understanding is possible. As Gadamer explains, "the miracle of understanding is not a mysterious communion of souls, but sharing in a common meaning" (1989, p. 292). That common meaning can arise only in a dialogue wherein one does not simply defend one's own beliefs or criticize what the other believes, but rather seeks to become clear about oneself, about one's own knowledge and ignorance (Molander, 1990). It is only if an engagement is a genuine conversation that one can engage in checking one's own prejudices. For, according to Dunne "the whole point of conversation is that I both allow some play to my own thinking and, in so doing, expose it to the counterweight of the other's contribution, which may confirm me in it or force me to amend or abandon it"(1993, p. 117).

It follows that in such an engagement, I seek to make sense of the other and to reach an understanding. However, as Wittgenstein pointed out, all attempts to make sense entail the risk of making no(n)-sense, and to understand is to take the risk of misunderstanding. This leads me to the final condition of understanding that I wish to clarify.

Understanding as Entailing the Risk of Misunderstanding

As much as we are currently in the grip of the text, we are in the grip of the denial of the possibility of error. To read the current methodological literature in qualitative inquiry is to learn of two attitudes toward error: Either (a) error is a non-issue because there are multiple interpretations among which no one is better than any other, or (b) error in interpretation is possible, but it can only be properly grasped in light of some new set of criteria—for example, action, voice, sacredness, positionality, community, or some such touchstone (Lincoln, 1995).

Through recourse to four ideas, I hope to show that both of these views are flawed. Consider first the notion of what objective knowledge means. It is commonplace in philosophy to argue that objective knowledge is not the result of a process whereby that knowledge was constituted. Rather, whether a claim is valid or objective has to do with the future, with the possibility that I might be wrong. My belief in p is objective when, despite the fact that I might now be fully justified in maintaining p, it is possible that I was wrong about p. In other words, my presumptive knowledge counts as objective when, even though I have been as careful as I can be in checking that p holds, I could still be surprised; I could still discover that p fails. Briefly put, my belief in p is objective when, apart from matters of language and justification, there is still something in p about which I might be making a mistake. My belief or knowledge is subjective when such surprises are ruled out. In our everyday life, we inhabit a world with real mistakes and surprises built in and, hence, objective knowledge built in. We live in a world in which such surprises are not ruled out, in which we fully recognize that some of our interpretations are mistaken, in which we admit to misunderstanding. If one admits to these possibilities of being "wrong," then it is hard to see how one could maintain that any one understanding is as good as any other.

Second, consider the notion of what it means to be intellectually virtuous. Lorraine Code argues that there is more to the matter of "getting it right," than simply having a "good score in terms of cognitive projects which come out right"(1983, p. 538). In her view, our efforts to navigate a world full of mistakes and surprises require a particular intellectual virtue that she characterizes as "a matter of orientation toward the world and towards one's knowledge-seeking self as part of the world. The intellectually virtuous person values knowing and understanding how things really are. He or she renounces the temptation to live with partial explanations where fuller ones are attainable and the temptation to live in fantasy or in a world of dream or illusion" (pp. 538–539). What Code is claiming is that our concern with getting it right has "more to do with our relation to the world than with the 'content' of particular actions or knowledge claims" (p. 538). What is it about this way we are in the world that suggests to us that "being mistaken" in our understanding of what others are doing or saying actually matters?

A third notion borrowed from Taylor (1988) helps us answer this question. In a well-known argument, Taylor claims that we are self-interpreting beings. This means "there is no answer to how things are with us that is quite independent of our interpretations" (p. 55). Stated somewhat differently, our finding an answer to the question "What shall I make of this?" in part is constituted by the kind of persons we are and the kind of persons we become. This fact of what it means to be human does not mean that problems of misunderstanding or error are irrelevant to the task of interpretation. Quite the contrary, it raises the stakes for what it means to misunderstand. Consider this example that I have adapted from Taylor: My brother and I have an argument and I am angry and resentful. My brother tries to get me to explain why I resent him, and perhaps in the process he is able to answer the story that I am now unfolding with his own version of the events. Perhaps he convinces me that there's another way of seeing things, one in which he is not as culpable, insensitive, and uncaring as I have portrayed him. Perhaps things go well, and I lose my resentment. Then the whole thing will fit into a certain story for us, the story of an original hurt, my smoldering feelings, and our talking it out to a new understanding.

Taylor argues that this negotiating of a new scenario is not at all incompatible with there being a fact of the matter of how I felt, of how my brother felt. On the contrary, the negotiation presupposes these facts of the matter. He puts it this way: "The basic constraint in which we live is not just that any interpretation was possible.... The founding assumption under which [this negotiation] proceeds is that there are answers to these questions about how people feel, what they want or think, what they meant by that gesture, and so on" (pp. 55–56).

In other words, this effort of my brother and I to make sense of the matter (to reach an understanding) presupposes, as a very condition of engaging in the activity, that we can be wrong. While what will count as a successful negotiation or sound understanding here (as elsewhere) cannot be fixed in advance of the contingencies of this actual engagement, we nonetheless have a way of understanding error and an incorrect interpretation.

Must we not still have some proper theory of error and associated criteria for identifying incorrect interpretations? The simple answer is no. One can have a theory of understanding that embraces the distinct possibility of misunderstanding (of getting it wrong, so to speak), yet requires no criteria. Consider, for example, Sokolowski's (1997) exploration of ways in which the kind of conversation or dialogue discussed above can fail. First, a partner in the dialogue may be too immature or mentally incapable of engaging in a conversation. Second, one party may understand the discussion but find the topic too disturbing and impulsively introduce a different issue. Third, a person may stay with a conversation but simply repeat the convictions that he has brought to it. Fourth, the words of a partner in the dialogue may be deceptive, seeming to move the conversation forward when they are in fact part of a strategy to mislead. Sokolowski holds that examining these possibilities (and others) for failure makes it more clear that hermeneutics "does not legitimate any and every projection of fantasy as valid" (p. 230). He adds:

> The very description of failure and success in hermeneutics, the description of how a conversation can stall as well as move on, shows that the [meaning] being manifested in a particular instance is not just any [meaning] at all. A conversation is not merely a human interaction, it is also a display of something, and the success or failure of the conversation is a success or failure in the manifestation of the [meaning] in question. The fact that failure can be recognized indicates the possibility of recognizing success and hence of recognizing the identity of the [meaning] being brought to presence by the conversation. (p. 231)

These possibilities for misunderstanding are not criteria for determining whether or not an interpretation is correct. Moreover, we cannot possibly decide in advance of any particular effort to engage in a conversation which of these ways may help us understand whether or not that conversation is going wrong. This is so because the conversation is an unrehearsed practical-moral adventure with no way of predicting how it will turn out or what will turn up. Thus, these ways of understanding how a dialogue might fail are just that, ways or possibilities of misunderstanding, not standards for what it means to have a correct understanding. There are no standards, no criteria of right and wrong, for dealing with the question of whether our concepts (our understandings) are understood and adequate for finding our way about (Molander, 1990).

Hence, we do not need a *theory of error* that specifies standards of right and wrong interpretation. However, we do need a *theory of understanding* that assumes we are seeking interpretations that are mutually understood and adequate for finding our way about the world. This is a theory of dialogue, about how to move together in a direction where all sorts of misunderstanding and error will be detected and found and addressed (Molander, 1990). Given such a theory we can make sense of the fact that every effort to understand runs the risk of misunderstanding, and every effort to interpret faces the possibility of misinterpretation. Furthermore, we can profitably deal with this situation without having a set of criteria that specify in advance what constitutes getting to the truth of the matter in answering the question "What shall I make of this?"

The hermeneutic phenomenology of understanding sketched above is not translatable into a set of methods for evaluation. It is possible, as Gadamer demonstrates, to show that achieving understanding is similar to acquiring the kind of practical wisdom called *phronesis* and to model a theory of understanding on practical philosophy. Neither of these efforts, however, relates closely to the kinds of concerns with method that characterize evaluation as a social science.

The occasion we call "understanding" can be best grasped when we think of notions like learning, conversation, and the possibility of misunderstanding. The phenomenon of understanding is not a methodological accomplishment, it cannot be captured in terms of a procedure or method and it is not governed by a set of criteria. Thus, one cannot take what I have been talking about as any kind of prescription for "how to do" evaluation. For what I have been describing is not a methodology, but an existential philosophy—understanding as characteristic of our "being" in the world—an account of a practice that we all engage in called the art of understanding, and the art of making ourselves understood to someone else.

6

Criteria or Human Judgment?

Much of the literature in evaluation is given to debates about the merits of rival positions X and Y. These might be two different evaluation methodologies or two different evaluative claims about a policy or program. It is often assumed in such debates that there must be some set of criteria independent of standpoint, personal disposition, and tradition for decisively arbitrating such disputes, that is, for showing that X is right and Y is wrong, or vice versa. These debates are an indication of the contemporary epistemological crisis in socio-political inquiry. The crisis is about defining what it means to behave rationally. The long-standing beliefs, principles, and methods of the logical positivist tradition supported the view that rational behavior was a matter of applying transhistorical criteria to the development and justification of epistemological claims. Only by doing so could we be free of bias and prejudice and thereby achieve objective knowledge. In the past fifty years or so, it has become increasingly apparent that these criteria are not to be found and, hence, our criteria-based conception of rationality is questionable.

In this crisis we face a philosophical conundrum that arises from the recognition that foundationalist epistemologies are no longer viable (e.g., Bohman, 1991b; Gordon, 1991). Philosophers of social science generally reject the epistemology of objectivism; they endorse the view "that there is no permanent, ahistorical framework to which we can ultimately appeal in determining the nature of rationality, knowledge, truth, reality, goodness, or rightness" (Bernstein, 1983, p. 8). Given the absence of indisputable rational or empirical foundations, how are we to decide among competing methodologies and different claims?

This chapter addresses the question of whether it is possible and desirable to define criteria uniformly applicable to adjudicating disputes between rival evaluation methodologies and rival evaluative claims. It explores two ways in which the question of criteria is currently addressed. The first approach draws on the resources of the very tradition that gives rise to the crisis. It defines the question as a philosophical problem requiring a criteriological solution. The second approach abandons the quest for criteria entirely. It defines the problem as one of how best to exercise moral and political judgment and seeks a solution through recovering concepts and insights from the pragmatic tradition of practical philosophy. I will suggest that criteriological solutions are fruitless and misguided, while attention to the tradition of practical reasoning holds promise as a means of successfully coping with the crisis.

Criteriology Defined

Criteriology assumes that "rational arbitration of differences needs 'criteria'" which provide "some externally defined standard, against which each [interpretation, claim, theory, and so forth] is to be weighed independently" (Taylor, 1995, p. 42, emphasis added). Criteria are considered to be decisive considerations that both parties to a dispute about competing claims must accept.

The logical positivists and the logical empiricists held that it was only by means of applying logical and empirical criteria that one was able to distinguish genuine, objective knowledge from mere belief. Their epistemology sought to realize the Cartesian dream of certain knowledge as the outcome of a rational individual's act of applying necessary and sufficient tests of truth. They were unwavering in their commitment both to the power of reason and to the certainty of empirical data. Their epistemological theory assimilated judgment to cognition.

It is widely accepted that the logical positivists' quest to establish permanent criteria and discover an indisputable foundation for knowledge proved to be unattainable. Even so, the spirit of that endeavor or, more precisely, the Cartesian dream of certainty, lingers on. Bernstein (1983, p. 71) argues that the lure or power of the quest lies in accepting a false dichotomy: *Either* we cling to the Cartesian hope that "with sufficient ingenuity we [can] discover, and state clearly and distinctly, what is the quintessence of scientific method and that we [can] specify once and for all what is the meta-framework or the permanent criteria for evaluating, justifying, or criticizing scientific hypotheses and theories *or* we must admit to a radical epistemological skepticism and, ultimately, radical relativism." This fear, or what Bernstein labels the "Cartesian anxiety," motivates the continuing quest for definitive criteria, although, generally, nonfoundational, fallibilistic epistemologies rule the day.

Criteriology then is the quest for permanent criteria of rationality founded in the desire for objectivism and in the belief that we can (or must) somehow transcend the limitations of our sociotemporal framework as individual knowers. Criteriologists argue that it is not only possible but absolutely necessary to develop regulative norms for the choice between methodologies, values, theories, claims, and conjectures. Without such norms, it would be impossible to determine whether one is behaving rationally. For criteriologists, the question of finding the right criteria is an epistemological problem. It is a question about what is true and how we can know it to be so. Correct cognition, particularly that of the individual agent, is the target of the criteriologist's inquiry.

In Pursuit of Criteriology

As shown in the following examples, criteriological solutions to the problem of rational behavior are evident in both meta-level theories of social science and evaluation (its nature and logic) and in methodological theories about the practice of social inquiry. The Tower of Babel provides us with an apt metaphor for the contemporary discussion of efforts to define criteria. It calls to mind the fact of multiple sets of criteria and raises the question of whether these multiple sets signal chaos, confusion, or an inevitable plurality of views. It speaks of the desire of some criteriologists to ascend to a god's eye point of view and thereby devise a set of universal criteria that will resolve the differences that are expressed in competing views. The confusion of Babel is analogous

to the relativists' comfort with intellectual chaos stemming from
the cacophony of multiple sets of criteria, none of which has any
legitimate claim to superiority.

Theories of Social Science/Evaluation

In the endemic debate in the social sciences between propo-
nents of *Geisteswissenschaften* and *Naturwissenschaften* it is common
to find a belief in methodological exclusivism: The view that there
exists but one proper aim and method (or set of criteria) for the
social sciences (Roth, 1987). Defenders of the unity-of-the-
sciences, for example, the strong naturalists Neurath, Nagel, Car-
nap, Popper, and Rudner as well as their critics, the anti-
naturalists Winch and Dilthey, are methodological exclusivists
and criteriologists.

Similarly, in the contemporary debate in the social sciences
between postpositivism and interpretivism, Phillips (1987; 2001),
the Popperian and defender of naturalism, is an exclusivist, as is
the anti-naturalist Taylor (1985). Each defends a one right definition, or a single set of criteria, that allegedly defines the nature of
the social scientific enterprise (although, of course, their respective
definitions or criteria are radically at odds with one another).

Other prominent examples of criteriology are evident in the
debate between qualitative and quantitative perspectives in
evaluation. In this quarrel over theories of evaluation, the works of
Guba and Lincoln (1989) and Rossi and Freeman (1993) present
two incompatible sets of criteria for defining what constitutes legitimate evaluation theory. In evaluation studies, and social science inquiry more generally, Guba and Lincoln are widely known
for their advocacy of methodological exclusivism. They explicate
what they call an axiomatic structure complete with competing
theorems through which they contrast conventional (also called,
positivist) and constructivist (also called, naturalistic) paradigms
for inquiry. They conclude that the assumptions of conventional
inquiry are ill-suited to the nature of socio-political phenomena
and claim that evaluation is best conducted using a set of constructivist assumptions and methodology. Rossi and Freeman, on
the other hand, are staunch defenders of evaluation as applied
(i.e., "conventional") social science. Moreover, Rossi (1994) has

recently argued for "separate turfs" or evaluation markets for the two opposing paradigms that he labels "connoisseurial" evaluation and "net-outcome" evaluation.

Theories About Practice

At the level of theories about practice, a variety of criteriological solutions are proposed for the problem of deciding whether a plan or design for inquiry, or whether the outcomes of an inquiry, are sound or justified. In short, there are many competing solutions to the problem of "getting it right." Several representative examples are presented below. In this discussion I consider criteria only and not the means or procedures that are advanced for achieving criteria. The criteriological solutions reviewed below are applicable to evaluation studies, even though not all specifically address evaluation studies. This is so because evaluation practice is typically viewed as a special application of social science research methodology. Criteria for deciding how to judge the relative merits of different inquiry methodologies (and, ultimately, the findings of those inquiries) apply regardless of whether the study's purpose is explanatory, descriptive, or evaluative; however, procedures or means for achieving criteria might be specific to different inquiry purposes.

'Universal' Conventional Criteria. A variety of researchers advocate applying standard, conventional criteria of validity and reliability to all forms of empirical social research regardless of specific methodology (e.g., Goetz and LeCompte, 1984; Kirk and Miller, 1986; Miles and Huberman, 1984; Phillips, 2001).[1] Particular procedures to assure the attainment of these criteria will differ depending on types of data, choice of research method, and so forth, but the criteria as ends-in-view remain the same. Yin (1994a), for example, claims that the criteria of construct validity, internal validity, external validity, and reliability are "common to all social science methods" (p. 33). He explains how these criteria (or what he calls "tests" of quality) are specifically addressed in case study designs for research and evaluation. Yin (1994b) has argued that the commonalities between qualitative and quantitative approaches to evaluation transcend their differences. He claims that both "fall within the same general rubric: social science" (p. 83), and that both share the following set of characteristics of what constitutes good evaluation: detailing evidence, addressing rival explanations, seeking results with significant implications, and demonstrating investigatory expertise in the subject matter.[2]

Alternative Criteria of Trustworthiness and Authenticity. Guba and Lincoln developed two sets of criteria for judging the quality of evaluation studies (and more broadly all social inquiries). One set, called "trustworthiness" criteria are "foundational ... because they are intended to parallel the rigor criteria that have been used within the conventional paradigm for many years" (Guba and Lincoln, 1989, p. 233). Furthermore, these are primarily "*methodological* criteria ... that speak to *methods* that can ensure one has carried out the process correctly" (p. 245). These foundational criteria of rigor are roughly the same as the conventional criteria noted by Yin above: internal validity, reliability, external validity, and objectivity. Guba and Lincoln's analogues are credibility, dependability, transferability, and confirmability.

These particular criteria, in Guba and Lincoln's view, are not entirely satisfactory for judging quality because they do not issue directly from the assumptions of the constructivist paradigm of fourth-generation evaluation. The constructivist theory of evaluation aims at developing a shared consensus (on claims, concerns, and issues surrounding a particular program) among stakeholders to the evaluation, who previously held different, and perhaps conflicting, constructions of the program. Hence, in Guba and Lincoln's view, it is more appropriate to judge the quality of evaluations based on constructivist beliefs and methodology in terms of "authenticity" criteria. According to Guba and Lincoln, these are "non-foundational" criteria and compatible with the epistemological and methodological assumptions of constructivism. These criteria do not speak solely to matters of method, but include "outcome, product, and negotiation [as] ... equally important in judging a given inquiry" (p. 245). Authenticity criteria include:

1) Fairness: "The extent to which different constructions and their underlying value structures are solicited and honored within the evaluation process."

2) Ontological authenticity: "The extent to which individual respondent's own constructions are improved, matured, expanded, and elaborated."

3) Educative authenticity: "The extent to which individual respondent's understanding of and appreciation for the constructions of others outside their stakeholding group are enhanced."

4) Catalytic authenticity: "The extent to which action is facilitated and stimulated by the evaluation process."

5) Tactical authenticity: "The degree to which stakeholders and participants are empowered to act" (Guba and Lincoln, 1989, pp. 245–50).

Pragmatic Criteria. Howe and Eisenhart (1990) have little patience with criteriological solutions that link criteria to the epistemological debate between positivism and interpretivism or constructivism. In their view, the continuing quarrel over choosing between alternative epistemologies (and consequently defining quality criteria in such terms) is pointless. Criteriology is best advanced by developing design and analysis standards that are "anchored wholly within the process of inquiry" and, hence, accommodate a variety of research methodologies (p. 3). In sum, Howe and Eisenhart, following Kaplan's (1964) well-known distinction, argue that standards should be developed in the context of research as logics-in-use rather than in terms of research as reconstructed logics.

Howe and Eisenhart acknowledge that, given the proliferation of legitimate research methodologies, any set of proposed standards must of necessity be stated at a very high level of abstraction. They propose that both qualitative and quantitative methodologies adhere to the following set of standards:

1) There must be a fit between research questions and data collection and analysis techniques.

2) Data collection and analysis techniques must be effectively applied, in a technical sense.

3) The research should demonstrate alertness to and coherence of background assumptions. In other words, assumptions derived from existing theory and/or the researcher's own dispositions and sub-

jectivity must be made explicit and it should be clear how such assumptions informed the research.

4) The overall warrant for the research findings must be made clear. The standard of overall warrant "encompasses responding to and balancing the first three standards ... as well as going beyond them to include such things as being alert to and being able to employ knowledge from outside the particular perspective and tradition within which one is working, and being able to apply general principles for evaluating arguments." (p. 7)

5) The researcher must attend both to external value constraints—i.e., considering the worth of the research and making conclusions generally accessible to the consumers of such research—and to internal value constraints—i.e., conducting the research in an ethical manner.

Subtle Realist Criteria of Validity and Relevance. Hammersley (1992), like Howe and Eisenhart, acknowledges that "while algorithmic and absolutely conclusive methods of assessment are not likely to be available, we can specify reasonable criteria that ought to be taken into account in making assessments [of the quality of social research]" (pp. 77–78). Hammersley's perspective on criteria is initially developed in the context of what constitutes good qualitative or ethnographic research. However, he claims that the criteria he identifies should be used to assess all social research.

Furthermore, like Howe and Eisenhart, Hammersley is not persuaded by Guba and Lincoln's approach to criteria. He also finds serious flaws with conventional criteria of internal and external validity and measurement reliability and validity. Hammersley's reformulation of criteria begins with the assumption that the purpose of social research is "to provide information that is both true and relevant to some legitimate public concern" (p. 68). Hence, on the basis of that definition, the two necessary and sufficient criteria in terms of which research should be judged are validity (or truth) and relevance.

The criterion of validity assumes what Hammersley calls a "subtle realism: An account is valid or true if it represents accurately those features of the phenomena that it is intended to describe, explain, or theorize" (p. 69). Although this implies a correspondence theory of truth, Hammersley argues that correspondence means "selective representation rather than reproduction of reality" (p. 69). Given that we can never know with certainty whether an account is true, "we must judge the validity of claims on the basis of the adequacy of the evidence offered in support of them" (p. 69). Hammersley offers three considerations for deciding whether the amount and kind of evidence provided is sufficient: the plausibility and credibility of claims; the centrality of the claim to the researcher's argument; the type of claim made (e.g., whether it is descriptive or explanatory).

In assessing relevance, the question of audience is important. If the inquiry is directed to the community of researchers, then aspects of relevance include the centrality of the topic studied to the substantive field and the extent to which the inquiry makes a significant contribution to the literature. When the research is addressed to an audience of practitioners, the same two aspects of relevance (importance and contribution) apply but with somewhat different implications.

Whither Criteriology?

Immanent criticism of criteriological solutions to the problem of behaving rationally reveals two major problems. First, what are often put forth as *criteria* are in actuality simply statements of important *procedures.* For example, Howe and Eisenhart proffer specification of overall warrant, alertness to and coherence of background assumptions, and so forth as criteria, yet these are actually *means* to some as yet unspecified criteria. Second, alleged criteriological solutions to the problem of choice among methodological claims (e.g., methodology X is better than methodology Y) actually provide little guidance. Assume for the sake of argument that Howe and Eisenhart have presented standards or criteria. Even if this were the case, these standards fail the test of good criteria: They are not decisive for deciding among competing claims about which is the better methodology.

Guba and Lincoln (1989) appear to solve this problem by offering two sets of criteria and by arguing "it is not appropriate to judge constructivist evaluations by positivistic criteria or standards, or vice versa" (p. 251). They base this claim on the argument that positivist and constructivist paradigms display irreconcilable axiomatic structures. However, it is hard to imagine alternative cultures or communities of inquiry on the model of alternative geometries. As Rorty notes, "alternative geometries are irreconcilable because they have axiomatic structures, and contradictory axioms. They are *designed* to be irreconcilable. Cultures are not so designed, and do not have axiomatic structures" (1985, p. 9). Guba and Lincoln commit what Rorty calls "the Cartesian fallacy of seeing axioms where there are only shared habits, of viewing statements which summarize ... practices as if they reported constraints enforcing such practices" (p. 251).

More serious problems arise from an external critique of the criteriological project. Consider, for example, that although all criteriological solutions disavow a naïve realism characteristic of empiricist methodologies, they still posit correspondence between reason (i.e., criteria) and reality as a necessary condition of rationality. This is most evident in the criteriology of Hammersley and Yin, but it is also implied in Guba and Lincoln's claim that conventional criteria are isomorphic with reality as defined by positivism, and constructivist criteria are isomorphic with reality as defined by constructivism.

Furthermore, assume for the sake of argument that criteriologists do provide a variety of viable criteria-based solutions to the problem of choosing between methodologies or choosing between competing claims. But how to decide which of *these* approaches is right? It will not do to say that all criteriological solutions share some common standards expressed in slightly different language. Suppose, for example, validity is held to be a central criterion. Validity is hardly held to mean the same thing by its defenders. Campbell's (1986) definition of this concept, for example, is not the same as Hammersley's that, in turn, differs from the Cronbach (1982) and Krathwohl (1993) interpretations, and so on. And none of these interpretations are the same as that of Guba and Lincoln. Hammersley emphasizes something similar to construct validity; Campbell places a premium on internal validity, particularly what he calls local molar causal validity. Cronbach, on the other hand, is more concerned with external inferences and argues that evaluation researchers should maximize relevance rather than internal validity. A notion like validity is discursive and can be variously interpreted from the perspectives of psychometrics, ethnography, the interpretive analytics of Foucault, and so on (Cherryholmes, 1988; Schwandt, 2001a). Whether one finds any of these particular discourses persuasive depends on political considerations as much as it does on traditional kinds of evidence and argument.

Criteriological solutions do not assume that, in foundationalist fashion, the assessment of competing claims is a simple matter of mechanical application of rules. Thus, they accept a nonfoundational epistemology. However, as J. K. Smith (1993) observes, the acceptance of nonfoundationalism does not cast doubt on the importance of the search for criteria in the epistemological project. The belief persists that rationality *must* be a matter of applying criteria, even given that any particular set of criteria are always to be regarded as provisional and subject to revision. Criteria are means for approximating regulative ideals like truth and objectivity—ideals for which we strive but which we can only imperfectly attain at any given time. To believe otherwise is to admit to skepticism or relativism (or worse, nihilism).

Those habits of intellectual life that characterize the endeavors of social scientists to define criteriological theories of and about social scientific practice are best regarded as "nurtured by the Enlightenment, and justified by it in terms of an appeal to Reason, conceived as a transcultural human ability to correspond to reality, a faculty whose possession and use is demonstrated by obedience to explicit criteria" (Rorty, 1985, p. 11). So conceived, criteriology is the bid to find an objective way out of the crisis of objectivism because it draws on the resources of the very project of epistemology that gives rise to the crisis to begin with.

Criteriologists do not give up hope of some meta-ground on which the debate between competing claims about methodologies (or about criteria themselves) can be settled. They regard the conflict over criteria as the result of error; error that must in the long run be eliminated if we are to achieve intersubjective agreement on the right criteria and, ultimately, the right interpretation. This belief in error elimination—that inquiry will eventually converge on the truth—is familiar to Popperians. It has recently been resurrected in the methodological strategy of critical multiplism in evaluation (e.g., Cook, 1985; Sechrest, Babcock, and Smith, 1993). Critical multiplism appears to be a kind of methodological pluralism—an endorsement of multiple research frameworks, strategies, methods, and criteria. On closer inspection, however, critical multiplism is not accepting of a plurality of points of view, for its

liminate different perspectives in the long run, converge
th, and thereby reveal the correct interpretation of some
itical phenomenon. A critical multiplist approach is perfectly ~ igned with criteriology.

This belief in the convergence of inquiry characteristic of criteriological solutions contrasts sharply with genuine methodological
pluralism. Defenders of pluralism accept that criteria are employed to determine "getting it right," but hold that there is no
single set of criteria by which to define what constitutes quality
research or evaluation. Rather, there are multiple sets, each inter-
nally valid with respect to the assumptions from which it is derived and the methodology it supports (Morgan, 1983; Roth,
1987). Supremacy is not claimed for any specific set of criteria for
defining what constitutes quality.

This pluralistic point of view is gaining popularity among
evaluators disaffected by the highly partisan ideological battles
that were waged in years past between defenders of so-called
qualitative and quantitative epistemological paradigms. Pluralists
define evaluation as a multi-paradigm, multi-methodological, and
multi-method practice. M. L. Smith (1994), for example, claims
that there is no last word in social science inquiry; that we need to
critique the methods and inferences of different approaches to
evaluation each on its own terms. She adds that there are multiple
ways to construe the validity of evaluation findings including
structural corroboration, ecological validity, catalytic validity,
consequential validity, and so forth.

Accepting multiple methodologies and criteria as a way of life,
as a situation that we must simply live with rather than get over,
as Rorty might say, means not equating pluralism with confusion,
chaos, or skepticism. Rather, it is an endorsement of a thorough-
going fallibilism. As salutary and refreshing as this view may be,
pluralism per se is more useful as a description of the current state
of affairs than a solution to the normative problem posed by Babel—a multitude of strange voices each advocating a different
point of view—how to choose?

define

Philosophy professor, coin
doctrine that nothing can be known for certain; that
is, there is no infallible knowledge, but there can still
be knowledge. We need not have logically conclusive
justifications for what we know.

An Alternative to Criteriology

The crisis in defining what it means to behave rationally in the face of multiple and conflicting methodologies and criteria cannot be solved using the resources of the epistemological project. The problem must be recast not as a problem of knowledge and truth but as an ethical-political problem of judgment and action under conditions of contingency and uncertainty. In so doing, it may be possible to see that behaving rationally is no more or less than a kind of "criterionless muddling through" (Rorty, 1985, p. 11). We might be able to imagine that what matters most is how we respond to or cope with the conflict of competing views, not that we achieve substantive permanent consensus on criteria.

From a philosophical point of view, an alternative to criteriology arises from the challenge of the pragmatic-hermeneutic tradition to the entire analytic project. R. J. Bernstein (1991) explains that this tradition accepts anti-foundationalism and a thorough-going fallibilism (but not epistemological skepticism) as an alternative to foundationalism. Further, it is keenly aware of and sensitive to "radical contingency and chance that mark the universe, our inquiries, and our lives" (p. 328). Finally, it accepts the fact that there is no escaping the plurality of traditions, perspectives, and philosophical orientations.

Redefining Social Inquiry

In the tradition of analytic reason, social inquiry is conceived of as a science characterized by the pursuit of empirical theory; the disinterested attitude of the empirical inquirer; the categorical separation of theory and practice or action; and, the categorical distinction between fact and value. All of these features figure prominently in portraying the social scientist's task as that of accurately and objectively explaining and describing socio-political phenomena but *not* making any prescriptive or normative claims (R. J. Bernstein, 1976). To accomplish that task well, social science has been in search of the correct method (a set of unambiguous criteria or rules), the correct application of which will lead to genuine knowledge claims.

A redefinition of social inquiry as a form of practical philosophy or practical reasoning challenges this conventional understanding in a number of ways. It thereby encourages a concomitant turning away from criteriological solutions to the problem of rational behavior. It criticizes the central preoccupation with method. Criteriology seeks to justify social scientific inquiry (including evaluation studies) by means of a theory of method that specifies objective criteria for both choice of methodology and assessment of knowledge claims; it is dedicated to finding the right criteria for making the right choice in each situation. It venerates method as the only legitimate grounds for the development of criteria for rationality. Recall that criteriology is premised on the belief that conflict between methodologies or between competing claims is the result of error. Formulating criteria of scientific method is held to be the best way to eliminate such error. This is so because method is regarded as an innocent or epistemologically neutral tool. Therefore, it is thought to be immune to criticism on the grounds of competing interests or commitments.

In this scenario, scientific rationalism is inescapably coupled with the *vita methodi* (Wolin, 1972)—the application of permanent, universal rules or criteria that demarcate genuine scientific knowledge from ideology or metaphysical concerns. Rationality on this view is procedural: To be a rational agent is a matter of observing or applying these rules or criteria. This view seeks to eliminate moral and political judgment from rational argumentation and to limit the latter to the correct exercise of procedural reason.

The new conversation about human rationality (R. J. Bernstein, 1983) abandons this theory-centered preoccupation with criteria and rules. It seeks to return to a practice-centered conception of rationality replete with the conflict of interests, values, and opinions. The everyday ideal of being reasonable or open to reason replaces the quest for a logical or scientific rationalism. This new conversation is premised on a return to a concern for practice. Aristotle (*Ethics*, book VI, chap. 5 and 8) argued that social inquiry, inquiry into moral and political life, is a distinctive form of human activity (*praxis*) that requires a kind of knowledge that can only be acquired through guided experience. This knowledge is *phronesis*, prudence, or practical wisdom and is not the same as scientific knowledge. Scholars across different disciplines (e.g., Bellah, 1983; R. J. Bernstein, 1991; Flyvbjerg, 2001; Gadamer, 1981; Rorty, 1982, 1983; Sullivan, 1983; Taylor, 1985) seek to recapture in various ways this Aristotelian vision of social inquiry as a form of practical reasoning. Sullivan (1983) summarizes the view as follows:

> Human investigation has an ineluctable moral, indeed political, as well as a philosophical dimension. This is because it not only takes place within the cultural matrix but has direct and indirect effects on the understanding of those living within the world it seeks to clarify. The objective of the human sciences is the deepening of our understanding of what it means to live a human life. That understanding conditions the whole matrix of questions and themes within which the investigation proceeds. (p. 304)

Conceptions of the aim of social inquiry are now being shaped not by the demand for a "neutral, objectifying science of human life and action" (Taylor, 1987, p. 472) or for *theoria* and *episteme*, but by the search for a better understanding of *praxis* and *phronesis*. The kind of investigation required here must attend to both ethical and political concerns (ethical because *praxis* [action] is defined by habits, modes of thought, customs, and mores; political because action is public, it is concerned with our lives in the polis (R. J. Bernstein, 1991). The rationality of everyday life (and the rationality of social scientific practice itself) is regarded as intrinsically dialogical and communicative. Of course, all of these ideas are subject to different interpretations (cf. Hiley, Bohman, Shusterman, 1991). At least we can see the outline of a different conception of social inquiry emerging.

Features of Social Inquiry as Practical Philosophy

By drawing on the tradition of practical philosophy it is possible to fashion a kind of human inquiry that is both descriptive and normative. This inquiry is concerned with "improving the rationality of a particular practice by enabling practitioners to refine the rationality of the practice for themselves" (Carr, 1995, p. 118). Various forms of action inquiry, collaborative inquiry, and critical feminist inquiry seem generally to embrace this view. Characteristics of social inquiry drawing on practical philosophy include the following:

First, the form of argumentation appropriate to practice is not that suggested by criteriology but what Taylor (1995) calls the *ad hominem* model of practical reason. In this way of reasoning, competing claims or interpretations are not evaluated against some external standard. Rather, we portray the passage or transition from one interpretation to the other as a gain in knowledge, "a step from a less good to a better understanding of the phenomenon in question" (p. 42). That gain takes the form of eliminating error or a confusion that a claim relies on, identifying or resolving a contradiction in a claim, or acknowledging the importance of some factor that the original claim screened out.[3]

When rationality is no longer defined as an act of applying criteria or following rules of method, it becomes possible to explore conversation and deliberation, conflicting opinions and choice as enduring characteristics of rational behavior in social inquiry. A focus on judgment, interpretation, and deliberation is, in R. J. Bernstein's (1983) view, a (the only?) legitimate response to fallibilism and "to the irreducibility of conflict grounded in human plurality"; that pluralism, in turn, requires "we seek to discover some common ground through debate, conversation, and dialogue" (p. 223).

Thus, a second characteristic of social inquiry as practical philosophy is that inquirers seek to establish a dialogical relationship of openness with participants in an inquiry. This is not simply a methodological and/or political move as it usually is defined in interpretive inquiry and participatory approaches to evaluation. Rather, this relationship reflects a commitment to rationality as dialogue, and thus it is a kind of moral-political framework that sets limits to the kinds of tasks to be performed in the inquiry and the ways in which they will be implemented (Smaling, 1995).

Third, inquirers view the participants in an inquiry (e.g., managers, administrators, teachers, laborers) as themselves engaged in performing a practical art (e.g., Amy, 1984; Barber, 1988; Holt, 1987; Schön, 1983). As such, the practice requires decisions based on what is judged to be good in a given situation. These decisions derive from interpretations of the case at hand, not from applying explanations (general knowledge) warranted by social scientific theory. This conception of practice emphasizes contextualism—a careful consideration of the immediate situation in which judgments are made—and it views the practice itself as proceeding pedagogically, not technically (Habermas, 1973).[4]

Fourth, the aim of such inquiry is not to replace practitioners' commonsense knowledge of their respective and joint practices with allegedly more sophisticated, theoretical, scientific knowledge but to encourage practitioners to critically reflect upon and reappraise their common-sense knowledge (e.g., Carr, 1995). This kind of inquiry involves teaching participants to engage in a type of reflection that is quite different from technical means-end reasoning. This form of reasoning is practical reasoning. The point of engaging in practical reasoning is to improve a particular practice by reflecting on the values (or internal aims or goods) of that practice. Elliott (1991) explains this as follows:

> Reflection directed towards the realization of values might be described as practical philosophy. Such a description directs our attention to the role reflective critiques of the value interpretations embedded in practice can play in improving it. Such philosophical critiques enable practitioners to continuously reconstruct their concepts of value in ways which progressively illuminate practical problems and possibilities. (p. 51)

When evaluators participate in such critiques, this reflective examination of practice ought to be symmetrical. That is, it ought to involve evaluators reflecting on *their* particular forms of social practice as a consequence of their involvement in helping participants in a study engage in reflection on their respective practice. In this way, social inquiry is not simply *research on* the practice or practical reasoning of its subjects. Rather, it is itself an exercise in practical philosophy. A concern with *praxis* and practical reasoning characterizes not only the object of investigation for inquiry, but the practice of inquiry itself. Stated a bit differently, social inquiry seeks to examine a dialogical encounter dialogically. It is inquiry as conversation about deliberation, conflicting opinions, and choice of the values or internal aims of a particular practice. These are enduring characteristics of rational behavior in both social inquiry and the practices social inquiry examines.

Finally, social inquiry as dialogical or practical reasoning is in part continuous with the project of modernity. It does not so much seek to overcome modernity as to give it new meaning (Carr, 1995; Taylor, 1995; Toulmin, 1990). We retain the Enlightenment insight regarding the importance of self-clarity about our nature as knowing agents or actors as a way to become rationally empowered to transform ourselves. However, we seek to adopt a better and more critically defensible notion of what this entails by criticizing the foundationalist Enlightenment narrative in which that ideal took shape.

Judging the Goodness of Social Inquiry as Practical Philosophy

To make this turn toward social inquiry as practical philosophy requires a different way of judging the goodness of this undertaking and its product. Traditional criteria-based solutions to judging legitimate knowledge are of little help when the central concern is the problem of political judgment and action under conditions of uncertainty. Rather than use the term "criteria," in what follows, I employ the term "guiding ideal" that shapes the aim of the practice and a set of "enabling conditions" that characterize the practice.

The guiding ideal that informs the aim of the practice of social inquiry as practical philosophy is quite opposed to the guiding ideal that informs traditional social scientific inquiry. Taylor (1985) notes that the "adoption of a framework for explanation [in socio-political] inquiry carries with it the adoption of the value-slope implicit in it" (p. 75). The value-slope of traditional social scientific inquiry is theory-centered, value-neutral, atomistic, disengaged, instrumental reason (although, of course, traditional social science claimed to have no value-slope whatsoever.) By contrast, the value-slope of social inquiry as practical philosophy is democracy, understood as a moral ideal not a set of formal procedures (R. J. Bernstein, 1985; House and Howe, 1999).

It is, of course, too simple to claim democracy as a moral ideal without acknowledging that what constitutes the practice of democracy is contested. In the United States, for example, there is much debate over whether democracy is best understood in terms of the merits of liberalism with its emphasis on negative liberty, in terms of the suppressed tradition of civic republicanism with its emphasis on participatory freedom, or as one of the versions of deliberative democracy. Stated simply, the guiding ideal or meta-value of democracy itself requires constant critique and evaluation. As R. J. Bernstein (1991) has pointed out in his critique of Rorty, we must be careful not to accept without question the idea of democracy as a set of historical practices. To do so is to substitute a historical myth of the given for what was under positivism the epistemological myth of the given. This is a subtle point, for Bernstein is not claiming here that there must be criteria, rules, or standards for deciding what constitutes democracy as a moral ideal. He is insisting that it will not suffice to cite various examples to define the ideal; we must confront the question "By virtue of what is some particular example an instance of democracy?"

Several kinds of enabling conditions are required both to sustain the debate over the constitution of the moral ideal of democracy itself and simultaneously to facilitate the dialogical encounter that is the exercise of social inquiry as practical philosophy. Of course, in keeping with the pragmatic, fallibilistic character of practical reasoning, all of these enabling conditions are themselves subject to revision. First, deliberation and dialogue are not simply an exchange of views or an effort to reach intersubjective agreement. Barber (1988) explains that judgment "entails not simply the congruence of opinions arrived at by independent individuals, but the integrity of a single whole judgment produced by the interaction of independent opinions" (p. 203). The feminist philosopher Seller (1988) adds that the kind of knowledge sought is the kind that requires contributions from all members in the encounter; knowledge is produced in the questioning and exchanging of views that take place within the conversation.

Second, the decision to engage in the act of deliberation through conversation is a moral and political commitment to a community of interpreters. R. J. Bernstein (1991) explains that to take one's own fallibility seriously means that we must be willing to listen to others without denying or suppressing the other or his/her views. We must not seek refuge in the framework of our own theories, expectations, past experiences, language, and so forth. "To the extent that this does happen," Bernstein claims, "it is primarily an *ethical* failure rather than a cognitive or linguistic one" (p. 336).

Third, the activity of deliberation is inescapably rhetorical in character. We aim to persuade other interpreters of a particular interpretation through a discourse that is characterized by such qualities as coherence, expansiveness, interpretive insight, relevance, rhetorical force, beauty and texture of argument, and so forth (Alexander, 1987). We do not simply affirm that the facts speak for themselves. The conversation among interpreters is an act of persuasion and involves using language infected by partisan agendas and interests. However, the free play of perspective, bias, and interest does not signal relativism, for as Mallioux (1990) explains: "We are always arguing at particular moments in specific places to certain audiences. Our beliefs and commitments are no less real because they are historical, and the same holds for our interpretations. If no foundationalist theory will resolve disagreements ... we must argue our cases. In fact, that is all we can ever do" (p. 134).

Fourth, the kind of argumentation characteristic of a community of interpreters is not principally adversarial and confrontational. Parties to the encounter are not viewed as opponents who seek to expose the weaknesses in each other's arguments. Rather, the conversation begins with the assumption that "the other has something to say to us and to contribute to our understanding. The initial task is to grasp the other's position in the strongest possible light. One must always attempt to be responsive to what the other is saying and showing .... The other is not an adversary or opponent, but a conversational partner" (R. J. Bernstein, 1991, p. 337).

Fifth, the discourse of dialogical interpretation requires supplementing a problem-solving style of cognition with a way of thinking that values imagination and possibility. Prawat (1993), a cognitive psychologist, has argued that problem-solving learning schemata downplay the transformative role of experience. They tend to define the world as a series of impediments or obstacles that the individual must overcome. Hence, the idea of practical problem solving readily lends itself to strategic knowledge and strategic thinking. Strategic or frame-based systems for learning, in turn, place a premium on assimilation of new ideas and information to existing schemata; they are structure-conserving processes of thinking. They allow little room for the possibility of speaking differently, of recognizing the ability of thought to transform itself, and so forth.

Finally, although not a set of enabling conditions per se, a new vocabulary may be used to express more adequately what it means to be reasonable without equating reasonableness and rationality with scientific rationalism. Goodman and Elgin (1988) respond to the epistemological crisis over defining rational behavior by suggesting that we "overhaul [our philosophical] conceptual equipment" (p. 154). They propose a new working vocabulary to replace notions of truth, certainty, and knowledge. They find the term *truth* to be an excessively narrow notion and propose *rightness* as a concept with greater reach: "Truth [of verbal statements] is but one among the factors—along with others such as relevance, effect, and useability—that sometimes enter into the rightness of what is said. Truth is an occasional ingredient in rightness" (p. 157). They suggest that the term *certainty*—"a pretentious muddle of the psychological and the pseudological—is unsalvageable" and propose that we use the term *adoption:* "We can adopt habits, strategies, vocabularies, styles, as well as statements .... Adoption is a matter of putting to work, of making or trying to make fit" (p. 159). Finally, they suggest we use the term *understanding* rather than *knowledge* because it is a more versatile term that allows us to refer to a skill, a process, or an accomplishment.

On the Social Role of Inquiry as Practical Philosophy

Left unsaid thus far is how to evaluate the outcomes of inquiry conceived independently of the quest for criteria and how to locate this kind of inquiry in the spectrum of professional social science. If rational behavior in social inquiry is not equated with scientific rationalism—that is, with the possession of some special method or criteria for discriminating genuine knowledge from mere belief—but founded instead in the ordinary actions of everyday people as they struggle to come to terms with conflicting views and opinions, then professional social inquiry cannot claim special status based on special knowledge. In effect, social inquiry as

practical philosophy decenters the cultural authority of the professional practice of social scientific inquiry. To the extent that we
do not privilege method or criteria, then "we shall be able to see
the social sciences as continuous with literature—as interpreting
other people to us, and thus enlarging and deepening our sense of
community" (Rorty, 1982, p. 203).

Of course, we cannot simply naïvely decree that social inquiry
is now synonymous with literature. We are not free to ignore how
the social sciences have served and continue to serve as conceptual practices of power. On the contrary, displacing scientific or
logical rationalism with the everyday ideal of being reasonable
should encourage us to examine how politics work in and through
and not simply on social science (Harding, 1992). Traditionally,
the concern with politics has been limited to examining how politics challenges the neutrality of social scientific practice and how
social science is incorporated into the political process of policy
making. As Smith (1990a) has shown, largely ignored is how
power and politics work *through* the dominant institutional structures, priorities, practices, and languages of social science to
shape our conceptions of society, social problems, solutions to
problems, and the like.

Decentering social scientific theorizing in society's efforts to
address social problems is described by Lindbloom (1990) as
moving from a scientifically guided society to a self-guided society. In the former, social science is at center stage and we assume
that "social problem solving, social betterment, or guided social
change … call above all for scientific observation of human social
behavior" (p. 214). However, in a self-guided society, social science plays only a supporting role in a more amorphous kind of
investigation undertaken by laypeople and functionaries. This
kind of problem solving is inescapably characterized by aesthetic,
prudential, and moral, as well as more conventionally scientific,
considerations. According to Lindbloom, it entails probing, often
simultaneously, into questions of means-end relationships, moral
considerations of how we should live, considerations of the capacities and limits of people and environments, and questions of
what to believe and what kind of evidence to require as a condition of belief. It is a "broad, diffuse, open-ended, mistake-making
social or interactive process" that is both cognitive and political

and requires "wide-spread inquiry and knowledge that even at their best will not look very scientific in the conventional sense" (p. 7). Against this backdrop we can point to three kinds of considerations that might be used to evaluate the goodness of the product or outcome of social inquiry as practical philosophy.

The first consideration, as suggested by Lindbloom (1990) and Pålshaugen (1994) is that social inquiry ought to generate knowledge that complements or supplements rather than displaces lay probing of social problems. Precisely what the relevant content of that knowledge should be requires more careful consideration. Gustavsen (1992), for example, argues that relevant content is information about the process of change and development. I suggest that it may well include teaching about practical philosophy and strong evaluation.

Second, the outcome of social inquiry as practical philosophy can be judged in terms of whether the social inquirer or inquiry team is successful at cultivating critical intelligence in parties to the encounter. May (1992) defines critical intelligence as the capacity to engage in moral critique. Typically, we think of social inquirers as cultivating forms of operational intelligence in their subjects. This kind of intelligence is instruction on means-end reasoning, on how to get to there from here. In contrast, critical intelligence is the ability to question whether the there is worth getting to. It requires not simply the ability to understand strategies and implement procedures but the willingness and ability to debate the value of various ends of a practice. The inquirer ought to teach in such a way as to encourage the development of this capacity for critical intelligence.

Third, as a contributor to the discourse on social science, the social inquirer qua practical philosopher can be evaluated on the success with which her or his reports of the inquiry enable the education of human judgment. The crucial issue in practical philosophy is the application of general principles to particular cases. As Aristotle (*Ethics*, Book VI, chap. 5) explained, moral and political life requires a sort of knowledge that can only be acquired through guided experience. This knowledge is practical wisdom or *phronesis*. There can be no scientific theory of practical wisdom or judgment. That is, we will not be able to state rules in propositional form that will direct us in linking the general to the particular or the theoretical to the practical. We can, however, train that kind of determining judgment through the study of particular cases. Hence, the social inquirer as practical philosopher must endeavor to prepare accounts that are useful in training the capacity for practical wisdom. These accounts "produce *regional,* or with respect to conditions, *relative knowledge*" (Feyerabend, 1987, p. 167).

It is unlikely that we will literally *resolve* the epistemological crisis of what it means to behave rationally in the face of competing methodologies or claims. Resolution denotes removing or explaining away doubts and bringing something to a conclusion. If dispelling doubt requires the drawing of sharp distinctions, the opposing of a one right way to all other inferior ways, and so on, then resolution is not likely imminent, for the very notion of resolution itself is part of the legacy of the epistemological project. It is more likely that we will simply get beyond or get over the crisis by learning that it is possible to recast the problem that lies before us. The problem now defined as the quest for criteria becomes the problem of how to cultivate practical reasoning. For this redefined problem we seek answers not in the following of procedures, the definition of first principles, the specification of criteria, and the like. Rather, we look to consequences and outcomes of our ways of deliberating.

Although the foundational, criteriological project of epistemology may be bankrupt that does not mean we can forgo the issue of defining, acting upon, and justifying a choice about the proper aim of social inquiry. Saying farewell to criteriology means looking to the practices, consequences, and outcomes of our ways of deliberating as a basis for forming a new kind of social inquiry. The greatest threat to this proposal is not relativism or cynicism, but the disbelief in shared values that make possible dialogical, interpretive, democratic communities of inquirers intent on improving their practices.

Notes

1   In the second edition of this book, LeCompte and Preissle (1993) qualify their earlier view and present the concept of validity in qualitative research as a complex matter. They claim that "Making the qualitative approach to validity analogous to that used in quantitative investigations may distort the very features of qualitative design that contribute something special to the human sciences" (p. 330). They explore the application of conventional notions of reliability and validity to qualitative research, but now claim that this examination is largely metaphorical and useful principally for examining the shortcomings in criteria and procedures across quantitative and qualitative approaches to inquiry.

2   The characteristics identified by Yin appear to be more like procedures than criteria. Echoing Yin's call for compatibility, Datta (1994) claims that we may be headed towards a third paradigm in evaluation; a mixed-methods (quantitative and qualitative) model of practice. However, whether conventional criteria or some set of criteria unique to this new paradigm would apply is not yet clear.

3   Taylor (1995, p. 52–53) offers the following example of what this reasoning looks like in everyday life: Imagine the case of a teenager, Pete, who is acting impossibly at home, screaming at his parents, being rude and arrogant with his younger siblings, and feeling resentment all the time. Pete's claim is that he feels a constant sense of being cheated out of his rights. He feels that something more is owed to him as the eldest, and he resents not getting it. Pete repeats this claim both to his parents and his social worker. Pete and his parents begin to talk out his claim (which is at once both cognitive and emotional) and Pete changes his view. He comes to a new view that his previous behavior was unjustified, and that one should not behave that way toward people. Taylor concludes that Pete has

> gone through a moral change; his views of what people owe each other in the family have altered. He's confident that this change represents moral growth, because it came about through dissipating a confused, largely unconsciously held belief, one that couldn't survive his recognizing its real nature... This is...the commonest form of practical reasoning in our lives... [It] is a form of argument where the appeal to criteria [to decide which of Pete's views is the 'correct' one], or even to the differentiated performance of the rival views in relation to some decisive consideration, is quite beside the point. Here the ad hominem mode of argument is at its most intense, and most fruitful. (p.53)

4   It is important to note here an approach to social inquiry that appears to
         take seriously this turn to human action and practical philosophy but does
         so only in a very limited way. An abiding concern for the life world—that
         is for various kinds of social practices and ways of life as they are actu-
         ally experienced (or lived, felt, and undergone) by participants in those
         practices or life ways—has long been the interest of interpretive social
         science approaches. By *interpretive* I mean those ways of conceiving of the
         human sciences that have their origins in Dilthey's *Lebensphilosophie*, We-
         ber's interpretive sociology, the phenomenology of Schutz and followers
         including the ethnomethodologists, and ideas drawn from the linguistic
         philosophy of Winch. These are the intellectual sources of much of the kind
         of social inquiry that is identified as ethnographic, qualitative, interpre-
         tive, phenomenological, field- or case-based, and so on. These inquiries,
         for the most part, cling to objectivating approaches in investigating lived
         reality. To be sure, these approaches advocate entering the world of human
         actors via participant observation and attending carefully to the ways in
         which participants define their situation. However, they treat human ac-
         tion as an *object* of understanding. Understanding the subjective meaning of
         human action is the result of some method of *verstehen* that demands a kind
         of closeness to the phenomena that facilitates access to actors' ways of
         meaning making. Giddens (1993), Habermas (1988), and Outhwaite (1975)
         have pointed out that interpretivist philosophies treat human action
         largely as meaning not as *praxis*. Human action is viewed as the object of
         the social inquirer's understanding. That understanding is forthcoming
         from grasping the meaning that resides in that action. Traditional interpre-
         tive social inquiry remains largely descriptive, objectifying, and theory-
         focused: descriptive in that it offers careful documentation of human action
         and life ways but does not engage in normative critique; objectifying be-
         cause it treats the meaning of human action as an object that stands over
         and against the activity of the knowing subject; theory-focused because it
         aims ultimately at empirical, explanatory theories of that action. (Of
         course, in postmodern ethnography all aspects of this traditional approach
         are being contested.) It is only with the advent of the philosophical herme-
         neutics of Heidegger and Gadamer and the critical hermeneutics of Haber-
         mas that the focus shifts away from method as the basis for knowing and
         that human inquiry is framed as action-oriented self-understanding.

7

Promises and Perils of the Evaluator as Strong Poet

In *The Call of Stories*, Robert Coles (1989) relates a story about his first year as a psychiatric resident at Massachusetts General Hospital. Coles was assigned to work with two senior psychoanalysts to discuss his treatment of patients, one of whom the residents called "the hiker." She was a tall, thin, intensely driven, black-haired woman, who paced the halls continuously and ate her food while standing upright, keeping her feet always moving.

One of Coles's supervisors, Dr. Binger, urged him to read more in the literature so that he could understand the nature of phobias and thereby derive an explanation for the particular fears that haunted this woman. Coles described Binger as vigorously analytic in his approach. He urged Coles to probe for the psychodynamics at work in the patient's mind, to formulate the problem and to get a fix on it by determining what factors or variables were at work, and then to decide on an appropriate therapeutic agenda.

At the same time Coles also reported to Dr. Ludwig, whom Coles thought to be a bit odd. In their first meeting, Ludwig told Coles he was going to tell him a story, and he proceeded to relate a tale of one of his own patients, a woman virtually paralyzed by her fears and worries. As Coles listened, Ludwig told of the events in this woman's life, how and where she met her husband, where she traveled and why, where she spent her spare time and with whom. By the time Ludwig finished, Coles was quite drawn into the tale of this woman's life, but he was puzzled by what any of this had to do with treating the patient.

At the close of their meeting Ludwig remarked: "The people who come to see us bring us their stories. They hope they tell them well enough so that we understand the truth of their lives. They hope we know how to interpret their stories correctly. We have to remember that what we hear is their story." Ludwig urged the young resident to focus his attention on the concrete details of his patient's narrative and to put aside for a while the idea of formulating the woman's problem.

Coles found this suggestion rather strange and did not know quite what to make of it in light of his training in psychiatric theory and symptomatology. After all, he reasoned, hadn't I already taken the patient's family and clinical history? Nonetheless, he followed Ludwig's advice. Haltingly at first, for he did not know how to question his patient in such a way that she would tell of her life, Coles managed to conduct a series of open-ended interviews with the woman, and she began to reveal aspects of her life of which she had never spoken before.

There is much more to this story, but for present purposes I need mention only that under Ludwig's tutelage, Coles began to explore other aspects of this narrative approach to psychiatric treatment, a way of healing that was so very different from formulating the patient's problem and searching for explanations using theoretical constructs as Dr. Binger encouraged.

This story offers a clue to a different way of thinking about the nature and practice of evaluation. Much current thinking about evaluation is preoccupied, to borrow a notion from Rorty (1989, p. 51), with the question, "How do you know?" Like Dr. Binger in Coles's story, evaluators seek explanations for how and why programs and policies work, or they aim to make statements of the value of such programs. In either case, the critical issue is the kind of knowledge claim that an evaluator is responsible for making and the kind of method that is offered as justification for that knowledge. The evaluator's model is the scientist who conceives of reasons for his explanations as warrants tied to claims of validity. The discourse that is taken most seriously is the discourse of technical expertise (Fisher, 1987).

Dr. Ludwig, on the other hand, like the poet and storyteller, stresses interpretation over the making of justified knowledge claims and invites us to consider a broader question, namely how we come to endow experience with meaning. We might imagine Ludwig's hero to be the antithesis of the modern analyst or consultant, or what Heidegger called the "calculative thinker, a person who 'computes'—weighs, measures, and counts—possibilities, benefits, and outcomes, but does not contemplate the meaning which reigns in everything that is" (Sullivan, 1986, pp. 65–66).

Familiar Terrain

Despite the existence of different models for evaluating educational and social programs, technical and scientific notions largely shape the ways we think about and conduct evaluation. Several features of that legacy bear emphasis.

For the most part, evaluation practice is defined as a cognitive activity. That is, its principal, and some might say only, concern is the production of *knowledge about* programs. To know about a program is to account for its activity and outcomes by means of a reductive explanation: The everyday lived experience and complexity of a reading program, a staff development program, a curriculum, and so forth are reduced to their analytic elements or component parts—that is, their dependent, independent, and moderator variables; the relevant demographic characteristics of their participants; their context; their outcomes; the decisions to be made by their developers, administrators, funders, and so forth.

Perhaps unwittingly for the evaluator in everyday practice, epistemological guidance here is provided by Hobbes for whom knowledge was something one has, not—as Aristotle claimed—something one does. In classical thought, knowledge of human affairs was an aspect of a *relationship* between the knower and the known. Knowledge was always a knowing *with* the other; it required a kind of participation and involvement. As Sullivan (1986) explains, Aristotle distinguished *techne* from *phronesis*:

> *Techne* refers to the kind of knowledge associated with a craft, in which the producer is in complete charge of his material and forms it in accord with a preconceived plan. By contrast, knowledge of human action, *praxis*, requires a kind of participation and involvement Aristotle called *phronesis* or prudence. Unlike *techne*, practical activity and practical knowing were understood as skills that cannot be set aside at will. That is, one does not, indeed cannot 'rest' from applying one's sensitivities about how to live. They have become essential parts of one's personal-

ity, so that a person is who he or she is only through exhibiting a kind of practical understanding and skill. Practical knowledge forms the personality of its practitioner and so is inseparable from his/her identity. (pp. 65–66)

The effect of Hobbes's project to redefine knowledge in the human sciences as knowing *about* objects was to exclude this moral dimension from the activity of knowing—that is, to divorce questions of ethics from matters of epistemology. Hence, the conception of knowledge in the social sciences and in evaluation today is much closer to the activity of Dr. Binger in Coles's story than it is to what Dr. Ludwig had in mind in his conversations with Coles.

The absence of this moral dimension effectively separates knowing from being (thereby honoring the calculative intellect over mere emotions). In terms of evaluation, the key activity thus becomes one of effectively employing what Bruner (1986, p. 13) calls the propositional mode of thought that "leads to good theory, tight analysis, logical proof, sound argument, and empirical discovery guided by reasoned hypothesis." The mystery of how best to live a moral-political life (the distinctive kind of human activity and the special kind of knowledge it demands) is no longer within the immediate purview of evaluation knowing defined in this mode.

Moral concerns are eclipsed from evaluators' rational-world paradigm and its discourse of argument. This point needs to be clearly understood. I am not saying that evaluators are indifferent or insensitive to moral concerns in the conduct of their work. They do address moral problems such as balanced reporting, the potentially harmful effects of the early release of information, the protection of respondents' rights, and so forth. Nor am I claiming that program administrators or managers, as individuals, are blind to moral dilemmas in their lives. What I am claiming is that given the legacy of seventeenth- and eighteenth-century thinkers like Hobbes and Locke, both evaluators and program managers view the enterprise of evaluation as well as the program to be evaluated as amoral instrumentalities—in other words, as simply means to an end. Programs are means to desired outcomes; evaluation is a means of determining whether desired outcomes are achieved.

The eclipse of the union of knowing and being is both constituted by and constitutes evaluators' modern role and their commitment to the instrumental use of evaluation. The modus operandi of the evaluator is spectator and scribe. The evaluator as spectator, as noted earlier, is generating knowledge about the program in question. Although empathetic with and respectful of program participants, evaluators remain apart from the program being investigated, invoking metaphors of vision to explain their work. Knowledge about the program being evaluated comes from "seeing," as the Greek root *eidos* remind us. The evaluator knows because he or she "observed," "inspected," or "focused on" the program, not because the evaluator participated in the lived experience of the program.

In keeping with this posture as spectator, the evaluator functions as the objective scribe—the official writer or clerk—who records observations about program activities and dutifully notes participants' impressions. As Nagel explains, the essential aspect of this objective stance is detachment: "The attempt is made to view the world not from a place within it, or from the vantage point of a special type of life or awareness, but from nowhere in particular and no form of life in particular at all" (1981, p. 208). This externalist stance—separating self from the object of inquiry—is essential, for the evaluator must be able to see and represent the program and participants as they really are.

Instrumental views of knowledge use flow nicely from this portrayal of role. Evaluation is predicated on the belief that we can use our evaluation instruments to probe, take apart, and reconstruct a social event such as an educational program, and in so doing understand it. That understanding can, in turn, be put to use in managing, controlling, predicting, or otherwise manipulating some state of educational affairs.

This then is the familiar terrain of evaluation. It is a ground that unites evaluators with the activities and aims of social scientists—with the economist, the psychologist, the political scientist, and with Dr. Binger in Coles's story.

New Terrain

In the past two decades or so we have witnessed the development of a different way to think about evaluation, one that does
not draw a sharp distinction between evaluation (or policy analysis, for that matter) and the kind of moral inquiry characteristic of
the humanities. This new conceptualization of evaluation is interested in recovering a sense of making and participating rather
than seeing and finding. Instead of pursuing ways in which
evaluation can be further rationalized or scientized, this new development suggests ways in which to "poeticize" the social practice of evaluation (Rorty, 1983). This signals efforts to draw the
practice closer to the everyday ways in which we go about our
business of understanding our lives together, making judgments,
and persuading others of the correctness of our views (Schwandt,
2001b).

The notion of poeticizing a practice like evaluation arises from
a strong critique of the rational-world paradigm with its accompanying emphasis on the tools of analytical logic and the method
of demonstration. The growing interest in narrative and story is a
concern for not simply a different textual form but a different
paradigm of understanding (Brodkey, 1987; Bruner, 1986, 1990;
MacIntyre, 1981; Marcus and Cushman, 1982). Fisher (1987) claims
that the rational-world paradigm for knowledge presupposes that:

> (1) Humans are essentially rational beings; (2) the paradigmatic mode of
> human decision making and communications is argument—discourse
> that features clear-cut inferential or implicative structures; (3) the con-
> duct of argument is ruled by the dictates of situations—legal, scientific,
> legislative, public, and so on; (4) rationality is determined by subject-
> matter knowledge, argumentative ability, and skill in employing the
> rules of advocacy in given fields; and (5) the world is a set of logical
> puzzles that can be solved through appropriate analysis and applica-
> tions of reason conceived as an argumentative construct. (p. 59)

For Fisher, the key notion here is argument, which in the rational-world paradigm is *"the* means of being human, the agency
of all that humans can know and realize in achieving their *telos"*
(p. 60, emphasis in original). In contrast, Fisher summarizes the
presuppositions of the narrative paradigm as follows:

(1) Humans are essentially storytellers. (2) The paradigmatic mode of human decision making and communication is 'good reasons,' which vary in form among situations, genres, and media of communication. (3) The production and practice of good reasons are ruled by matters of history, biography, culture, and character.... (4) Rationality is determined by the nature of persons as narrative beings—their inherent awareness of *narrative probability*, what constitutes a coherent story, and their constant habit of testing *narrative fidelity*, whether or not the stories they experience ring true with the stories they know to be true in their lives.... (5) The world as we know it is a set of stories that must be chosen among in order for us to live life in a process of continual re-creation. In short, good reasons are the stuff of stories, the means by which humans realize their nature as reasoning-valuing animals. (p. 31)

Empiricist epistemology is the philosophical ground of the rational-world paradigm, while hermeneutics as practical philosophy is the ground for a narrative mode of knowing. Fisher's emphasis here on reasoning with an audience through a text or an utterance rather than arguing the merits of a proposition places this thinking about narrative squarely within the Aristotelian tradition of practical wisdom. Following Gadamer and others, Fisher subscribes to the notion that it is in the context of dialogue and conversation that knowledge arises and is to be understood.

The tradition of philosophical hermeneutics emphasizes the situatedness, contextuality, and contingency of all knowledge and action. Hermeneutics is not a method that the inquirer employs to generate objective knowledge of human lives, in the way that scientific method properly employed yields objective knowledge of the natural world. Rather, it is a condition of our being-in-the-world; it emphasizes that the social world is itself a multivocal interpretation:

Our capacity to understand is rooted in our own self-definitions, hence in what we are. We are fundamentally self-interpreting and self-defining, living always in a cultural environment, inside [what Charles Taylor called] a "web of signification we ourselves have spun." There is no outside, detached standpoint from which we gather and present brute data. When we try to understand the cultural world, we are dealing with interpretations and interpretations of interpretations. (Rabinow and Sullivan, 1987, p. 7)

While the notion of narrative knowing has its antecedents in the widespread critique of the naturalistic interpretation of the social sciences, the recovery of interest in hermeneutics, and the blurring of the boundaries between the humanities and the social sciences, it is not synonymous with all so-called qualitative approaches to evaluation. It is characteristic of qualitative approaches to be responsive to the concerns of evaluation stakeholders, to gather data in the form of words rather than numbers, to write up thick descriptions instead of barren technical reports, and so forth. However, one can make all these procedural changes and still think of evaluation practice as applied social science, that is, as a kind of instrumentality and a means of knowing about programs.

Narrative knowing and poeticized evaluation signal a more radical change in thinking. Instead of grounding evaluation knowledge in the making of propositions as described above, this new conception of evaluation embraces what Bruner calls the "narrative" mode of knowing. Unlike the former, whose imaginative application leads to sound arguments (recall Dr. Binger's approach to treating Coles's patient) the imaginative application of narrative leads (as Dr. Ludwig might suggest) to good stories that portray the human condition and lead to new understandings. Sarbin (1986, p.11) has argued that narrative is an organizing principle for human action: "our plannings, our rememberings, even our loving and hating, are guided by narrative plots." Narrative, as Bruner points out, is built upon concern for the human condition: Stories reach sad, comic, heroic, or absurd outcomes, whereas arguments are simply conclusive or inconclusive. "Arguments convince us of their truth," Bruner reminds us, "stories of their lifelikeness" (1986, p. 11).

Applied to evaluation, the narrative mode directs us toward portrayals, stories, and cases that reveal how people who live a program or policy endow that experience with meaning (Abma, 1999). Narrative focuses on the particular—the specifics of program participants and program setting, the details of their actions, intentions, feelings, and the like. There is at least an implicit bid here to (re)present participants' understanding of their participation as a central focus of evaluation reporting. This way of thinking about evaluation is continuous with literature. That is, evaluation is viewed as yet another way of helping us interpret and reinterpret ourselves to ourselves.

A narrative mode of knowing and of representing what one knows is explicitly concerned with "knowing with" rather than "knowing about." As a result, in a narrative portrayal the evaluator is always in and part of the story she or he tells. The evaluator gives shape to what she or he hears and sees. As the semiotician Eco points out, "To tell a story is to take a stance towards events and, rather than to reflect a world, to create a world"(1979, p. 90). The evaluator operating in the narrative mode must reveal that stance in writing about a particular program. This means more than revealing how one is empathetic and respectful; it means that in the writing, the evaluator does not take the detached, autonomous voice of authority (or what one of my student's called the third-person invisible). To honor the idea of "knowing with" rather than "knowing about," the evaluator must explain how she or he was involved in the process of making meaning. The evaluator's own lived experience is not a liability to be exorcised but a precondition for knowing.

Thus, in this new conception of evaluation, the evaluator can neither be spectator nor scribe. Dr. Ludwig taught Coles this lesson. Coles came to recognize that he brought his own story both to his evaluative encounter with patients and to the seminar room where he interacted with his supervising teachers. The stories he constructed in those settings were affected by his listener's habits and predilections. He saw that his version (his evaluation) of his patient's stories was a retelling. The way he looked at patients' lives, the matters he chose to emphasize, the details he considered important, and the imagery used to make his interpretations all gave shape to what he heard as he remade his patients' stories into something of his own.

Caveats

A poeticized approach to evaluation that leads to gripping stories, cases, and narrative portrayals provides a welcome antidote to a preoccupation with arguments and propositions in evaluation. However, endorsing the importance of immersion in and a narrative recounting of participants' experience with evaluation also require attention to possible troubles with this approach. Difficulties may arise with the validity or correctness of narratives—both narratives generated by participants in some program being evaluated and those told by the evaluator—and the generalizability and use of these portrayals of the particularities of experience.

Validity

Of course, the validity of narratives per se is not always an issue. In some situations, we may wish simply to be entertained by a good story. But in the case of evaluation, where, as Phillips (1993, p. 7) points out, "something of significance hangs in the balance, when further action or intervention is called for, when policy is about to be made ... we are more likely to act successfully if we act on the basis of correct information." Thus, the issue of the validity of narratives cannot be made to disappear by calling it a matter of "misplaced verification," as Bruner (1986, p. 14) does, and arguing that what matters in judging narratives is only that they be plausible, credible, coherent, and gripping stories. We all know from experience that stories based on experience may have all such qualities and still be quite untrue. I can tell a convincing story in which I am resolute in my belief that my daughter dyed her hair purple simply to spite me, and despite my genuinely believing this to be true, I could be quite wrong (and perhaps detrimentally so for our relationship). A participant in an educational program may tell a credible story (and genuinely believe) that the program failed to achieve success because the program director was malevolent, and this may simply be untrue. Hence, validity is at stake in using stories in evaluation, for the evaluator takes as evidence stories that participants generate and, in turn, fashions her or his own narrative that, at least implicitly, claims to be bearing knowledge and explanation. Kvale (1995) has suggested several ways in which the validity of narratives the evaluator uses as evidence can be established. An *experiential* reading of a narrative entails questioning whether a story told by a participant in a program does in fact reflect the participant's experience. This kind of check is done by not necessarily taking a story at face value, but by questioning to clarify understandings and meanings said to have been experienced. A *veridical* reading of a narrative entails checking the truth of claims made by storytellers by seeking corroborating as well as disconfirming evidence. And a *symptomatic* reading of a narrative places it within the domain of a rationale for the participant's actions and beliefs. The validity of a narrative about the failure of an educational program, for example, might be checked by pursuing the related nexus of a participant's beliefs about the actions of other participants with whom he or she is involved. Kvale notes that not all of these readings are always necessary, for it depends on the kinds of questions the evaluator is asking and the uses to which the narrative is to be put in the evaluator's report.

Generalization and Use

Assuming that the evaluator has attended to the issue of the correctness of narratives told by participants, it remains to consider what to do with these tales of particular, situated experiences that the evaluator subsequently fashions. The standard answer to the question of how cases or portrayals of specific situations can be used in evaluation is case-to-case transfer (Lincoln and Guba, 1985). On this view, it is the evaluator's responsibility to provide a portrayal in sufficient detail such that a reader of the case can engage in reasonable but modest speculation about whether the case contains lessons that are applicable to the situation in which the reader finds herself. A similar idea is advanced by Stake (Stake and Trumbell, 1982) who argued for the importance of styles of evaluation reporting that conveyed holistic impressions; that revealed the inherent uncertainty and ambiguity that typically accompany any effort to understand the activity, accomplishments, issues, strengths, and shortcomings of a program that was the object of evaluation; and, that created vicarious experience for readers making it possible for them to combine this understanding with their previous experience so as to reach new "naturalistic generalizations." Both of these views appear to be something like a scientific analogue to the novelist's bid to render experience inviting. The novelist aims to craft a narrative in such a way that it engages readers by drawing them into empathetic identification with the human experiences of pain, sorrow, joy, hope, irony, tragedy, and the like that are being portrayed through the lives of specific protagonists. There also seems to be at least a partial parallel here to Geertz's notion of thick description—the obligation to inscribe the meaning of actions to actors (Geertz, 1973.)

Although thick description is necessary, it is not, as Geertz explains, sufficient. The interpreter faces a dual task to "uncover the conceptual structures that inform our subjects' acts, the 'said' of social discourse" *and* to "construct a system of analysis in whose terms what is generic to those structures ... will stand out against the other determinants of human behavior" (p. 27). In Geertz's opinion, unlike the novelist, the researcher (and, we might add, particularly, the evaluator) assumes an obligation to diagnose as well as to describe, that is, "to set down the meaning particular social actions have for the actors whose actions they are, and [to state], as explicitly as we can manage, what the knowledge thus attained demonstrates about the society in which it is found and, beyond that, about social life as such" (p. 27).

If we accept Geertz's advice, then the evaluator qua interpretive researcher is more than a teller of tales of particular experiences. Cases of the particular or the local must be made to speak to larger social issues. Cases become the means by which the personal experiences of program participants in some specific site are connected to the public policies and institutions that have been created to address those personal problems (Denzin, 1989). Failing to make this kind of extension leaves interpretive work vulnerable to the common complaint that "you either grasp an interpretation or you do not, see the point of it or you do not, accept it or you do not. Imprisoned in the immediacy of its own detail, [the interpretation] is presented as self-validating, or worse, as validated by the supposedly developed sensitivities of the person who presents it" (Geertz, 1973, p. 24).

A second way to envision the relationship between a narrative approach to evaluation and issues of generalizability and use follows as a consequence from a particular way of envisioning evaluators as teachers. Evaluators may define their responsibility as that of teaching various kinds of practitioners (teachers, managers, social workers, nurses, and so forth) to develop conceptions of wise practice or the ability to deliberate well in particular circumstances. Wise practice is a kind of practical-moral knowledge. It is an ability to evaluate and interpret the situation at hand and, consequently, to adopt a course of action that is both effective and appropriate in the situation. Having the knowledge of wise practice is having what we might call good judgment.

The critical issue is how does one acquire this capacity for good judgment? How can it be taught? Surely, one cannot be taught a theory of human judgment—that is, a theory of how to be a human being in situations of various kinds. The particularity, indeterminacy, and mutability that characterize situations in daily life make life inaccessible to rule-bound procedure or formal generalization. How I respond to a situation demanding good judgment today may guide but surely will not predict how I might respond to a similar situation tomorrow. Hence, what matters most is having the capacity for good judgment or the ability to deliberate well on a case-by-case basis. This capacity can be cultivated through the study of particular cases. Through such study, one learns how to recognize the morally relevant features of a situation and how to recognize the ways in which standing commitments, principles, traditions, and the like might shed light on the deliberation. Well-crafted cases or narratives can be used for this purpose. The evaluator-as-teacher provides practitioners with such cases and thereby indirectly helps them educate their own perception and cultivate their capacity for wise practice. Cases are often used this way in training the interpretive perspicuity of clinicians and lawyers. In effect, cases are used to help practitioners acquire the ability to be good interpreters.

A third means of using cases is suggested by a conception of the evaluator as social critic. Here, Walzer's (1988) discussion of the distinguishing features of social criticism is instructive: Criticism is a kind of reflexive ethnography, predicated on the assumption that it is a mistake to believe that we must escape our situation in order to describe it accurately. Critics seek to remain close to ordinary life and everyday understandings. They seek intimacy with readers and listeners: "The primary or natural language of criticism is that of the folk; the best critics simply take hold of that language and raise it to a new pitch of intensity and argumentative power" (p. 9). Furthermore, criticism is always moral in character.... Its crucial terms are corruption and virtue, oppression and justice, selfishness and the commonweal. When 'something is rotten in the state of Denmark,' the rot is some wrongful policy or practice or set of relationships. What else could it be? The special role of the critic is to describe what is wrong in ways that suggest a remedy. (pp. 9–10)

Conversely, when some policy, practice, or set of relationships is working well, the evaluator, as social critic, would celebrate such an occasion in the narrative he or she creates. Finally, the practice of social criticism is "founded in hope; it cannot be carried on without some sense of historical possibility" (p. 17). Following Walzer's advice, an evaluator might use cases in the service of broader social criticism.

Bruner (1986) and others have pointed out that how one talks comes eventually to be how one represents what one talks about. The more evaluators talk about knowledge as a tool for fixing or improving human affairs, the more they tend to believe that they are actually talking about the way "things really are." That is, they come to believe that contested human affairs are a set of "problems" that can be "fixed." The narrative mode of expressing what one knows is conversational and deliberative; it leads to a deeper understanding of the common good being sought via a program, or to what Rorty (1979, p. 204) calls the "widening and deepening of our sense of community and the possibilities open to that community." As Bruner (1986, p. 69) claims, "our sensitivity to narrative provides the major link between our own sense of self and our sense of others in the social world around us."

It is salutary that some evaluators are supplementing the preoccupation with procedures for establishing the empirical proof of propositional claims with a concern for narratives that express the lived reality of participants. Evaluation grounded in narrative and the idea of knowing *with* rather than knowing *about* draws attention away from the idea of manipulative improvement and toward notions of self-understanding and edification.

But in turning to narrative, the evaluator's obligation does not end with the consideration of the qualities of a good story. The evaluator as poet must, of course, explore how to achieve verisimilitude or lifelikeness in stories and portrayals, how to establish narrative fidelity, and how to achieve an invitational quality in the construction of the story or portrayal. Evaluators must also examine carefully how aspects of author and respondents' voice, writing style, and audience help shape the telling of the case. When operating in the narrative mode evaluators must do all this and more. When evaluators look to the character of Dr. Ludwig and the strong poet for inspiration of their own practice, then they must also find a way to link the telling of tales to efforts to say something significant beyond the case at hand.

Part III

Moral, Ethical, and Political
Perspectives

8

Reading the Landscape of Values in Evaluation

In the past decade, matters of value and ethics in U.S. evaluation practice have risen to the foreground. The evidence here includes renewed efforts to purge evaluation of the lingering effects of the meta-theory of value-free social science (House and Howe, 1999; Scriven, 1991), attempts to link evaluation practice specifically to issues of social justice (House, 1993) and critical theory (Sirotnik, 1990), systematic examinations of the role of values in theories of evaluation practice (Shadish, Cook, and Leviton, 1991), endorsement of standards for evaluation practice (Joint Committee on Standards for Educational Evaluation, 1981, 1994), and the development and adoption of ethical principles for evaluators (Shadish, Newman, Scheirer, and Wye, 1995). Discussion of ethics in professional evaluation practice has been a regular feature of the annual meetings of the American Evaluation Association over the past few years. The organization's main journal, the *American Journal of Evaluation*, contains a regular feature, "Ethical Challenges," where evaluators offer responses to particular ethical dilemmas encountered in practice.

Even accepting the fact that a concern with ethics is a mark of emerging professionalism, this values discourse is somewhat remarkable because public discussions of ethics and values in professional practices is a difficult undertaking for several reasons. First, and not least, in the West and particularly in the United States, evaluation (as well as other professions involved in social policy, programming, and administration) is heavily influenced by the tradition of value-free social science. In this theory of science, ethics and values are defined as irrational, subjective, emotive, and attitudinal matters and, hence, not part of a properly scientific practice.

This state of affairs is compounded by a second problem. As many commentators have noted, the modern self struggles with the grip of an epistemology of disengagement from and control of the social world (Taylor, 1989). This way of knowing squeezes out the realm of the personal, the intuitive, the perceptual, and the emotive, all characteristics of moral engagements. This loss is reflected in the modernist tendency in social science and management practice to convert what are essentially moral and ethical problems to technical and administrative ones. Third, some scholars have argued that the marketplace exerts great pressure on professionals of all kinds to place careerism and self-interest over beneficence, and erodes the sense of a profession as a vocation or calling in service to the public good (May, 1992; Pellegrino and Thomasma, 1993).

Fourth, discussion of ethics and values has been particularly difficult in evaluation because the field for at least the last fifteen years or so has been preoccupied with the quantitative-versus-qualitative methods debate that often obscured consideration of moral issues. Ironically, in its European origins, this debate was very much about the interconnections between social science epistemologies, theories of society, and the moral and political obligations of social scientists. However, in the U.S., the debate took the form of quarrels about the merits of different types of data, methods, and designs. In focusing largely on matters of methodology, the debate often ignored more profound criticisms of social science epistemology and related questions of the proper aim, subject matter, and obligations of evaluation as a social practice (House, 1993; 1994).

Fifth, we have difficulty speaking about ethical issues because notions of moral neutrality, moral pluralism, and amoralism seem to have replaced the kind of moral anchors that once were provided by a vocabulary of civic republicanism and a public theology. As a nation, we struggle with finding a moral vocabulary rich and nuanced enough in which to discuss moral issues in public forums. Virtually every attempt to develop such a language has met with serious objections. For example, the language of justice and rights is criticized for lacking any conception of the good, for its atomistic conception of the self, and for its concern for protecting only negative liberty; discourse ethics emphasizing conditions for democratic dialogue is criticized for being abstract and rationalistic; and, the language of civic virtue is charged with being wedded to neoconservative concerns with privatism and political apathy in the public realm.

Finally, ethical discussions are difficult because of the tentative, searching nature of moral beliefs. We seem to be comfortable with tentativeness and fallibilism in our epistemology, holding that our empirical claims about the social world can be reasonably warranted although never certain; at the same time we are profoundly uncomfortable admitting the same about our claims of moral value.

Nevertheless, despite these myriad difficulties, a thoroughgoing examination of value questions is a particularly important aspect of the social practice of evaluation. Evaluators have a special obligation to examine values as they relate to the objects they evaluate, and they are also especially obliged to submit their own practice to normative scrutiny. These responsibilities emerge from the evaluation community's claim that its expertise lies in its special knowledge of theory of evaluation. Ideally, evaluators are not simply social researchers with methodological expertise and political acumen but are obliged by the very nature of their work to make claims about the value of some practice, program, policy, project, or technology. Judgments of value are warranted interpretations of a particular evaluand as good, good enough, poor, or corrupt (Everitt, 1996). Moreover, these assessments of value cannot help but entail assumptions about what ought to be done or avoided or what it is right to do. Through making interpretations of the value of programs and policies, evaluators not only inform the means by which human or social good is realized but shape our definition of the social good as well.

Because evaluators lay claim to a special knowledge of the means and purposes of valuing, they ought to be capable of using that expertise to evaluate their own practice. This kind of meta-evaluation includes not only assessing the worth of various methodologies (a common enough undertaking) but assessing the values assumed and promoted in the practice itself. This assessment takes us into the realm of political morality, an arena of exploration in which the spheres of politics (and its issues of justice, fairness, and equity) and ethics (and its issues of moral character, virtue, and moral judgment) cannot be neatly decoupled in considering the purpose of a practice and the role of practitioners in the society they serve.

The Landscape of Values in Evaluation

With these considerations in the foreground, I turn to a descriptive and evaluative reading of values and ethics in the contemporary landscape of evaluation. My aim is to make a small contribution to the growing public discussion of the normative aims and character of evaluation practice. I begin with two generally well-recognized avenues for examining values in evaluation practice.

Values as Professional Ethics

Perhaps the most commonly understood values discourse in evaluation practice is concerned with what constitutes ethically responsible professional conduct. For example, after extensive discussion at its annual meetings and considerable work on the part of a special task force, the membership of the American Evaluation Association endorsed the *Guiding Principles for Evaluators* in 1994. (A number of other national professional evaluation associations including the Canadian Evaluation Society and the Australaisan Evaluation Society have also adopted ethical codes of conduct.) These principles are neither specific rules for conduct nor codified as something to which evaluators must take an oath of allegiance. They are guidelines, not standards or prescriptions, and they are not used to monitor or sanction individual practitioners. The scope and depth of the coverage of these principles is disputed, but that is not necessarily a shortcoming, for they are mainly intended to raise awareness of ethical issues in practice and to stimulate debate about right conduct. These principles are evidence of a community of evaluation practitioners searching for norms of professional behavior including, but also extending beyond, the usual concern for methodological competence.

Values in the Use of Evaluations

At issue here are the standard moral questions stemming from external political pressures on the work of evaluators as well as in the applications made of evaluation knowledge. There is a substantial literature spanning two decades that reflects upon these kinds of moral questions. It includes the work of Lee Cronbach on the fit of evaluation to political systems of accommodation versus command; Carol Weiss's extensive work on the politics of evaluation; Daniel Stufflebeam and William Webster's efforts to distinguish pseudo from legitimate evaluations; the work of Barry Mac-Donald and others on democratic evaluation; and Eleanor Chelimsky's concerns for protecting the independence of evaluators in the political arena by taking steps to guard against their vulnerability to partisan attack.

Most, if not all, of this work is framed by the assumption that the evaluator is (or ought to be) an impartial, objective analyst dedicated to the pursuit of practical knowledge regardless of whether that knowledge is intended to serve purposes of accountability, organizational development, or theory building (Chelimsky, 1997). However, much recent discussion (e.g., Scriven, 1997; Stake, 1997) centers on the question of the evaluator's role as advocate and whether self-proclaimed impartiality is but a professional ideology obscuring the expanding influence of the policy analyst and evaluator (Fischer, 1987). I take up this issue more directly below.

Values as Properties of the Evaluation Object

Applied ethics in evaluation encompasses the questions of what values are relevant subject matter in evaluating the goals, operation, and outcomes of policies, programs, projects, and technologies and whether and how these values are to be taken into account in an evaluation judgment (Scriven, 1991).

Consider first the problem of identifying and defining the relevant values bearing on the evaluand. Imagine, for example, that the object of evaluation is a program designed to provide in-home health care to physically disabled individuals. What meta-values are important here: Fairness and equity in services provided? Absence of any additional harm in the act of providing the service? What practical values are important: Efficiency? Physical appearance of health care personnel? Or consider a case of evaluating the ethical conduct of the evaluator: What set of values should be brought to bear here? The story of the controversy surrounding the inclusion in the *Guiding Principles* of the fifth principle, Responsibilities for General and Public Welfare (which holds that the evaluator's obligations extend beyond meeting clients' needs and encompass the public interest and good) (Shadish, et al., 1995) illustrates the struggle to identify a primary value—i.e., in this case, the ethical obligation to consider the public good—and warrant its inclusion in judging 'good' evaluation practice.

A more significant part of the problem concerns whether and how to take such values into account in making an evaluative judgment. Suppose an evaluator is successful in identifying relevant values related to justice, equity, respect for persons, and so forth in the circumstances of a particular program evaluation. Then the question becomes, how do those values figure in the overall assessment of the value of the program? Here, generally, there are two positions, each offering a different answer to the question. The two positions display considerable disagreement on the moral proposition that the evaluator ought to be making summative value judgments.

The *objectivist position* assumes that there is a professional moral imperative for evaluators to evaluate. It holds that values are rationally and objectively determinable (House and Howe, 1999). On this view, values function as criteria for judging the merit and/or worth of the evaluand. They are taken into account through a variety of means, including needs assessments, logical analysis of the function of an evaluand, and careful argumentation for those general ethical principles that, in part, constitute the socio-political context in which the evaluand was conceived and in which the activity of evaluation unfolds. The objectivist maintains that an evaluator simply is not engaging in the activity of evaluating if he or she does not consider all relevant values bearing on the performance of the evaluand and does not subsequently render a summative judgment based on those values.

The *descriptivist position* disagrees. It acknowledges that it is insufficient simply to generate factual data about the performance of an evaluand and that value-related data must be uncovered as well. However, it argues that values are subject to pervasive disagreement and cannot be rationally determined (House and Howe, 1999). Hence, the evaluator's professional obligation should be confined to describing the various values held by stakeholders and showing how different value perspectives may lead to different conclusions about the merit of the evaluand. In this view, it is the responsibility of primary stakeholders (not the evaluator) to make the final judgment of the merit or worth of the evaluand (Shadish, 1994).

The defense of the descriptivist position rests on at least two arguments. The first, what House and Howe (1999) call the radical undecidability of values thesis, can be stated as follows: The evaluator cannot make warranted claims about the value of an evaluand because there is no generally agreed upon moral theory that supplies an unquestioned justification for particular moral claims. Rather, we have a proliferation of moral theories (theories of justice as defined, for example, by Locke, Kant, and more recently Rawls; theories of virtue as advanced by neo-Aristotelians such as MacIntyre; feminist ethical theories of care as defended by Noddings or trust as explained by Baier), no one of which is regarded as clearly superior. However, there is a serious flaw in this argument: the debate over which is the best moral theory or which theory provides the best justification for particular moral claims need not be settled before we can identify what has moral value and make justified moral judgments. That would be equivalent to saying we cannot engage in the activity of relating in meaningful ways to others in society until we first have agreement on the best theory of society. The same empirically well-supported moral claims—that one should always help those in need, that honesty in one's dealings with other humans is good, that safety is an absolute requirement in children's toys, and so on—are compatible with but receive different justifications in different moral theories.

A second argument given in support of the descriptivist position might be called the subjectivist thesis. It can be stated as follows: When the evaluator specifically is charged with making a value judgment, it is likely that the evaluator's own values will

become the basis for the judgment; hence, evaluators should not
make summative judgments. This conclusion is not necessarily de-
rivable from its premises. Values as criteria can come from many
sources, but they need not (and should not) arise from the evaluator's personal tastes or preferences. To be sure, evaluators are
typically citizens in the same society wherein an evaluand is being
examined. In this way, the identification of relevant values is, in
some way, admitting that the evaluator-as-citizen personally
holds the values shared by all citizens in the society. However,
said values are not the property of the evaluator's personal taste,
nor are commonly held values somehow the sum or average of the
values held by all individuals. Rather, values are intersubjective—that is, they are part of what constitutes the life-world in
which the evaluator-evaluand-stakeholders are all a part. What
the evaluator is doing in identifying values and basing a judgment
of program merit on shared values evident in needs analyses, cost
analyses, and so on is making an interpretative justification—a
warranted argument based on evidence (Fraser, 1989)

Values Constituting the Ethical Aim of Evaluation

Current concerns about the moral-political stances of parti-
sanship, value neutrality, and advocacy in evaluation—evident,
for example, in the exchange between Stufflebeam and Fetterman
over empowerment evaluation (Fetterman, 1994, 1995; Stufflebeam, 1994) and in the contrary views about advocacy expressed
by Stake and Scriven (in Chelimsky and Shadish, 1997—reflect
considerable disagreement on the moral end-in-view or the human
or social good that evaluation practice is intended to serve. This is
a question of the political morality of the practice, and, in my
judgment, the least understood and the least examined part of the
portrait I am sketching. This is so because most answers to the
question, to what purpose or in whose interest should evaluation
practice be conducted? are given in epistemological and/or political terms. However, there are ethical claims at stake in answers to
this question as well—claims about the nature of the moral life;
claims about agency, authority, identity, and human interaction;
claims about the way society ought to be and the ways professionals ought to serve that society, and so forth. In other words,

there is an important sense in which the framework for thinking about the epistemology and politics of a practice is wedded to the morality of that practice (Taylor, 1987).

The remainder of this chapter is devoted to exploring three ways in which this union is conceived using a set of terms introduced by Rein (1983) in his examination of policy studies. I begin by describing an ethics for social inquiry that, paradoxically, claims to keep epistemology and political morality distinct by maintaining an amoral, apolitical stance. Then I discuss an emancipatory ethical aim, and finally the ethical aim of fostering practical wisdom. What I present here is something like ideal types that various kinds of practices of evaluation aspire to. These types do not comprise a template by which practices can be neatly sorted, and above all they do not map onto the so-called qualitative-quantitative debate in evaluation methodology.

An Analytical, Value-Neutral Framework. In this conception of the ethical aim of the practice, the purpose of evaluation is to generate a particular kind of social scientific knowledge that can be used to ameliorate social problems. The moral claim made here is that, in generating that knowledge, evaluation practice ought to be neutral with respect to the ways in which that knowledge can be used to serve different ends that society values. In other words, the knowledge produced in professional evaluation should be principally empirical not normative. The evaluator qua social scientist has no business making evaluative conclusions; he or she should be disinterested and, in that sense, value-neutral with respect to different conceptions of a good program, a good society, and so on. Social inquirers can describe various value positions held by members of society, but they should never engage in judging which is the best. This is necessary, the argument goes, because while reason is a valuable guide to adjudicating claims about matters of empirical fact, it is useless for deciding among competing values.

This framework for defining evaluation practice is evident in several perspectives, including the fact-gathering, or monitoring, approach to evaluation, as well as the descriptivist valuing approach, including what Scriven (1993) calls the weak decision support and the relativistic views of evaluation. This framework derives from the Weberian and Mertonian claim to a disinterested or value-free social science (Merton, 1973) and is predicated on what Weber (1963) called the unbridgeable distinction between the work of the social scientist and the work of the ordinary, evaluating, acting person:

> To apply the results of this (scientific) analysis in the making of a decision is not a task which science can undertake; it is rather the task of the acting, willing person: he (sic) weighs and chooses from among the values involved according to his own conscience and his personal view of the world. Science can make him realize that all action, and naturally ... inaction, imply in their consequences the espousal of certain values and ... the rejection of certain others. The act of choice itself is his own responsibility. (p. 359)

Various defenses of this position have been made over the years and the strong critique of this view as an inappropriate metatheory for evaluation (House and Howe, 1999; Scriven, 1993) and social inquiry in general (Bernstein, 1976; Hollis, 1994; Root, 1993) is well known.

Paradoxically, this framework claims to be amoral—that is, it has no moral aim other than upholding the view that the good of society is best served by the production of valid, reliable, impartial information on the part of social inquirers. Though not indifferent to the idea of improving society or social life, this framework is based on the belief that that goal is best accomplished by clearly limiting the expertise of the professional social inquirer to empirical matters. In fact, in empirical matters, the authority of the inquirer is regarded as (relatively) absolute because of the special knowledge he or she possesses about methodology. The ethic of this perspective is principally scientific and concerned with what counts as responsible behavior in the generation and analysis of data. It is an ethic that governs not *engagement with* but *disengagement from* the normal, customary flow of partisan, emotive, subjective meaning schemes that characterize human interaction and social life generally (Sievers, 1983). Hence, the kind of trust that the use of the analytic framework engenders between the analyst/evaluator and client is anonymous and institutional as opposed to personal and face-to-face (Porter, 1995).

As a stance toward society, the analytical framework defines social problems in an apolitical, scientific manner. Social policy is seen more or less as an exercise in social technology. Karl Popper's idea of piecemeal social engineering is perhaps the most famous expression of this framework. In program evaluation, this theory of practice is most evident in Donald Campbell's (1969, 1982) notion of the experimenting society. More recent explanations of this framework emphasize that the social scientist must be politically astute in understanding ways in which scientific information can be fed into the policy making process. Carol Weiss (1983, 1987), for example, has been particularly concerned with how social scientists and evaluators introduce their empirical work into the mix of interest, ideologies, and information characterizing the policy environment. Her belief is that social scientific information can be introduced into the mix to help resolve conflicts in ideologies and interests. In this way, evaluation knowledge is less likely to be directly or instrumentally applied but rather used to "enlighten" policy makers and program planners.

Arguably, this theory of the political morality of the practice of evaluation (and social science practice more broadly) is the most dominant framework in the West. It has served both the utilitarian, technocratic conception of democracies that was prominent in the 1960s and 1970s as well as the more recent versions of pluralist-elitist-equilibrium theories of democracy (House, 1993). It has become virtually a background ideology that dictates both the understanding of social problems and the knowledge required to solve them. To borrow a turn of phrase from Sullivan (1983), in this ideology, social scientists aspire to be something like scientific shepherds who lead or at least wish they led a highly rationalized flock. In contemporary defenses of this analytical framework in evaluation practice, one hears at least an implied lament that scientific rationality must always regrettably cope with the messy world of political rationality.

In the United States, this theory of practice has been fairly comfortably allied with economic and social laissez faire approaches to the polity. Its defenders claim they are acting in the service of individual freedom, providing information that makes the marketplace of ideas a more secure—that is, rational—place in which competing interests can bargain. As Shadish (1996, p. 4) observed, evaluation informed by this theory of practice, "serves a system-enhancing role" by "giving all stakeholders the information they need to fight their battles in the political and social arena."

In the foreseeable future, it seems likely that this framework for evaluation practice will continue to complement the new managerialism arising across the West that seeks to transform the culture of public services through devolution and decentralization (Clarke, Cochrane, and McLaughlin, 1994; Pollitt, 1995). This development is paradoxical, because the new managerialism, in part, grows out of a reaction against the authority of professionals to direct social problem identification and treatment. The movement (if that is the correct term) emphasizes depoliticizing social policy, going beyond national political debates to produce rational and efficient decisions about the deployment of social resources at local levels. This avowedly apolitical character, coupled with a strong interest in allegedly neutral criteria of economy, efficiency, and effectiveness, is likely to make the new managerialism resonate strongly with the analytical, value-neutral perspective in social inquiry. The difference will be that social scientists and evaluators will turn away from serving the state with its messy partisan world that makes use of scientific information difficult to serving the needs of managers.

An Emancipatory, Value-Committed Framework. The analytical, value-neutral framework arose out of sustained criticism of inherited, unquestioned authority. It championed the critical scrutiny of empirical evidence to reach reasoned conclusions about appropriate possible courses of social action. The value-committed framework arises largely out of criticisms that the analytical, value-neutral framework has lost its emancipatory, liberatory, and democratic origins. The familiar argument is that the analytical framework with its goal of enlightening policy makers has become wedded to a cognitive-instrumental-technical outlook, lacks a critical purchase, and has become a rationale for an elitist science that serves existing structures of power. Evaluation informed by a value-committed framework also seeks a particular kind of social scientific knowledge. However, this knowledge is not at all disinterested.

Value-committed frameworks display considerable variety depending on whether they are grounded in participatory, democratic, feminist, or critical social science perspectives. Nonetheless, all share a view of human agency at odds with the analytical, value-neutral framework. Value-committed perspectives take political rationality as the primary starting point or arena for conceiving of evaluation practice. Negotiation, conflict, disagreement, and ideological struggle is the stuff with which evaluation practice must come to terms. However, this does not mean that evaluation is conceived solely in terms of political rhetoric. Rather, it signals a different ethic of engagement. The value-neutral, analytic perspective on evaluation practice emphasizes breaking from ordinary interactive relationships in favor of scientific rationality, nonpartisanship, and neutrality with respect to ethical values embedded in human actions (e.g., policies, projects, programs) that are under examination.

In contrast, emancipatory practices seek to be continuous with human interaction and reflect a commitment to everyday life. Flacks (1983) summarizes this commitment as follows:

> a morally guided social science must have the goal of enabling people themselves to make their own history, of breaking down the structures and motivational frameworks that sustain elitism and privatism, of achieving social arrangements in which communities can engage in the formulation of the terms and conditions of daily life as an integral part of daily life itself. (p. 349)

Giddens (1991, p. 210) explains that the central ethic of emancipatory approaches is to "liberate individuals and groups from constraints adversely affecting their life chances." He argues that the political morality of emancipatory inquiry is best characterized as

a) a politics of others—it is concerned with division between human beings made on the basis of class, gender, ethnicity, ruling versus subordinate, rich versus poor, and so on;
b) concerned with power and the reduction or elimination of exploitation, inequality, and oppression in social relations; and,
c) having the primary imperatives of justice, equality, and participation.

There are many variations of evaluation practice that share this general framework, and they differ widely on what precisely is the emancipatory end-in-view and on the way it should be achieved. Mertens (1995), for example, argues from a feminist perspective that evaluation practice ought to recognize silence or marginalized voices; analyze power inequities; and, be linked to political action. Approaches to evaluation practice informed by neo-Marxist critical theory likewise reflect an emancipatory aim (Sirotnik and Oakes, 1990). These practices emphasize that a program evaluation should be designed in relationship to, and provide an understanding of, the broader socio-political and economic context in which the program unfolds, embrace explicitly the stance of social justice, and ameliorate unjust social conditions (Richardson, 1990).

A value-committed perspective is also evident in the objectivist view of evaluation that aims at revealing the truth of the matter when it comes to judging the merit, worth, or significance of some evaluand. House and Howe's (1999) explication of deliberative democratic evaluation is an excellent case in point. Like Scriven (1997), House and Howe endorse the view that evaluation can be objective in the sense of "working toward unbiased statements [of fact and value] through the procedures of the discipline, observing the canons of proper argument and methodology, maintaining a healthy skepticism, and being vigilant to eradicate sources of bias" (House and Howe, 1999, p. 9). Their view also accords a special role for the expertise and authority of the evaluator, not simply as a skilled interpreter with a refined ability to make reasoned judgments, but also as an advocate for democracy and the public interest. They argue that evaluation ought to be committed to a conception of deliberative democracy wherein, through processes of including multiple views and legitimate interests, promoting dialogue, and fostering deliberation, the evaluator reaches unbiased, impartial, objective conclusions about the value of an evaluand. This particular value-committed perspective thus promotes two primary sets of values. The first has to do with defending a type of cognitivism with respect to values: Disputes about values are capable of (at least provisional or temporary) resolution through rational, reasoned argumentation that takes place in communicative exchanges. The second set is concerned with defending a theory of the polity (deliberative democracy) in which such a process can best unfold. This approach, like all value-committed perspectives, champions reason and rationality and thereby opposes all forms of ethical skepticism.

A Value-Critical Framework. This framework shares with the value-committed approach its emphasis on the primacy of everyday life and its rejection of the radical undecidability thesis (the view that values disagreement is endemic, hence we cannot rationally determine which are the best values). It also shares with both value-neutral and value-committed frameworks a belief in the possibility of improving the rationality of human practices. However, it differs sharply in its view of the nature and aim of social inquiry and the role that professional inquiry plays in clarifying and shaping the contours of social discourse.

Evaluation practices guided by value-neutral and value-committed frameworks endeavor to keep professional social inquiry at or near the center of social life (Lindbloom, 1990). They do so in two ways: first, by defining that which is to be evaluated as an "object" about which knowledge is to be generated by professional inquiry, and second, by defining social research as a systematic, methodical process for acquiring positive knowledge of these objects that can, in turn, be used to direct society. Although the notion of a scientifically guided society is certainly the strongest in the analytical perspective, scientific social inquiry also plays a crucial role in emancipatory practices in helping members of society see how they have been wrongheaded, misguided, unclear, or even delusional in their policies, practices, and technologies.

In contrast, evaluation practices based in a value-critical framework decenter this conception of the aim, nature, and place of social inquiry in social life. They do so by redefining social inquiry as a dialogical and reflective process of democratic discussion and philosophical critique (Carr, 1995). A value-critical perspective abandons the nearly exclusive preoccupation of social inquiry with generating methodical (i.e., method-driven) knowledge about the rationality of human practices (projects, programs, policies). It does not regard what is to be evaluated as an "object" about which theoretical knowledge must be generated. Rather, what is evaluated is a human practice or action in which human beings are engaged. The activity of producing social knowledge of objects through the application of method is replaced with a conception of social inquiry aimed at cultivating practical wisdom that, in turn, is not *about* the practice but constitutive of the practice itself. In this way, a value-critical framework removes professional social inquiry from the center of society and replaces it with a focus on *praxis* and the cultivation of practical wisdom.

Improving *praxis* by enabling practitioners to refine the rationality of their practices is the aim of evaluation conducted in a value-critical framework. This can only be achieved by helping practitioners develop a kind of educative, critically reflective self-knowledge that makes it possible for them to question the beliefs and unstated assumptions which sustain decision making within a particular practice of education, management, social service, health care, and so forth (Carr, 1995). Evaluation practice oriented by the ethical aim of cultivating practical wisdom aims to help practitioners develop what the philosopher Pendlebury (1995) calls perceptive equilibrium. Pendlebury's argument can be briefly explained as follows. We begin with the premise that evaluators seek to help practitioners (teachers, program administrators, policy makers, and so forth) make sound judgments about what constitutes good practice or excellence in a human endeavor like a policy, program, or project. The critical question is, how is that practical wisdom best achieved?

One answer is that it is best achieved through a procedure that meets certain criteria:

- we are to distrust any judgments we might make that stem from fear, anger or other emotions;
- we must distrust any judgments from which we might stand to gain in some way;
- the principles we use in our reasoning must be general in form, public and universal in character;
- these principles ought to impose a general ordering on conflicting claims about excellence; and,
- these principles should be decisive as a court of last appeal for practical reasoning.

In this way of thinking, sound judgment is best achieved by making some set of principles authoritative over day-to-day practice.

A second way of answering the question of how best to culti-vate practical wisdom or sound judgment is to say that rational deliberation should be undertaken not by applying principles to cases but by being immersed in the particularities and emotional attachments of situations. Practitioners develop sound judgment by using their ability to discern salient features of those situations, being spontaneously perceptive and responsive, and so forth. Here, practitioners are encouraged to act habitually from immer-sion in the details of practice. Unfortunately, this exclusive atten-tion to specifics and concrete circumstances often overwhelms any sense of commitment to principles and standing commitments.

Evaluation practices aimed at cultivating practical wisdom seek to bring standing commitments, theories, and principles on the one hand, and details of particular situations on the other hand, into equilibrium. Human endeavors such as educating, man-aging, providing health care and social services, and so forth are constructed around standing commitments to what is good and right; they are oriented toward agreed-upon social aims. At the same time, these endeavors or practices are essentially character-ized by their mutability, indeterminacy, and particularity that make it impossible to use systems of general rules and principles to judge their goodness. Judging the merit or worth of a particular practice—that is, whether it is good, good enough, poor, or cor-rupt—thus requires cultivating perceptual awareness of concrete particulars. However, one cannot ignore standing commitments and general principles that form the traditions of various prac-tices. In addition, because of the mutability and indeterminacy of practices, one cannot engage in some process of weighing alterna-tive goals, values, criteria, and the like that reduces judgment of what constitutes good practice to calculation. Rather, we must engage in strong evaluation, judging the qualitative worth of dif-ferent aims of our practices by bringing into simultaneous critical examination the perceptual knowledge of the concrete details of a practice and the conceptual knowledge of principles that have traditionally shaped the goods of that practice.

The task for an evaluation practice in a value-critical frame-work is to help clients cultivate this capacity. The notion of evaluation expertise is not abandoned in this undertaking, but it is redirected to teaching about what it means to engage in a kind of

153

. is constitutive of the exercise of practical-moral
luators use their special knowledge about what it
aluate and how to come to warranted conclusions of
f human practices to add to and encourage practitioner.   ive, conversational critiques of the value commitments
embeau.d in their practices. An evaluator's knowledge is used in
a complementary or supplementary manner. It is not knowledge in
the form of a pronouncement about an evaluation object from an
allegedly detached, objective, and disinterested observer who en-
lightens practitioners or seeks to emancipate them from the chains
of false consciousness, erroneous reason, and the like. Moreover, it
is not knowledge in the form of partisan concern exclusively for
local narratives and attention to fine-grained particularities of local practice. Rather it is a kind of knowledge that supplements or
complements the knowledge of practitioners. Evaluation practices
informed by this ethic of cultivating practical wisdom thus take
different pedagogical forms than those practices characterized by
enlightenment and emancipatory aims. Examples include the dialogue conferences characteristic of some forms of Scandinavian
action research and the modeling of evaluation on Socratic dialogues (Elden and Levine, 1991; Gustavsen, 1992; Karlsson, 1996,
1998).

In summary, what I have sketched here are three different
ways of conceiving of the ethical aim of evaluation practice. To
argue that one's aim is to enlighten, to emancipate, or to cultivate
practical wisdom is not simply to make a cognitive claim—that is,
a defense of a particular kind of evaluation knowledge or a particular way of warranting an evaluation claim. It is also to take an
ethical stance on the question of how one ought to *be* as an evaluator in society and to make a claim about the goods or ends served
by the particular human practice we call evaluation.

The point of this brief portrait of ways in which ethics and
values are manifest in evaluation practice is really a quite simple
one. Ethical discussion aims at making us more critically aware of
what we are doing. It brings us back to thinking about what it is to
be a good evaluator, and to asking in whose interests should we
be acting and to what purpose. These are ethical questions, and
they should take precedence over technical questions of how to do

evaluation. They take precedence in the sense that they are an indispensable requirement for any genuinely educational practice like evaluation. To paraphrase an observation by Carr (1995, p. 99), it is only by virtue of a self-conscious desire to be guided and informed by philosophical beliefs about the value of a particular practice that the educational character of that practice can be recognized and sustained. This concern with the primacy of ethical questions in understanding (and reforming) a social practice is not a kind of philosophical or moral imperialism as Patton (1997) has claimed. Rather, it is an acknowledgment that the assumed neutrality of technique does not allow us to escape difficult questions about the moral and political meaning of our practice for the society in which we work.

The social science legacy of evaluation practice is undeniable; it cannot be undone. What can be done is to recognize the limitations on conceptions of evaluation practice imposed by that tradition. Perhaps the greatest limitation is that one is easily convinced that what matters most about what it means to do "good" evaluation are models, methods, and methodology and resolving quarrels over whether evaluation is best conceived as utilization-focused, objectivist, naturalistic, or quasi-experimental. One ought not let these concerns overwhelm consideration of the ethics and political morality of evaluation practice. And this statement, of course, is itself a moral claim.

9

Dialogue and the Moral Point of View

In the past few years, the field of evaluation has shown considerable interest in participatory and collaborative forms of evaluation. In these practices, the evaluator behaves less like an independent third party who renders a judgment of the value of some social or educational program and more like a facilitator or collaborator who supports the efforts of practitioners to evaluate their own practices (Cousins and Earl, 1992, 1995; Fetterman, Kaftarian, and Wandersman, 1996). The term *dialogue* figures prominently as a trope in these new ways of thinking about evaluation (e.g., Ryan and DeStefano, 2000). It signals a particular ethical and moral stance on the part of the evaluator—i.e., promoting inclusion of all relevant stakeholders; a particular responsibility on the part of the evaluator—i.e., facilitating meaningful engagement with stakeholders in an evaluation; and a commitment to a democratic means—i.e., making decisions about the merit and worth of a social or educational program via deliberation. This chapter explores two broad meanings of the concept of dialogue and suggests how each of these meanings is related to different frameworks of morality. The relationships to be discussed are represented in the marked cells of table 2. The chapter concludes with some reflections on the implications of this analysis for conceptions of collaborative and participatory evaluation.

Procedural Conceptions of Dialogue and Ethics

It is commonplace to think of dialogue as a tool of reason. In procedural terms, dialogue is an instrument or means to some end. It is a matter of *how* to proceed rationally in the exchange of messages for the purposes of gaining information, bringing some state of affairs to pass, reaching agreement, settling a dispute, and so on. In Western thought, persuasion dialogues or critical discussions are generally regarded as the ideal or normative model of a

Table 2: Relationship Between Dialogue and Ethical Frameworks

	Ethical/Moral Framework	
Conception of Dialogue	*Universalistic*	*Proximal*
Procedural	X	
Substantive		X

"good" dialogue because they are built upon standard rules—a(n) (informal) logic of argumentation—that establish how critical discussion should take place. Hence, in the literature on arguments, there is extensive treatment of what comprises valid arguments, what role appeals to emotion and authority play in argumentation, and how to identify logical errors, biases, and fallacies (Walton, 1989). This conception of logical argumentation, persuasion, or critical discussion lies at the heart of what in Western thought is assumed to be reasonable and rational behavior. Moreover, a procedural notion of dialogue is regarded as central to democratic forms of government. Nussbaum's (1997) claims are illustrative of many others to this effect:

> The case for preferring democracy to other forms of government is weakened when one conceives of democratic choice as simply the clash of opposing interests. It is very much strengthened by conceiving of it in a more Socratic way, as the expression of a deliberative judgment about the overall good…. Logical analysis is at the heart of democratic political culture. When we do wrong to one another politically, bad argument is often one cause…. Logical analysis dissipates confusions. It unmasks prejudice that masquerades as reason. Doing without it would mean forfeiting one of the most powerful tools we have to attack abuses of political power. (pp. 27, 36)

Nussbaum points to the symbiotic relationship between dialogue regarded as a type of procedural rationality and liberal democratic theories of political morality. The latter reflect a procedural conception of ethics and morality. As Newman and Brown (1996) correctly point out in their introduction to ethics for evaluators, the dominant paradigm for theorizing morality and ethics focuses on logic and reasoning. The standard answer to the question, "What is ethics and morality about?" is "rule-guided reason." The ideal moral person is rational and disinterested. He or she brackets away impulses and emotions so as to construct a careful argument for moral behavior. This ideal is readily evident in both Scriven (1995) and House and Howe's (1999) explanation of how, in determining appropriate criteria on which to base a judgment of value, one must distinguish genuinely morally weighty needs from wants that may be afflicted by desire and passion. Their views echo Rawls's (1971) claim that fairness must not be held at the mercy of existing wants and interests. Stated somewhat differently, as rule-guided reason, the moral point of view abstracts from context—from the motivations, particular situations, and lifeways of the moral actors in question (Noddings, 1996; Vetlesen, 1997)—and strives for an impartial, universalizable perspective based on rules or procedures for correct moral reasoning.

An additional characteristic of this view is that ethical rules must be based on clearly defined principles that serve as foundations for moral choices. Baier (1958, quoted in Bauman, 1993, p. 66) expresses this requirement as follows:

> A man cannot be said to have adopted the moral point of view unless he is prepared to treat the moral rules as principles rather than mere rules of thumb, that is, to do things on principle rather than merely act purposively, merely to aim at a certain end. And, furthermore, he must act on rules which are meant for everybody, and not merely for himself or some formed group.

This view is evident in evaluation. Scriven (1991), for example, defines ethics as optimally the set of rules governing behavior and attitudes based on the principle of prima facie equal rights. Newman and Brown (1996) develop a theory of ethical decisionmaking based on the principles of autonomy, avoidance of harm, beneficence, justice, and fidelity. House (1993) claims that the proper principles for an evaluation ethics are mutual respect, noncoercion, nonmanipulation, and support for democratic values and institutions.[1]

This view of ethics and morality embraces a common core of ideas: that morality is deontological (primarily concerned with moral obligations and commitments); that the moral point of view is marked by its impartiality and universalizability; and that conflicts of rights and obligations are open to argumentative resolution. Taken collectively, these ideas comprise a largely formalistic understanding of morality. *Formalistic* here means that the moral point of view is defined in terms of formal criteria. Alternatively, we might say that form is privileged over content as Vetlesen (1997) explains:

> Universalizability, impartiality, and impersonality—the formal criteria instrumental in defining the 'moral point of view'—now function as the features a given item must possess in order to qualify as actually having moral content. In other words, only issues, questions, problems, and dilemmas lending themselves to adjudication and consensual resolution by means of [these] formal criteria ... are allowed to qualify as "moral" in content. (p. 4)

When a procedural conception of dialogue is wedded to this framework for thinking about ethics and morality, morality is a matter of justice and the conflict of rights open to argumentative resolution by means of deliberative democratic dialogue.

It is not uncommon to hear arguments to the effect that abandoning the foregoing procedural account of the union of dialogue and morality invites relativism, or worse, nihilism. For if the moral point of view is not characterizable in terms of its universality and impartiality and if moral choices are not open to argumentative resolution, then moral choice is but a matter of local or individual custom, preference, interest, or desire. The form of this argument for relativism is as follows: "[A]ll knowledge is interpretation; interpretations are always value-laden; values are ultimately expressions of some heterogeneous non-cognitive faculty, process or event (such as the mechanics of desire, history, or the will to power); therefore truth claims are ultimately expressions of that non-cognitive faculty, process or event" (N. H. Smith, 1997, p. 16).

This is the view of those radical postmodernists and radical social constructionists who hold that claims about what is true and right are but a plurality of fictions, reason but the infinite play of différance. These scholars are deeply suspicious of the power of reflection and find it impossible to trust in conversation or dialogue (Gallagher, 1992). Their pervasive skepticism about the veracity of all cognitive and moral claims derives, in part, from the belief that since there appear to be no sure foundations on which to ground our claims about what is true and what is right, it must therefore be the case that all such claims are constructed from individual or communal perspectives and thus are relative to the practices, beliefs, and values that constitute those perspectives. In short, knowledge of what is true, what is good, what is right, and so on is, by definition, always partial, situated, and idiosyncratic.

If radical social constructionism is the only substitute for the standard account of dialogue and morality sketched above, then there is nothing left to say. If we level all distinctions between truth and falsehood; if right or wrong, good or bad are completely arbitrary; if we subscribe to a "logic of disintegration" (di Leonardo, 1991, p. 24), then there is no place for any morally evaluative or politically committed stance. At best, we would have to content ourselves with deconstructing the ethical practices and claims of evaluators absent any apparent purpose for such an activity.[2]

Substantive Conceptions of Dialogue and Ethics

An alternative to both the standard account of dialogue and morality and to the radical social constructionist critique becomes apparent when we begin to consider dialogue substantively. Substantive conceptions of dialogue are not concerned with dialogue as an instrument or tool; rather they define dialogue as a fundamental or characteristic aspect of human existence. Charles Taylor (1991a), for example, speaks of the "dialogical self":

> We cannot understand human life merely in terms of individual subjects, who frame representations about and respond to others, because a great deal of human action happens only insofar as the agent under-

> stands and constitutes himself or herself as integrally part of a 'we.'
> Much of our understanding of self, society, and world is carried in
> practices that consist in dialogical action....[O]ur identity is never sim-
> ply defined in terms of individual properties. It also places us in some
> social space. (p. 311)

Martin Buber's philosophy also deals with dialogue substantively,
as a basic ontological premise—human existence is always existence in relation, in dialogue; we become who we are in relation
with others (Friedman, 1996a). In the philosophical hermeneutics
of Hans-Georg Gadamer (1989), dialogue is the characteristic
structure of human understanding. At the heart of this notion lies
the idea that understanding happens to us. Understanding is
something like an unending interpretative undertaking, something never "finished"; it is a dialogic event that we participate in
as historical beings, not a means or instrumentality over which we
have complete and objective personal control.

The key to realizing a genuine event of understanding is that
through dialogue with another (be it a person, a text, or a tradition) we allow the other to speak to us. This means that we do not
simply debate "our" view versus "their" view (thereby simply
reproducing, restating, and continuing to argue for our current
understandings) but that each party to the event of understanding
genuinely risks her or his own self-understanding and thereby is
open to the possibility of a mutually evolved new and different
understanding. This is a profound and hazardous undertaking, as
Garrison (1996) explains, for it

> requires us to recognize that historically and culturally conditioned
> prejudices constitute our personal identity. These prejudices provide the
> forestructure that makes [understanding] possible. To listen to others
> different from ourselves we must remain open and that means parts of
> our interpretive forestructure is rendered at risk. Said differently, active
> listening requires personal vulnerability. Risking self-identity is dan-
> gerous. Advocates of dialoguing across differences, such as multicul-
> turalists and democratic pluralists, rarely acknowledge this danger. (p.
> 449)

Noddings (1984) situates dialogue as the heart of an ethic of closeness, care, proximity, or relatedness. In this way, dialogue with
the other opposes impersonality and universalizability as charac-

teristics of the moral point of view. Dialogue signals that morality must be theorized from an *experiential* basis, specifically in the experience of the I-thou or the one-caring and the one-cared-for relationship.

In these views, neither dialogue nor morality is conceived in procedural terms. Dialogue is not a matter of moving argumentatively forward through the opposition and interaction of different views, but an encounter between genuinely other persons (Friedman, 1996b). Morality is not defined by its formal criteria; rather, "the moral issues which preoccupy us most and which touch us most deeply derive not from problems of justice in the economy and the polity, but precisely from the quality of our relations with others in the 'spheres of kinship, love, friendship, and sex'" (Benhabib quoted in Vetlesen, 1997, p. 4). These relations demand what Nussbaum (1990, p. 162) characterizes as attentiveness—"an openness to being moved by the plight of others"; the willingness "to be touched by another's life." Normative attention, in turn, requires a way of knowing that is contextual and narrative rather than formal and abstract. Context refers both to each individual's specific history, identity, and affective-emotional constitution and to the relationship between parties in the encounter with its history, identity, and affective definition. These two elements are linked by narrative.

Moreover, because these relations are highly contingent and contextual, the moral act itself, as Bauman observes (1993, p. 181) "is endemically ambivalent, forever threading precariously the thin lines dividing care from domination and tolerance from indifference." The inherent fragility, precariousness, and incurable ambivalence of morality means that the moral life is not about decisionmaking, calculation, or procedures. Rather, it is "that unfounded, non-rational, unarguable, no excuses given and non-calculable urge to stretch towards the other, to caress, to be for, to live for, happen what may" (Bauman, 1993, p. 247). Bauman (1995, p. 66) adds that what the moral life amounts to in this view is a "never-ending string of settlements between mildly attractive or unattractive eventualities." Here, the notion of settlement differs from a calculating decision. It is not a conclusion one reaches based on applying principles; it has no fixed procedure.

Completely absent in this way of thinking of the moral life is the notion that morality is about argumentative resolution of competing moral claims. The moral encounter does not mean rule-following, but expression and communication. Furthermore, in this framework, there is no teleological, liberalist idea of moral progress driven by a vision, albeit imperfect, of social betterment, or a belief that our values and our moral abilities are evolving to some improved form.

In this alternative framework, ethical relationship is grounded in the notion of being-for the Other. The relationship of being-for is prior to intentionality, prior to choice. Morality in this alternative framework is not voluntary. Moral orientation comes before any calculating action on the part of the moral agent; it is prior to purposefulness, reciprocity, and contractuality. Morality, in the first instance, is not about a kind of moral decision making that precedes moral action. Morality is not optional. Being-for is a kind of responsibility that is prevoluntary, unremovable, noncontractual, nonreciprocal, and asymmetrical. As Vetlesen (1997, p. 9) explains, "the core of being-for is neither right nor rights, neither the happiness nor the good of those concerned. Its core is responsibility. Responsibility not as freely assumed, not as socially or politically or legally sanctioned; and yet as coming from outside rather than inside, as originating from what is exterior not interior to the agent." He adds that matters of justice, goodness, happiness all matter, but come later, and they do not "taken together or singly, define morality the phenomenon, responsibility the task."

Implications for Collaborative and Participatory Evaluation

Issues critical to understanding the agency/role of the evaluator and the very purpose of the practice of collaborative and participatory evaluation will be addressed differently depending on the justification offered for the practice. For the sake of ease of reference, consider justification P to be based on a procedural conception of dialogue coupled with a universalistic moral point of view, and justification S to reflect a substantive conception of dialogue wedded to a proximal moral point of view. The distinction in conceptions of the evaluator's agency or role given these different justifications can perhaps best be understood by examining the meaning of the terms *dialogue* and *dialectic* as explained by Friedman:

> As the prefix *dia* suggests, both dialogue and dialectic imply the alternation between two different points of view. In the case of dialogue, this also means real meeting with the unique otherness of the other, whereas in the case of dialectic the alternation may take place within the head of a single thinker, and the points of view may remain disembodied and hypothetical.... *Dialogue recognizes differences and never seeks for simple agreement or unanimity. Dialectic, in* contrast, begins with the categories of 'the same' and 'the other,' but excludes the reality of 'the between' and with it the recognition of real otherness as that which can be affirmed even in opposing it. Thus both the original assumption and the goal of dialectic is a unified point of view. The dialectician's faith in logic as the arbitrator and common denominator not only of his inner reflections but also of the dialogue between person and person is essentially single-voiced, monological, and pseudo-universal. (1996b, pp. 17–18, 20–21)

When collaborative or participatory evaluation is based in justification *P*, the evaluator-as-agent adopts the roles of facilitating, enabling, and, where necessary, controlling the dialogue and process of deliberation so that legitimate stakeholder interests are uncovered, discussed, and debated in a fair and just manner (House and Howe, 1999). Although the "dialogue" here is unquestionably an act of exchange or sharing of views, it effectively remains what Taylor (1991a, 1995) calls a monological act or a nonparticipatory relation. Thus *dialectic* is the more proper characterization of the agency and role of the evaluator in justification *P*. Dialectic brings in other people, but it is fundamentally the evaluator as interlocutor who presses through the differences of views to reach some agreement. Dialectic more accurately characterizes the evaluator's agency (as well as the agency of all parties to the collaborative evaluation) in terms of notions of disengagement (in the sense of impartiality), procedure-governed reason, and argumentative resolution of disputed moral claims. This kind of agency or role must, of course, be exercised in an ethically responsible manner. Hence, the fundamental moral point of view here is one of impartiality, respect, noncoercion, and nonmanipulation. Under justification *P*, collaborative and participatory forms of evaluation are unquestionably a kind of dialectic; they are based on a process of deliberation that aims at resolution. The parties to the dialectic affirm one another only indirectly via the roles each plays (as, for example, evaluator, program manager, program director, program recipient, program funder) in the process of deliberation. Collaboration and participation are instrumental means to an end.

When collaborative and participatory forms of evaluation are grounded in justification S, however, a different conception of evaluator agency and identity is entailed. First, each party to the evaluation recognizes the other directly, not in terms of social role, but in terms of the other's uniqueness. The relationship is genuinely dialogical in the sense described above by Friedman in that it is not merely a reciprocal exchange or a matter of equity and balance among views expressed, but a genuine mutuality and a commitment of the parties to be present, responsive, and responsible to each other and to the relationship (Graf-Taylor, 1996). Noddings argues that recognizing one's primary accountability to the Other creates a paradoxical form of agency:

> I still do things—must do things—but my moral agency is in a deep sense subject to the Other. My agency no longer swaggers about the world planning, controlling, dominating, and totalizing. There is a recognition that a basic relatedness in which the Other plays an essential role lies beneath all forms of association created by particular cultural patterns. (1996, p. 262)

Second, when grounded in this sense of human agents as dialogically related, notions of collaboration and participation in evaluation practice denote not a means but an end or way of being. Dialogue refers not simply to a participatory relationship characterized by directness, involvement, mutuality, responsiveness, and presentness. It also signifies an ethic of proximity and engagement and a fluid way of knowing through relationship and listening (versus disengagement and argumentation). On this account, knowledge, in the first instance, derives from an encounter in which the other's difference is affirmed and not necessarily assimilated into a mutually unified point of view. Moreover, as Walker (1992) explains, the moral point of view here is wedded to an epistemology that struggles with a union of knowing and being, thinking and feeling. One does not necessarily set aside a critical rational faculty or the capacity to be appropriately moved by reasons in favor of caring. Nor does one ignore lived experience with its emotions, contingent relations, and so forth in favor of attention to objective, procedural rule-governed knowing. In other words, dialogue signifies a living "in between."

The two different justifications are likely to be associated with dissimilar ways of reporting and expressing evaluation judgments. Justification P assumes that some unitary concept of value can be reached via deliberation. Consequently, it is not uncommon that forms of collaborative and participatory evaluation informed by justification P would favor a reporting format that clearly displays the procedures employed in reaching that unitary judgment (e.g., how parties to the deliberation were constituted, how the criteria of merit (value) that each promoted were identified, how the different criteria were justified in terms of evidence, how the criteria were combined to reach a unified or synthetic judgment). Justification S, however, assumes that alternative conceptions of value cannot necessarily be expressed in some common units of calculation and thus rendered commensurable. It is thus more compatible with a reporting format that renders judgments in a language of qualitative contrasts (Taylor, 1985). In a genuine dialogic (versus dialectic) evaluation, parties to the dialogue would be aiming to understand their differences about the value of the practice under examination. Accordingly, distinctions between what is good or bad, right or wrong about the program or what is regarded as action that is base or noble, courageous or cowardly, honest or duplicitous, and so on would be rendered contrastively. Each item in one of the above pairs can only be understood in relation to the other. Collaborative and participatory practices grounded in justification S would more likely employ a language of evaluative distinctions, not a language of calculation. This language of qualitative contrasts is "most at home and has its most telling exemplars in narratives"; therefore, judgments of lived practice require narrative redescription: "[A] story which relates obstacles overcome or still looming large; conflicts resolved, displaced, or deepened; turning points for better or worse; climaxes and culminations" (Pendlebury, 1995, pp. 63–64). It is by means of these carefully crafted accounts or stories that evaluators

would aim to engage the already elaborately constructed interpretations of value held by stakeholders and other readers of an
evaluation report.

There is both an inevitable and necessary connection between
justification P and justification S, between dialectic and dialogue.
Life is characterized by the twofold movement of self relating to
other and distancing self from other, of I-Thou and I-It, of subject-
subject and subject-object, of caring and justice. The problem at
hand is thus not one of overcoming one of these views, but of recognizing that dialogue is the source of our understanding that
makes dialectic possible. Attending to justification S for collaborative and evaluative practices can serve as a reminder that justification P is not our *primary* way of being in the world. We too easily forget that disengagement, the monological point of view, the
first-person singular self are not "the primary locus of understanding ourselves," but simply "islands in the sea of our unfor-
mulated practical grasp on the world" (Taylor, 1991a, p. 308).
Collaborative and participatory evaluation practices grounded in
justification S—in substantive conceptions of dialogue and proximal conceptions of the moral point of view—help keep us humble
in our aspirations to determine dialectically the value of human
practices.

Notes

1   Henry and Julnes (1998) avoid endorsing any particular set of ethical
        principles, preferring to steer a course between the extremes of ethical
        relativism and ethical absolutism. They are highly critical of the pro-
        found relativism of radically constructionist views that claim all values
        are arbitrary and that choice is a matter of individual taste. They argue
        that it is both necessary and desirable "to develop a reasoned stance on
        values." In their view, that reasoned stance is not to be found in any sin-
        gle, formal moral theory that purports to serve as an infallible guide to
        ethical choices. Rather, they defend a process of "natural valuation"
        through which values emerge over time as human needs evolve. This

process of evolution is the result of analysis and critical examination informed in the long run by the telos of social betterment through democratic means. The fact that there is this kind of disagreement in the evaluation community on the right set of principles for an evaluation ethic does not invalidate the claim that the search for foundational principles of morality is critically necessary in this framework.

2   It is possible, however, to endorse a social constructionist insight without drawing a radically skeptical postmodern conclusion about the meaning of that insight. Moderate social constructionism is equivalent to moderate skepticism that is informed by a pragmatic temperament (Bernstein, 1991). Ethical choices and value claims of social inquirers are contingent, fallibilistic, and plural. These claims are also reflexive in that they partly constitute their object. Yet, this kind of social construction is tempered by a belief that the object (the program, policy, etc.) exists independently of the claims that evaluators make about that object. While respecting historical difference and change in what constitutes knowledge and value and recognizing that knowledge and value are always developed from a particular contingent stance, this view refuses the more radically skeptical claims that we are trapped in a prison house of language and that knowledge and value claims have no determinable relation to extra-linguistic referents. As di Leonardo (1991, p. 29) claims of this moderate view, "although we recognize that our Archimedian point may be historically contingent, it is nonetheless real and we stand on it as we move the world." This more moderate version of constructionism is assumed in much contemporary writing about epistemological and ethical concerns in evaluation including Conner's (1998) social ecological view of evaluation and Weiss' (1998) observation that constructionism does not necessarily entail radical particularity.

10

Contingency, Power, and Choice: Reflections on Postmodernist Thinking in Evaluation

Theorizing the implications of postmodern intellectual developments for the social practice of evaluation is oddly ironic, for the activity itself constitutes a distinctly modern undertaking. Treating social activities, social practices, or the very idea of the social as an object of reasoning, theoretical reflection, and abstract knowledge is a preoccupation traceable to the work of the French and Scottish *philosophes* whose work ushered in what came to be known as the Age of Enlightenment (Smart, 1996). As if that were not trouble enough, theorizing about the implications of postmodernity can be a perilous undertaking because of the controversial definition of postmodernism (cf. Best and Kellner, 1991; Denzin, 1986; Harvey, 1989). Hence, some point of departure must be provided.

In this chapter I assume that to theorize a practice after postmodernity means coping with the consequences of living in a world "which is thoroughly constituted through reflexively applied knowledge" (Giddens, 1990, p. 39). Smart (1996) draws on this observation to conclude that

> The circularity of the relationship between social knowledge and social realities, the fact that social knowledge constitutes a resource which unavoidably, and unpredictably, contributes to the transformation of the social objects analyzed, has meant that knowledge is of necessity continually subject to revision, and in consequence no longer to be characterized by certainty. (p. 422)

What this kind of reflexivity signals is fallibilism and not necessarily radical skepticism—the refusal to grant that there is any knowledge or justification. However, fallibilism is accompanied by a mood or stance of incredulity and disbelief, or, in short, post-modern doubt. Burbules' (1996) explication of this notion is help-ful here. Burbules is concerned with understanding the meaning of the term *incredulity* in the oft-quoted Jean-François Lyotard char-acterization of postmodernism as "incredulity toward metanarra-tives." He argues that, as a philosophical stance, incredulity does not mean denial, rejection, or refutation of modernist conceptions of language, science, ethics, reason, justice, and so forth, but some-thing more like doubt, instability, and uncertainty:

> Denial or refutation place one outside of the view being rejected, beyond and above it. But what is our stance to be toward ways of thinking that for us are necessary, that we do not know how to live entirely with-out—but in which an unshaken confidence is no longer possible? (p. 40).

Doubt is not denial, but a loss of faith in and the inability to believe in what have been long-taken-for-granted presuppositions and procedures. Postmodernism is this mood or attitude of doubt. It is not an exposure of errors to be corrected, narratives to be fixed, concepts to be replaced; in sum, it is not doubt in the ser-vice of seeking certainty. As Giddens and others have pointed out, contemporary social life provides the circumstances for this doubt. Two of the sources identified by Burbules are of particular interest here: first, "the understanding that certain dynamics of asymmetrical power which distort and compromise even the best of human intentions are inherent to the institutional and informal patterns of life in which humans are engaged," and, second, "the particular way in which discourse—language in use—colors and shapes our ways of living and being in the world" (1996, p. 42). My aim in this chapter is to suggest ways in which one might be justified in doubting the taken-for-granted institutional politics and discourse of the practice of evaluation.

Evaluation as a Social Practice of Power

Cook and Shadish (1986, p. 194) have proclaimed that evaluation is a worldly science because it fully embraces the "whole messy world of social programming." Does it, though? Undoubtedly they are correct in claiming that it is naïve to assume that evaluation fits neatly into a problem solving model characterized by rigid procedural rationality. Evaluators nowadays are considerably more attuned to the social and political realities of policy making and social programming. However, evaluation continues to be "otherworldly" to the extent that it remains ignorant of its normalizing practice. Whose interests do evaluators serve? What "world" of social problems and solutions to those problems do evaluators as social agents actually create through their practice?

To answer these questions I begin with a particular perspective on human action that assumes that social *praxis* is fundamental to understanding human action (Cohen, 1996). In other words, this analysis of what it means to perform evaluation practice shifts from a traditional focus on individual *consciousness*, or individual mental acts directing conduct, to *practice*, or performance of social conduct. For many years, discussions of evaluation practice have privileged the conscious processes of individual knowers (e.g., calculation, interpretation, normative commitment) and associated virtues (e.g., rationality, responsibility, impartiality). Talk about what it means to evaluate has been cast largely in terms of the mental acts of individual agents who face a world of objective constraints that the mind must take into account.

Consider, for example, Scriven's (1980) explication of the logic of evaluation. The principal concern here is with improving the ability of the evaluator to reason well, for "reasoning is the basis of what evaluators do and what they tell their clients to do" (Fournier, 1995, p. 1). The notion that evaluation practice is largely the province of the individual scientific practitioner and her or his conscious capabilities is also evident in the stated purpose of the impressive volume, *Foundations of Program Evaluation* (Shadish, Cook, and Leviton, 1991): "This book is meant to encourage the theoretical dispositions of practitioners by expanding their repertoire of methods, challenging the assumptions behind their methodological and strategic decisions, and creating a broader conceptual framework for them to use in their work" (p. 35).

This way of portraying evaluation theorizes the activity of evaluation practice largely in terms of the epistemological acts of individual agents. Evaluators are viewed principally as knowers who must cultivate a certain set of mental capacities and intellectual virtues. Through an analysis of these capacities and virtues we come to understand what it means to do evaluation. However, when *praxis* becomes the conceptual tool for analyzing evaluation, then there is far less focus on individual mental acts and more on social enactments, tacitly enacted practices—that is, routines that reproduce familiar forms of social life (Cohen, 1996). Accordingly, evaluation practice is cast less in terms of the collective activities of individual conscious agents and more in terms of social performances, social agency, or ongoing iterative social practice (Bourdieu, 1990; Giddens, 1984).

This makes it possible to view evaluation, as House (1993) explains, as an economic, socio-political, and cultural institutional practice. As an institution in its own right (or as a significant part of other cultural institutions), evaluation practice accrues and exercises power to define the socio-political world. With a few notable exceptions, including House (1993), Cronbach and associates (1980), and the work on democratic theory of evaluation undertaken by Barry MacDonald and colleagues in England (for an overview see Simons, 1987), investigation of evaluation as a sociopolitical institution is notably absent from textbooks and journals, especially in the U.S.

At first glance, this assertion may seem to be curious and weakly supported, because current understanding of evaluation practice is informed by considerable empirical and conceptual research on the politics of evaluation. Furthermore, this body of knowledge has been growing since the publication of Weiss's (1973) seminal paper, and the comprehensive review of evaluation theories by Shadish, Cook, and Leviton (1991) gives a prominent place to an evaluation-specific social programming knowledge base. This knowledge base addresses the critical role that external (i.e., social, political, economic) context plays in shaping and constraining a program, as well as the necessity of understanding theories of social change and the links between social change and program development.

However, these socio-political considerations are largely cast as objective aspects of a social world that constrain the epistemological (mental) activity of the conscious, responsible, rational, autonomous evaluator-as-knower. This knower aims to produce a particular kind of empirical social scientific knowledge about the merit or worth of policies, projects, programs, and technologies that, in turn, is used to enlighten society or to emancipate it from its misconceptions. The mental processes necessary to generate reliable and valid knowledge of this kind are constrained, and in some cases threatened and compromised, by the vicissitudes and contingencies of real-world management and administration. Hence, the evaluation practitioner must be attuned to the politics of conducting evaluative inquiries and the interest- and ideology-laden world of policy making and social programming.

The primary concerns in this perspective are how political context constrains the evaluator's task of knowing about and reporting on a program; how politics affect the use of evaluation knowledge; and how the appearance of an evaluative mandate in the political arena itself is interpreted as a political move and threatens the autonomous, responsible actions of the evaluator. More precisely, what is going on here is a discussion of how politics act *on* the institution of evaluation to compromise its epistemological authority. What is missing here is discussion of the manner in which politics act *through* the social practice itself to create this authority in the first place.[1]

Central to this different understanding of evaluation politics is the notion that the institution of evaluation is one of the "ruling apparatuses of society"—"those institutions of administration, management, and professional authority and of intellectual and cultural discourses which organize, regulate, lead, and direct capitalist societies" (D. E. Smith, 1990b, p. 2). House (1993) makes a similar claim about the emergence in modern market societies of evaluation (and social science more generally) as an institution with distinct cultural authority. Lindbloom (1990) concurs and suggests that contemporary industrialized societies tend to be "scientifically-guided societies" that look to the expertise of social scientists for social problem solving, social betterment, and guided social change. It is because we invest authority in social science institutions like evaluation that they have a normative force for us.

Tacitly enacted practices reproduce themselves because actors take their behaviors and the meanings of their behaviors for granted. As Bellah and colleagues explain (Bellah, Madsen, Swidler, Sullivan, and Tipton, 1991), from a sociological point of

view, practices or institutions are patterned ways of living together. These patterns are comprised of rights and duties, power
and responsibilities that make the institution—e.g., social science,
politics, the economy, the family, the church, the corporation—a
normative force in our lives. It is through institutions that we extend meaning to events of daily life and hence "institutions mediate the relations between self and world" (p. 287). Evaluation is
thus not simply what individual practitioners do, but is an institutional practice that mediates the relationship between citizens and
their social world.

   One way in which this mediation takes place can be explained
as follows: As a practice or institution, evaluation (and, more
broadly, all social scientific) enterprises participate in what D. E.
Smith (1990b, p. 6) calls "relations of ruling"—"the complex of
extra-local relations that provide in contemporary society a spe-
cialization of organization, control, and initiative." Evaluation,
like other professions (or disciplines or near professions), participates in the construction of ruling relations not by exercising social
authority to command obedience or control decisions about policy
but by virtue of its epistemological or cognitive authority (Addelson, 1983). This is a conceptual practice of power: a power to define the socio-political world through objectified knowledge (D. E.
Smith, 1990a). Starr (1982) refers to this authority of professions
as cultural authority—the probability that a given profession's
particular definitions of reality and its judgments of meaning and
value will prevail as true and valid. Borrowing Starr's notion,
House (1993) explains that evaluation answers the appeal of governments (and private agencies, as well) to scientific authority;
hence, evaluation is a new form of cultural authority. Governments
and private agencies use evaluation to legitimate, inform, and control.

   This conceptual practice of power is exercised not simply in
the scientific pronouncements (journal articles, written evaluation
reports, oral briefings, and so forth) of social science professionals
but through the metaphysical commitments that are reflected in
social scientific activity itself. In other words, evaluators and social scientists do not simply teach others their scientific views,
they also convey their beliefs about the socio-political world. An
illustration in the arena of disability research is provided by

Oliver (1992). He points out that social researchers working for the British government promoted the view that disability is a problem "in the person" by asking survey questions such as: Are your difficulties in understanding people mainly due to a hearing problem? Have you attended a special school because of a long-term health problem or disability? Oliver maintains that if the researchers had taken the view that the problem of disability is "in society," then they might have asked instead: Are your difficulties in understanding people mainly due to their inabilities to communicate with you? Have you attended a special school because of your education authority's policy of sending people with your health problem or disability to such places? A second illustration about how social inquiry does not discover the nature of the social world as much as construct it is provided in Addelson's (1983) explanation of how the functionalist Merton and the symbolic interactionist Becker defined the phenomenon of deviance very differently:

> Merton looked for the *cause* of deviant behavior ... and found the cause in social structures exerting a definite pressure on some people. Becker asks about deviant behavior as behavior defined under *ban*, and so he asks about who does the banning, how the ban is maintained, and what effect the ban has on the activity itself. On the basis of interactionist metaphysics, he doesn't assume that deviance is something there for the natural scientific eye to discern. Whether something is deviant or normal in a society is a question of power and perspective within the society. (p. 176)

In evaluation practice, House (1983) explained how cognitive authority in evaluation is exercised via the teaching of metaphysical commitments implicit in the language used to describe the social world. He revealed how these commitments are intertwined with theories and statements about social and educational programs in the use of particular metaphors for social programming, social policy, and social program evaluation. He illustrated how the language of evaluation does not simply describe the socio-political world but constructs its meaning.

Towards Questioning the Social Practice of Power

To address the nature and consequences of the politics that act through the practice of evaluation, one must resist the tendency to depoliticize evaluation as a conceptual practice of power. The paradoxical use of this term is explained by Fuller (1988): To depoliticize a practice of cognitive authority is to close the question of authority in favor of the experts, while to politicize the expertise of social science professionals is to open the question of cognitive authority to the critical scrutiny of society at large. Harding (1992) concurs and explains that the kind of politics that act less visibly and less consciously through the dominant institutional structures, priorities, practices, and languages of science paradoxically function as a kind of depoliticalization. A depoliticized practice, in Harding's view, "certifies as value-neutral, normal, natural, and *not political at all* the existing scientific policies and practices through which powerful groups can gain the information and explanations that they need to advance their priorities" (pp. 568–69, emphasis added).

A depoliticized practice is unaware of its own conceptual practice of power. It fails to examine how it produces objectified knowledge. D. E. Smith (1990a) explores how relations of ruling in our society are done by means of abstract concepts and symbols that social science professionals help create. That is, notions like mental illness, poverty, violence, crime, work satisfaction, employment, educational achievement, disability, and so forth are constructs of the practice of government. They are objectified forms of knowledge that organize our everyday world. "Objectified" here means that these concepts are made into synthetic objects of the knowledge discourse in social science, evaluation, and policy making. This is accomplished by severing these concepts from their grounding in the actualities of people's experience.

This is readily evident in the official knowledge of administrative processes: Physical metaphors and images are used to refer to processes that are actually communicative and cultural; for example: span of control, information flow, input, output, and so forth. Viewed concretely, systems of administration are largely symbolic systems; their forms, structures, and oppressions are symbolically mediated impressions (Young, 1990). D. E. Smith

(1990a) provides the following illustration of how objectified knowledge means that *who* acts and *how* disappears:

> Take, for example, a passage such as this from the work of a social scientist: "Structure can be defined as the design of organization through which the enterprise is administered. This design, whether formally or informally defined, has two aspects. It includes, first, the lines of authority and communication." In this passage, the term 'structure' identifies a conceptual order. It is the 'design of an organization.' What might be actually observed as what people do in an organization is treated as mere appearance; the conceptual reality is to be discerned through that appearance.... The actualities of living people become a resource to be made over into the image of the concept. The work becomes that of transposing the paramount reality into the conceptual currency in which it is governed. (p. 53)

There are numerous other ways in which the social locations and priorities of the institutions and conceptual schemes within which evaluation practice occurs are not questioned. The one, and often only, way in which this has been discussed in evaluation is in terms of the managerial bias of evaluation—its tendency to give priority to the questions, needs, and perspectives of functionaries, program managers, and the like. Even so, this is only the most obvious aspect of the social location of the practice. House (1993) identifies a far subtler and unexplored bias in the affiliation of evaluation as an institution with the prevailing pluralist-elitist-equilibrium theory of political democracy.

A number of other aspects of the social location of evaluation practice in need of exploration are suggested by Lindbloom (1990) in his critique of professional social science. To be sure, Lindbloom is examining social science disciplines, not the practice of evaluation per se. Even so, many evaluation practitioners have their roots in, and share professional affiliations with, these disciplines and make their careers therein. Hence, it is reasonable to assume that the following impairing influences on the ability to probe into social problems extend to the practice of evaluation:

- the white middle class bias in professional practice;
- the inability of social scientific professions in general to overcome presumptions in favor of hierarchical forms of social organization in family, school, work organizations, and politics;

- the dominant or standard views in disciplines; for example, econo-
  mists call attention to the beneficial consequences of economic organizations without noting that a function and accomplishment of an
  economy is to permit a relatively small segment of a population to
  enjoy disproportional income and wealth and to direct the productive activities of a less qualified mass of people; political science advances a narrow, benign interpretation of politics—that political
  parties are basic institutions for translating mass preferences into
  public policy and that politics has the function of coordinating the
  learning processes of a whole society—as opposed to viewing political parties as institutions that control citizens' views or politics
  as a process by which elites impair the probing of citizens; or sociology's benign view of socialization as a process of learning to con-
  form to social norms when in fact socialization processes often pro-
  tect some groups at the expense of others, and little attention is paid
  to how socialization of particular groups, say working-class children, is a matter of accepting the norms of superiors;
- the bias of social science in general that places the burden of proof
  on dissenting views; Lindbloom observes: "Such a [burden] makes
  sense in circumstances in which the agreed or conventional professional belief has emerged from well-conducted professional inquiry,
  often the case in the natural sciences.... Frequently, however, in the
  social sciences, established agreement has never been processed in
  that way and may itself represent an untested, impaired professional
  agreement" (p. 209);
- the affiliation of professional social scientists with elites: their de-
  pendence on elite grants, their employment with elites, their tendency
  to pass into the ranks of social and political elites;
- the centralist bias of professional social science—the assumption of
  the necessity of central power and coordination for social order.

There is very little examination of how these social arrangements and social locations of the practice of evaluation are implicated in its cognitive authority. Likewise, there is little, if any, discussion of evaluation expertise as the power to define the experiences of others and to (re)present them to other authorities. To
understand this power, we need to consider the ways in which the
enterprise of evaluation (and the individual evaluation practitioner) acts as a "recontextualizing agent" (B. Bernstein, 1986). In recontextualizing the experiences (i.e., the lived realities) of program
stakeholders, the actual conditions of their experience are delo-
cated from their original site and relocated into a new pedagogic
situation. In so doing, the agent of the relocation or recontextuali-

zation (i.e., the evaluator) changes the way in which the experience of stakeholders with a particular program is positioned in relation to other aspects of stakeholders' experience. For example, participation in, say a job training program, an educational innovation, or a welfare program is intimately interwoven with all the life experiences of said participants; their experiences in the program are not simply experiences as "program participants." The experience is no longer theirs but becomes part of the professional discourse of evaluators—that is, it is redescribed as effects, outcomes, participants' views of the program, variables, and so forth. What once was part of the discourse of program participants becomes the discourse of the expert.

In this new context, the original experience or participants' knowledge is integrated around a different set of political and cultural needs and priorities dictated by the professional's reference group, not the participants'. Finally, the experience of participants is refocused and repositioned so as to change its use. For example, the experience of stakeholders in a program designed to improve workforce literacy may have been part of their efforts to gain power and control over their lives. This experience is relocated and rewritten by evaluators for use in determining whether program funders' expectations for gains in on-the-job reading and computing skills were met. The ways in which the expertise of the professional evaluator is implicated in the politics of the symbolic control of public knowledge bear closer scrutiny.

Finally, we must examine the cognitive politics of the assumption that the evaluator must be politically neutral or unbiased, and in that sense objective. The common view is that the professional evaluator must be nonpartisan and avoid advocating the political (or moral) views of any special stakeholder group. This is equivalent to holding that the evaluator (and evaluation knowledge) must be nonideological, for ideology identifies the biasing of statements or claims by special interests or perspectives. D. E. Smith provides us with one view of how ideology and objectivity (or neutrality) are typically opposed in social science, a view which we can readily apply to evaluation practice: "If the perspectives and concepts of the knower [i.e., evaluator] are determined, for example, by class interests, by gender or racial standpoints, then sociological [i.e., evaluative] claims to objective knowledge are invalidated" (1990a, p. 32). She further observes that this neutral, nonideological, objective stance of the social scientist (or evaluator) "is to be guaranteed by the detachment of the social scientist from particular interests and perspectives; it is not guaranteed by its success in unfolding actual properties of social relations and organizations" (1990a, p. 32).

But whose interests does this stance of neutrality serve? House (1993) argues that in the absence of the evaluator's advocacy for minority group interests, majority elite views will dominate. In addition, Harding (1991, 1992) explains that objectivity as neutrality fails to provide any resistance to the production of inquiry claims that reflect the institutional politics of scientific elites. She and others who argue for standpoint epistemologies hold that to criticize values and interests sedimented in dominant conceptual schemes, institutions, and practices we must start from outside those structures by beginning our inquiries in the lives of individuals marginalized by those structures. Mertens (1995), for example, has argued that evaluation should ensure that "groups traditionally marginalized in society" are heard in an evaluation, that power inequities inherent in social relationships defining planning, implementing, and reporting evaluations should be carefully examined, and that evaluation should be linked to political action.

By shifting our conceptual lens such that we focus less on evaluation as a matter of particular cognitive capacities and virtues of individual knowers and more on evaluation as *praxis*—routines or processes socially enacted—we are better able to reflect on the taken-for-granted politics and discourse of evaluation as social practice. Reflection helps us understand that the practice of evaluation invariably contributes to the construction of our social world. Further, it reveals that this activity of construction is inevitable yet never wholly satisfying or innocent. We cannot do entirely without social construction via enacted practices, yet we cannot be entirely comfortable with or confident and certain of our constructions.

Where Do We Go from Here?

The mood or attitude of postmodern doubt may lead to this recognition of the problematic discourse and politics of evaluation, but then what? Do we, fundamentally, have no choice but to "live with the ruin"? (Ian Stronach, personal communication, January 2, 1997). The postmodern habitat (Bauman, 1992) is constituted by what R. J. Bernstein (1991, p. 329) calls "a plurality of traditions, perspectives, philosophical orientations." For the postmodernist, there is no escaping this situation, no way to transcend it; we must simply learn to live with it.

Learning to live with the ruin means avowing a kind of humility in the face of the plurality of perspectives. This is not necessarily a bad thing. It means recognizing that to express a particular perspective can also mean to make an honorific gesture about it—one that can "privilege the claimant's own perspective and exclude others" (N. H. Smith, 1997, p. 16). A postmodern posture challenges this kind of honorific pronouncement in evaluation and makes space for diversity, heterogeneity, and difference. How this space can be created is suggested by Burbules who argues that the "conflicted, unstable outlook, an outlook of sustained tensions and of disenchanted hopes" brought on by postmodern realizations can be made "somewhat livable" by turning to three narrative tropes that provide "ways of coping with the paradox of doubting the very things one can hardly do without"(1996, p. 43). Of the tropes irony, tragedy, and parody, "each begins with the embracing of apparently contradictory or self-undermining positions, but turns that realization into a larger vision of possibility within a conflicted, uncertain world" (p. 44). Although Burbules is principally concerned with the implications of postmodernism for education, his observations might well be extended to evaluation practice:

> Education [and evaluation as well?] involves engagement, among persons and between persons and the matters to be explored.... Playing with the tropes of irony, tragedy, and parody are among the ways that we can avoid taking ourselves as teachers [and as evaluators?] too seriously. We can adopt certain stances without fully endorsing them. We can question our authority, and invite others to question it, even in contexts that arrogate authority to us whether we wish it or not.... Such a stance al-

lows for both a respect and appreciation for perspectives and approaches that broaden our understandings, but also a wary suspicion of
the tendency for teachers [evaluators?], texts, and methods to become hy-
postasized, entrenched. (pp. 45–46)

However, as salutary as this posture of playfulness may be for
disturbing taken-for-granted frames of reference and perspectives,
it is not adequate for facing the existential condition of contingency. Radical postmodern reflexivity challenges all received
ideas, arguments, epistemologies, and sociopolitical developments
and reveals them to be nothing but the product of "the unwar-
ranted assumption of privileged analytic and political positions"
(Smart, 1996, p. 423). In this posture, reason, identity, cognition,
and morality are all fundamentally contingent. Any effort to aspire beyond this condition to something that is transcendentally
true, real, or good is thought to be contingency-negating and,
hence, detrimental to proper intellectual conduct (N. H. Smith,
1997). To the extent that the posture of playfulness embraces this
radical reflexivity it may actually disable us from arguing compe-
tently about our choices of what it is right to do and good to be. It
may foreclose the possibility of deciding which among competing
interpretations is better, at least for now.

The danger of the radical postmodernist way of coping with
the contingency of all efforts to explain ourselves to ourselves
stems from its mistaken assumption that there are only two modal
responses: Either we are rational and reasonable by virtue of our
ability to grasp foundational claims about truth, reality, or goodness, or we disavow reason as nothing more than a strategy
through which some groups exercise power and control, and, thus,
we surrender to relativism and radical skepticism. This is an im-
poverished conception of rationality.

On the one hand, it is necessary to acknowledge the "ruin,"
that is, as R. J. Bernstein claims, to cultivate an "awareness and
sensitivity to radical contingency and chance that mark the universe, our inquiries, our lives" and to accept a "thoroughgoing fallibilism where we realize that although we must begin any inquiry
with prejudgments and can never call everything into question at
once, nevertheless there is no belief or thesis—no matter how fundamental—that is not open to further interpretation and criti-

cism" (1991, p. 326). On the other hand, this acknowledgment need not entail abandoning political responsibility, ethical decision, and the necessity of continuously making a choice and taking a stand (Smart, 1996).

Rational choices are possible if we adopt a model of rationality that avoids the either-or extremes of pure transcendental foundations and pure contingency noted above. On a model derived from practical philosophy, to be rational is to be capable of engaging in perspicuous articulation. Taylor (1989) argues that rational accounts (and rational actions) perspicuously display epistemic gains and losses in particular concrete cases by identifying and resolving contradictions in some original interpretation, or by pointing to a confusion that the interpretation relied on, or by acknowledging the importance of some factor which the interpretation screened out. It is precisely on these grounds that we can criticize, in particular cases, accounts of evaluation that ignore it as a conceptual practice of power.

In reviewing an earlier draft of this chapter, Ian Stronach (personal communication, January 2, 1997) asked,

> How does such writing on cognitive authority, on the conceptual practice of power, on the social location of evaluation practice, authorise itself without tacitly and illegitimately cleansing itself from the taint of such power/knowledge? How does it avoid the charge that it does what it forbids, enlisting an exemption clause for its own discourse?

Implicit in these questions is the assumption that we are playing a zero-sum game: Either this account can authorize itself or it cannot. What I am suggesting here is that conceiving of the problem as one of choosing between the alternatives of "certainty of authorization" versus "contingency-affirming play" is mistaken. We can offer an interpretation of evaluation practice, refracted from a different angle, revealing it to be in many instances a conceptual practice of power, and argue that such an interpretation offers a gain in our understanding of the practice.

Notes

1   Proctor (1991, pp. 269–270) argues that the failure to come to terms with social (and natural) science as a political power is largely an outcome of the ideology of value-neutrality: "The principle of neutral science, together with the doctrine of subjective value, constitutes the fundamental political ideology of modern science. Science in this view is neutral and public; values are subjective and private. Science is the realm of public reason, values the realm of persona whim. The choice of ends is personal and arbitrary; the means for meeting those ends are public and rational. Science progresses best when governed least: *laissez-innover* in science is the counterpoint to *laissez-faire* in market relations. Science in this vision is a neutral instrument, useless in itself, useful only when applied. The scientist discovers, society applies; values are implicated in the latter but not the former."

11

Notes on Being an Evaluator

There is a growing sense within the field of evaluation that it can finally get on with the business of doing good work now that decades of wrangling over the merits of so-called qualitative versus quantitative approaches to evaluation have finally subsided. The methodological debate seems to have abated in view of claims that a logic of warranted judgment underlying all research transcends any differences in method, and that a third paradigm is emerging that will offer a synthesis of the two it is replacing; specifically, a mixed-methods approach that combines the strengths and compensates for the shortcomings in any individual method (Greene and Caracelli, 1997; Reichardt and Rallis, 1994).

Whether or not one regards these particular claims as persuasive, it is difficult to imagine that anyone now seriously doubts that quasi-experimental as well as fieldwork methods, qualitative as well as quantitative data, and narrative as well as statistical forms of analysis and reporting are all useful in evaluation. To put the point more in terms of the enduring philosophical argument about whether the social sciences are best conceived of as explanatory or hermeneutic, it would be hard to find many who would argue against the view that an adequate social science of evaluation should seek both to understand the meaning of human action and to grasp the causes, connections, and consequences that lie beyond the horizon of meaning of everyday practice (e.g., Fay, 1996).

Moreover, even though postmodernism has made some inroads into evaluation thinking (e.g., Mabry, 1997), there appear to be few if any evaluators willing to make the strong holistic argument that because the kinds of claims made in social science are interpretations, one can never determine whether one interpretation is more correct or better than another (Bohman, 1991a). In other words, although embracing fallibilism and the inevitability of limiting conditions on our ability to know, few in evaluation have gone so far as to embrace radical interpretive skepticism. The postpositivist scene in social science has revealed a horizon of troubling issues about reflexivity, aesthetic and narrative form, agency, authority, and representation. However, in evaluation it has not meant, what Calinescu called a radically skeptical "epistemological impossibilism" or "a pervasive sense of a radical, unsurpassable uncertainty, a sort of epistemological nihilism" (1987, p. 305).

My intention in this chapter is not to resurrect the methodological debate, nor to offer a new proposition that will touch off more acrimonious arguments. Rather, I want to suggest that recognizing the utility of a catholic conception of method and design in evaluation, as important as that may be, does not mean that all serious differences in the practice have been resolved.

An important issue that has yet to receive careful direct attention has to do with the identity of the evaluator. By identity, I mean the moral image that evaluators have of themselves as professionals or experts of a particular kind. What do they think it is right to do and good to be as an evaluator? A few years ago, this issue came to the fore in the point-counterpoint American Evaluation Association presidential addresses of Yvonna Lincoln (1991) and Lee Sechrest (1992). Although typically read as another quarrel between constructivist and empiricist paradigms, this exchange presents an opportunity to examine the question of who evaluators are or should be. Sechrest himself suggested this reading in a subsequent rejoinder to Lincoln's address (Sechrest, Babcock, and Smith, 1993).

Both past presidents had an image in mind of the identity of the evaluator. Lincoln invited evaluators to consider the arts of program evaluation as a counterbalance to an overreliance on a cult of scientific expertise. She concluded with the suggestion that evaluators should "become less like priests and more like shamans, in a cultural sense" (1991, p. 6). Sechrest somewhat wistfully lamented a "generation gap." He called for a return to the "first generation" of evaluation—that is, to an image of an evaluator as scientist who has mastered the quantitative tools of description and analysis. He directed his criticism at those who would suggest a different identity for the evaluator, what he called "a new creature so unlike us" (1992, p. 2).

The issue in question here is evaluator identity—a matter of what it means to be an evaluator—and it concerns at base a question of self-definition and the embodiment of the aims of evaluation practice in the person of the evaluator. If human beings are, as Geertz, Gadamer, Taylor, and others claim, self-interpreting narrative beings suspended in webs of significance they themselves have spun, then evaluator identity (as well as the identity of teachers, nurses, managers, lawyers, and so on) is about creating a narrative—a story—of who they are and what they should be as professionals of that kind. Telling such a narrative is inescapably to take a moral stance (Bruner, 1990; Taylor, 1989). That is, to tell a story of who we are, how we have become, and where we are going we must have a sense of what it is good to be.

MacIntyre provides a useful conceptual tool for the analysis of stories of identity. He argues for the presence of central characters in modern society. A central character is a rationalization of an identity that reflects the moral ecology of a society. MacIntyre defines a *character* as "an object of regard by the members of the culture or some significant segment of them. He [sic] furnishes them with a cultural and moral ideal" (1984, p. 26). Characters are a very special type of social role because of the way their existence embodies both moral and metaphysical ideas and theories. A character's role in society is infused with these characteristics. MacIntyre was particularly concerned with the character of the manager and the therapist in contemporary society. For present purposes, I will define the character of the evaluator as the protagonist in a story that evaluators tell about themselves and about the purpose and role of evaluation in society.

There can be little doubt that the central character, the social and moral representative of what it means to be an evaluator in our culture, is the technically competent, politically astute social scientist. It is this character that I surmise Professor Sechrest had in mind in calling for a return to the first generation of evaluation. This character personifies a concatenated set of metaphysical and moral beliefs that have been spelled out in previous chapters; hence I will only summarize them here.

The central character of the evaluator qua social scientist embodies the general belief that the primary task of the evaluator is description and explanation, not normative criticism. The latter is regarded as largely a philosophical matter and, hence, without merit in the conduct of evaluation. For example, consideration of the values, ends, or goods to be served by a social or educational program are beyond this character's concern, except as value preferences that are held by stakeholders and thus subject to empirical description and inventory. To be sure, the evaluator as citizen may be concerned about the general social welfare, but as social scientist he or she is obligated to adopt the disinterested, nonpartisan, scientific attitude both during the course of and toward the object of his or her study.

While mindful that the fruits of his or her labor lend themselves more readily to the enlightenment of decision makers than to social engineering, this character nonetheless embraces and promotes what Lindbloom (1990) calls the image of a scientifically guided society. According to Lindbloom, in this vision of society, "social problem solving, social betterment, or guided social change ... calls above all for scientific observation of human social behavior such that ideally humankind discovers the requisites of good people in a good society and, short of the ideal, uses the results of scientific observation to move in the right direction" (p. 214). Accordingly, this character represents the belief in technological gain as the criterion of genuine knowledge and elevates the importance of the work of the artificer or craftsman over that of the philosopher and critic. To be a good evaluation craftsman means to possess and to use techniques and skills of the highest descriptive and analytical prowess: "our best science and accompanying quantitative analysis" as Professor Sechrest (1992) so succinctly stated.

Procedural considerations dominate substantive ones in this character in other ways as well. For example, rational behavior for this character has little to do with the kind of moral discrimination or correct vision of the good so essential to everyday life. Rather, rationality in the character of the evaluator-as-social-scientist is defined in procedural terms as a kind of style or method of thought (e.g., the correct methodology correctly applied). Because substantive matters of human purpose or the social good are outside the scope of this character's concerns for his or her practice, moral obligations are defined solely in terms of the content of professional responsibilities and obligations. The scope of moral concern here, as Taylor expressed it, is "purely with what it is right to do rather than with what it is good to be" (1989, p. 79).

The contemporary character of the evaluator embodies the aim of scientific evaluation. The latter is nicely captured in this observation by Sechrest: "If we want to have the maximum likelihood of our results being accepted and used, we would do well to ground them, not in theory or hermeneutics, but in dependable rigor afforded by our best science and accompanying quantitative analysis" (1992, p. 3). Defined in this way, evaluation practice is a disembodied cognitive enterprise. The character of the evaluator promotes in belief and action a vision of a good society that is best achieved by scientific investigation that follows the rules of evidence and that objectively filters out extrascientific or nonscientific considerations. A central message of much contemporary theorizing about the social sciences is that the sciences and arts of human inquiry are human artifacts often deeply implicated in political and social interests (Jacob, 1992; Proctor, 1991). However, the character of the evaluator screens out this awareness by treating such interests not as constitutive of investigations but as intrusions on the scientific evaluation process and as threats to the scientific integrity of her or his findings.

Professor Lincoln suggested that a new story of evaluator identity was in the making. The central theme of this developing story is how to reunite cognitive and moral concerns in the identity and practice of evaluators (and of social inquirers more generally). A new (dare I say) generation of evaluators is exploring how to engage in a kind of evaluation practice that is at once descriptive and normative, that incorporates the moral and political dimensions of everyday life into the activity of defining social problems and evaluating social programs as solutions to those problems, and that regards evaluation practice as a form of social self-understanding or interpretation in the tradition of public philosophy (Bellah et al., 1991). These explorations are yielding images of the character of the evaluator very unlike the "creature" of what Professor Sechrest calls the first generation.

Reuniting cognitive and moral concerns in a redefinition of the aims of evaluation practice and defining the new character of the evaluator is not an easy task and it is beset with several dangers. The story is unfolding in the telling, and it is subject to incoherence, blind alleys, confusion, and ambiguity. One stumbling block on the road to restorying is to fall victim to the intentional fallacy—moral kind. The fallacy is this: If you intend a moral result, set up a moral device (e.g., training in ethics and values); send evaluators through the device and they will have achieved moral vision. There are systematic ways of talking and thinking about socio-political and moral problems, and we should learn such means of investigation and argumentation. However, these problems are extremely complex and require moral sensibility and moral imagination that can only be acquired through sustained examination of a phenomenon over time. We cannot expect to cultivate this kind of understanding simply by adding a course on moral issues or moral reasoning to the evaluation curriculum much like we would add a course on structural equation modeling or fieldwork methods.

Toward this end the education and training of evaluators must be refigured. Not the least of these refigurations is the need for better education in theories of political morality and in social theory that explores the meaning and role of scientific expertise in society. The current character of the evaluator is readily marked in the main by the possession of a special methodological expertise and a highly refined set of technical skills in problem formation, data gathering, and data analysis. The social practice that this character represents consists largely in the exercise of applying these special tools of description and analysis. In preparing for the practice, one first learns the tools and the rules for their use and then applies them to the analysis of any evaluation object. Following Aristotle's advice, I suggest that we reverse our priorities here. We can only understand the evaluative dimensions of a human endeavor by first becoming familiar with that endeavor; hence, well-developed sensibilities about the moral and political dimensions of the practice are a prerequisite to good evaluation.

We must also be careful not to substitute, as protagonist in the story, one high priest for another—replacing the evaluator qua social scientist with the evaluator qua cultural watchdog or humanist. Echoing Weber, Geertz reminds us that as we refigure social thought, "the specialist without spirit dispensing policy nostrums goes, but the lectern sage dispensing approved [value] judgments does as well. The relation between thought and action can no more be conceived of in terms of wisdom than it can be in terms of expertise" (1980, p. 178). Both wisdom or moral vision and expertise or technical prowess must be reconciled in the character of the evaluator. This is not a matter of combining two sets of skills, those of Lincoln's shaman and Sechrest's scientist, for example. Rather, it is a matter of forming a new character in whom both moral and cognitive concerns are united in a view of evaluation as social philosophy.

The postmodern predicament of the evaluator (and the human inquirer more generally) is a crisis of identity and character and the struggle to tell a different story about what it means to evaluate that features a different protagonist. We may long for a story of the way it was, but wishing will not make it so. Of course, neither will wishing make it possible to create a new narrative of evaluation. That will require far more careful analysis of the story that evaluators have been consistently telling themselves about who they are. Some aspects of that story need to be exploded as myth—the separation of cognitive and moral concerns chief among them. Other aspects of that story are perhaps worth preserving if but significantly reshaped in the retelling. One such element is the plotline—the notion that we are capable of improving our practice by subjecting it to scrutiny and radical criticism. It will also require far more careful attention to the search for a new vocabulary that signals a new way of understanding social practice.

Professor Sechrest calls for evaluators to return to their roots in the first generation of evaluation practitioners, but in so doing he is only half right. He would have us retell a story wherein the metaphysical, the moral, the philosophical are irrelevant to constructing and performing an identity and role as evaluator. I too wish for a return to roots, but to recovery and retelling of a story line in which such considerations were inescapably part of what it meant to engage in self-definition, judgment, and the study of others and ourselves.

Postscript

Many commentaries on the conditions of contemporary society express a deep concern with the deformation or distortion of the notion of *praxis*. This situation results from the inappropriate extension of method-driven knowledge to the problems of moral-political life. It arises from repeated attempts to transform what are essentially moral-political judgments into technical exercises. The technology of evaluation contributes to this problem via its aim to rationalize, through the application of scientific information or procedures, the evaluative judgments required in teaching, providing social services, delivering health care, and the like. As currently conceived, evaluation is one of those human endeavors like administration, management, health care, and education which reflect a strong belief in the manageability of everything human, and in which knowledge generated via a special set of methods is increasingly allowed to define and circumscribe our entire view of the world. Gadamer (1992) makes this point in the following way:

> What appears to me to characterize our epoch is not the surprising control of nature we have achieved, but the development of scientific methods to guide the life of society.... The scientific tendencies of thought underlying our civilization have in our time pervaded all aspects of social praxis. Scientific market research, scientific warfare, scientific diplomacy, scientific rearing of the younger generation, scientific leadership of the people—the application of science to all these fields gives expertise a commanding position in the economy and society. And so the problem of an ordered world assumes primary importance. (p. 165)

As we increasingly look to a science of evaluation for guidance in overcoming the quotidian problems of evaluating our actions in everyday life, there emerges the expectation of the mastery of social life by scientific reason (e.g., Bauman 1987; Gadamer, 1992; Lindbloom, 1990). It is here that we begin to experience the misconstrual of *praxis*. The expert, which the evaluator-as-social scientist claims to be by virtue of his or her superior knowledge, is invested with an exaggerated authority: "The expert is the one we look to for giving us true directives for acting, that is, for the discharging of the practical, political, and economic decisions one needs to make, instead of relying on our own practical and political experience" (Risser, 1997, p. 111). Experts do little to dissuade practitioners of the importance of scientific expertise and authority. In fact, they encourage it by promoting the view that their knowledge is superior in many respects to the knowledge of practitioners. It is held to be superior by virtue of the fact that it is based on method, and thus not encumbered by human limitations such as various cognitive and emotional biases. Scientific knowledge is regarded, at the very least, as a significant improvement in lay understanding, and therefore authoritative in some respects over it.

One aim of the preceding chapters was to demonstrate that evaluation is first and foremost a lived moral-political and interpretive practice, not a technical endeavor. It is an activity undertaken by practitioners of all kinds in which they seek to judge again and again, from one occasion to the next, whether they are doing the right thing and doing it well. The judgments they reach in each case are constitutive of their sense of what it means to be a good practitioner of one sort or another. As lived, engaged *praxis*, evaluation requires judgment (*phronesis*), wisdom, and practical application of understanding to oneself. I have suggested that the possibility of restoring the primacy of evaluation as *praxis* lies within recovering ideas from the tradition of practical hermeneutics, including a reconceptualization of the meaning of notions such as engagement, rationality, dialogue, knowledge, and identity. This does not mean casting aside social scientific knowledge. However, the restoration of evaluation as *praxis* does call for more than a fallibilist epistemology and the virtue of humility on the part of those who argue for the overriding importance of generating social scientific knowledge in evaluation.

The kind of knowledge and rationality demanded by *praxis* is *sui generis*. It is not merely personal judgment or an expression of taste, nor an inferior form of scientific knowledge and reasoning (Berlin, 1996). No amount of increased attention to improving an epistemology based on method will yield insight into the nature of this knowledge and its requirements of engagement and wise judgment. In fact, such attention is inimical to such a realization. The study of scientific reasoning, the continued exploration of better or improved scientific methods, and the examination of social scientific progress through the application of scientific knowledge provide little insight into understanding the lived reality of evaluation because these undertakings are about the production of scientific knowledge. They are not about the business of understanding and improving the natural human capacities to deliberate, to reach agreement in language, and to persuade others of our point of view.

Hence, we must look to other intellectual traditions for guidance in understanding what is entailed in grasping and improving the lived reality of evaluation *praxis*. This investigation will reveal that the belief in transforming everyday practice by bringing it under the rule of method and scientific rationality is a mistake—one of confusing a kind of knowledge appropriate to one human activity as the kind of knowledge appropriate for *all* forms of human activity. However, this does not mean that knowledge generated via method is completely irrelevant to *praxis*. Evaluation decision making is like the kind of decision making found in clinical medicine and in case law. It is a kind of diagnosis made by practitioners—an evaluative judgment about the right and appropriate action in a given situation. This capacity simultaneously demands intimate familiarity with the relevant features of the case at hand, knowledge of and reliance on general principles (often in the form of a taxonomy of cases), argument by analogy from more or less well-understood cases (e.g., general principles reflected in well-documented cases) to the less well-understood, always disputable, case at hand. Knowledge generated via scientific method can be helpful in the activity of practical reasoning, but it cannot *replace* the knowledge required for finding one's way in the details of what is the right evaluative judgment about this program, this project, this student (client, employee, and so forth) in these circumstances (Jonsen and Toulmin, 1988).

Having the right scientific knowledge or the right expert at one's disposal will not rescue managers, teachers, nurses, or human service agency workers from the contingencies of the evaluation decisions that they face and allow them to treat moral-political problems as if they had technical solutions. While of course practitioners would like to have at hand the best general, scientific knowledge they can acquire, the corrigibility, ambiguity, and circumstantiality of everyday evaluative judgment cannot be eliminated, replaced, or refined by relying on scientific method and its associated rationality. The virtue of having method-driven, objective, systematically produced general knowledge becomes a vice when we are led to mistakenly believe that such knowledge is sovereign with respect to practice.

The *praxis* of teaching, or of managing or providing social services or health care, is characterized by the inevitable and ineradicable conditions of plurality, uncertainty, and difference. In contrast, the social scientific conception of evaluation, informed by the ideology of social progress through the application of scientific knowledge, is unabashedly aimed at removing uncertainty, reducing diversity, eliminating ambivalence and difference. In this modern scenario, social scientific experts of all kinds (including evaluators) act as "legislators of reason" (Bauman, 1987). They believe that they can establish the standards for knowledge and value, arbitrate what constitutes genuine knowledge, and rescue social life from its inherent contingency, diversity, localized practices, and the like. They aim to silence all that falls short of scientific reason and rationality, fostering the advancement of social control through strategies of surveillance and medicalization of behavior in social institutions of all kinds including government, schools, factories, prisons, and hospitals.

This ideology of evaluation expertise in the service of social scientific progress receives too little attention. The unspoken assumption of the field seems to be that social progress through the application of scientific evaluation knowledge is simply a good to be taken for granted and that the most significant problem faced by the field is how to produce and apply such knowledge (whether through refinements in quasi-experimental, field-based, participatory, or mixed methods). In advocating a renewed interest in *praxis*, my aim has been to disturb this taken-for-granted assumption about the aim of evaluation as a social science and its associated conception of the expert evaluator.

My intent has been to recover and subsequently revitalize both responsibility and moral accountability for evaluation in the daily activity of practitioners. That daily activity is characterized by ambiguity, uncertainty, ambivalence, contingency, the endlessly critical, and the disruptive. This is a call for evaluators to accept (rather than seek to overcome) these features of evaluation decision-making while they simultaneously aim to help practitioners wrestle with making sound evaluative judgments in social practices that by their very nature are always instantiated in multiple and often conflicting forms. This of necessity means decentering the authority of the evaluator as scientific expert capable of pronouncing judgment on the value of practitioners' activities. As this authority is relinquished, the evaluator can come to serve as a teacher and an interpreter, helping practitioners better understand one anothers' understandings and judgments. This is not a call to abandon reason and rationality in evaluation but to recover an understanding of these notions suited to grasping evaluation as a moral-political rather than a technical undertaking.

Bibliography

Abma, T. A. (1999). Introduction: Narrative perspectives on program evaluation. In T.A. Abma (Ed.) *Telling tales: On evaluation and narrative. Vol. 6: Advances in Program Evaluation* (pp. 1–27). Stamford, CT: JAI Press.

Addelson, K. P. (1983). The man of professional wisdom. In S. Harding and M. B. Hintikka (Eds.) *Discovering reality* (pp. 165–86). Dordrecht, The Netherlands: D. Reidel.

Alexander, J. (1987). The centrality of the classics. In A. Giddens and J. H. Turner (Eds.) *Social theory today* (pp. 11–57). Stanford, CA: Stanford University Press.

Amy, D. J. (1984). Why policy analysis and ethics are incompatible. *Journal of Policy Analysis and Management*, 3(4): 573–91.

Bahktin, M. M. (1984). *Problems of Dostoevsky's poetics*. C. Emerson, Ed. and Trans. Minneapolis, MN: University of Minnesota Press.

Baier, K. (1958). *The moral point of view*. Ithaca, NY: Cornell University Press.

Barber, B. (1988). *The conquest of politics*. Princeton, NJ: Princeton University Press.

Bauman, Z. (1987). *Legislators and interpreters: On modernity, postmodernity and intellectuals*. Ithaca, NY: Cornell University Press.

———. (1992). *Intimations of postmodernity*. London: Routledge.

———. (1993). *Postmodern ethics*. Oxford: Blackwell.

———. (1995). *Life in fragments: essays in postmodern morality*. Oxford: Blackwell.

Bellah, R. N. (1983). The ethical aims of social inquiry. In N. Haan, R. N. Bellah, P. Rabinow and W. M. Sullivan (Eds.) *Social science as moral inquiry* (pp. 360–82). New York: Columbia University Press.

Bellah, R. N., Madsen, R., Sullivan, W. M., Swidler, A., and Tipton, S. M. (1975). *Habits of the heart*. Berkeley, CA: University of California Press.

———. (1991). *The good society*. New York: Knopf.

Benhabib, S. (1986). *Critique, norm, and utopia: A study of the foundations of critical theory*. New York: Columbia University Press.

Berk, R. A., and Rossi, P. H. (1977). Doing good or worse: Evaluation research politically reexamined. In G. V. Glass (Ed.) *Evaluation studies review annual: Vol. 2*. Beverly Hills: Sage Publications.

Berlin, I. (1996). On political judgment. *New York Review of Books* (October 3): 26–30.

Bernstein, B. (1986). On pedagogic discourse. In J. G. Richardson (Ed.) *Handbook of theory and research for the sociology of education* (pp. 205–40). New York: Greenwood Press.

Bernstein, R. J. (1976). *The restructuring of social and political theory.* New York: Harcourt Brace Jovanovich.

———. (1983). *Beyond objectivism and relativism.* Philadelphia: University of Pennsylvania Press.

———. (1985). Dewey, democracy: The task ahead of us. In J. Rajchman and C. West (Eds.) *Post-analytic philosophy* (pp. 48–59). New York: Columbia University Press.

———. (1991). *The new constellation: The ethical-political horizons of modernity/postmodernity.* Cambridge, MA: MIT Press.

Best, S., and Kellner, D. (1991). *Postmodern theory—Critical interrogations.* New York: Guilford Press.

Bohman, J. F. (1991a). Holism without skepticism: Contextualism and the limits of interpretation. In D. R. Hiley, J. F. Bohman, and R. Shusterman (Eds.) *The interpretive turn* (pp. 129–54). Ithaca, NY: Cornell University Press.

———. (1991b). *New philosophy of social science.* Cambridge, MA: MIT Press.

Bourdieu, P. (1990). *The logic of practice.* Cambridge: Polity Press.

Brodkey, L. (1987). Writing ethnographic narratives. *Written Communication,* 4: 25–50.

Bruner, J. (1986). *Actual minds, possible worlds.* Cambridge, MA: Harvard University Press.

———. (1990). *Acts of meaning.* Cambridge, MA: Harvard University Press.

Buker, E. (1992). Rhetoric in postmodern feminism: Put-offs, put-ons, and political plays. In D. R. Hiley, J. F. Bohman, and R. Shusterman (Eds.) *The interpretive turn* (pp. 218–44). Ithaca, NY: Cornell University Press.

Bull, B. L., Fruehling, R. T., and Chattergy, V. (1992). *The ethics of multicultural and bilingual education.* New York: Teachers College Press.

Burbules, N. C. (1993). *Dialogue in teaching.* New York: Teachers College Press.

———. (1996). Postmodern doubt and philosophy of education. In *Philosophy of education: 1995* (pp. 39–48). Urbana, IL: Philosophy of Education Society.

Burbules, N. C., and Rice, S. (1991). Dialogue across differences: Continuing the conversation. *Harvard Educational Review,* 61(4): 393–416.

Calinescu, M. (1987). *Five faces of modernity.* Durham, NC: Duke University Press.

Campbell, D. T. (1969). Reforms as experiments. *American Psychologist,* 24: 409–29.

———. (1982). Experiments as arguments. In E. R. House, S. Mathison, J. A. Pearsol, and H. Preskill (Eds.) *Evaluation studies review annual: Vol. 7* (pp. 117–27). Beverly Hills, CA: Sage.

———. (1986). Relabeling internal and external validity for social scientists. In W. M. K. Trochim (Ed.) *Advances in quasi-experimental design and analysis.*

Vol. 31: New Directions for Program Evaluation (pp. 67–78). San Francisco: Jossey-Bass.

Carr, W. (1995). *For education: towards critical educational inquiry.* Buckingham, UK: Open University Press.

Chelimsky, E. (1997). The political environment for evaluation and what it means for the development of the field. In E. Chelmisky and W. R. Shadish (Eds.) *Evaluation for the 21ˢᵗ century* (pp. 53–68). Thousand Oaks, CA: Sage.

Chelimsky, E., and Shadish, W. R. (Eds.). (1997). *Evaluation for the 21ˢᵗ century.* Thousand Oaks, CA: Sage.

Cherryholmes, C. H. (1988). *Power and criticism.* New York: Teachers College Press.

Clarke, J., Cochrane, A., and McLaughlin, E. (Eds.). (1994). *Managing social policy.* London: Sage.

Code, L. B. (1983). Responsibility and the epistemic community: Woman's place. *Social Research, 50*(3): 537–55.

———. (1991). *What can she know? Feminist theory and the construction of knowledge.* Ithaca, NY: Cornell University Press.

Cohen, I. J. (1996). Theories of action and practice. In B. S. Turner (Ed.) *The Blackwell companion to social theory* (pp. 112–42). Oxford: Blackwell.

Coles, R. (1989). *The call of stories.* Boston: Houghton Mifflin.

Conner, R. (1998). Toward a social ecological view of evaluation use. *American Journal of Evaluation, 19*(2): 237–242.

Cook, T. D. (1985). Postpositivist critical multiplism. In L. Shotland and M. M. Mark (Eds.) *Social science and social policy* (pp. 458–99). Newbury Park, CA: Sage.

Cook, T. D., and Shadish, W. R., Jr. (1986). Program evaluation: The worldly science. *Annual Review of Psychology, 37*: 193–232.

Cooper, D. E. (1996). Modern European philosophy. In N. Bunnin, and E. P. Tsui-James (Eds.) *The Blackwell companion to philosophy.* Oxford, England: Oxford University Press.

Cousins, J. B., and Earl, L. M. (1992). The case for participatory evaluation. *Educational Evaluation and Policy Analysis, 14*: 397–418.

———. (Eds.). (1995). *Participatory evaluation in education: Studies in evaluation use and organizational learning.* London: Falmer.

Cousins, J. B., and Leithwood, K. A. (1986). Current empirical research in evaluation utilization. *Review of Educational Research, 5*(3): 331–64.

Cronbach, L. J. (1982). *Designing evaluations of educational and social programs.* San Francisco: Jossey-Bass.

Cronbach, L. J., and associates. (1980). *Toward reform of program evaluation.* San Francisco: Jossey-Bass.

Datta, L. (1994). Paradigm wars: A basis for peaceful coexistence and beyond. In C. S. Reichardt and S. F. Rallis (Eds.) *The quantitative-qualitative debate: New perspectives. Vol. 61: New Directions for Program Evaluation* (pp. 53-70). San Francisco: Jossey-Bass.

————. (2000). Seriously seeking fairness: Strategies for crafting non-partisan evaluation in a partisan world. *American Journal of Evaluation, 21*(1): 1–14.

Denzin, N. K. (1986). Postmodern social theory. *Sociological Theory, 4*: 194–204.

————. (1989). *Interpretive interactionism.* Newbury Park, CA: Sage.

————. (1997). *Interpretive ethnography: Ethnographic practices for the 21ˢᵗ century.* Thousand Oaks, CA: Sage.

di Leonardo, M. (1991). Introduction: Gender, culture and political economy: Feminist anthropology in historical perspective. In M. di Leonardo (Ed.) *Gender at the crossroads of knowledge: Feminist anthropology in the postmodern era* (pp. 1–48). Berkeley: University of California Press.

Dunne, J. (1993). *Back to the rough ground: 'Phronesis' and 'Techne' in modern philosophy and Aristotle.* Notre Dame, IN: University of Notre Dame Press.

Eco, U. (1979). *The role of the reader.* Bloomington, IN: Indiana University Press.

Eisner, E. W. (1991). *The enlightened eye.* New York: Macmillan.

Elden, M., and Levine, M. (1991). Cogenerative learning. In W. F. Whyte (Ed.) *Participatory action research* (pp. 127–42). Newbury Park, CA: Sage.

Elgin, C. (1996). *Considered judgment.* Princeton, NJ: Princeton University Press.

Elliott, J. (1991). *Action research for educational change.* Buckingham, England: Open University Press.

Everitt, A. (1996). Developing critical evaluation. *Evaluation, 2*(2): 173–88.

Fay, B. (1996). *Contemporary philosophy of social science.* Oxford: Blackwell.

————. (1987). *Critical social science.* Ithaca, NY: Cornell University Press.

Fetterman, D. (1994). Empowerment evaluation. *Evaluation Practice, 15*(1): 1–15.

————. (1995). In response. *Evaluation Practice, 16*(2): 179–99.

Fetterman, D., Kaftarian, A. J., and Wandersman, A. (Eds.). (1996). *Empowerment evaluation: Knowledge and tools for self-assessment and accountability.* Newbury Park, CA: Sage.

Feyerabend, P. (1987). *Farewell to reason.* New York: Verso.

Fischer, F. (1987). Policy expertise and the 'new class': A critique of the neoconservative thesis. In F. Fischer and J. Forester (Eds.) *Confronting values in policy analysis: The politics of criteria: Vol. 14 Sage Yearbooks in Politics and Public Policy* (pp. 94–126). Newbury Park, CA: Sage.

Fisher, W. R. (1987). *Human communication as narration: Toward a philosophy of reason, value, and action.* Columbia, SC: University of South Carolina Press.

Flacks, R. (1983). Moral commitment, privatism, and activism: Notes on a research program. In N. Haan, R. N. Bellah, P. Rabinow and W. Sullivan (Eds.) *Social science as moral inquiry* (pp. 343–59). New York: Columbia University Press.

Flyvbjerg, B. (2001). *Making social science matter.* Cambridge, England: Cambridge University Press.

Fournier, D. M. (Ed.). (1995). *Reasoning in evaluation: Inferential links and leaps. Vol. 68: New Directions for Evaluation.* San Francisco: Jossey-Bass.

Fournier, D. M., and Smith, N. L. (1993). Clarifying the merits of argument in evaluation practice. *Evaluation and Program Planning, 16*(4): 315–23.

Fraser, N. (1989). Talking about needs: Interpretive contests as political conflicts in welfare state societies. *Ethics, 99*: 291–313.

Freire, P. (1975). *Pedagogy of the oppressed* (M. Bergman Ramos, Trans.) New York: Herder and Herder.

Friedman, M. (Ed.). (1996a). *Martin Buber and the human sciences*. Albany, NY: State University of New York Press.

———. (1996b). Martin Buber's "Narrow Ridge" and the human sciences. In M. Friedman (Ed.) *Martin Buber and the human sciences* (pp. 3–25). Albany, NY: State University of New York Press.

Fuller, S. (1988). *Social epistemology*. Bloomington, IN: Indiana University Press.

Gadamer, H.-G. (1977). Theory, technology, practice: The task of the science of man (H. Brotz, Trans.) *Social Research, 44* (3): 529–61.

———. (1981). *Reason in the age of science*. (F. G. Lawrence, Trans.) Cambridge, MA: MIT Press.

———. (1989). *Truth and Method* (2nd rev. ed.) (J. Weinsheimer and D. G. Marshall, Trans.) New York: Crossroad.

———. (1992). The limitations of the expert. In D. Misgeld and G. Nicholson (Eds.) (L. Schmidt and M. Reuss, Trans.) *Hans-Georg Gadamer on education, poetry, and history: Applied hermeneutics* (pp. 181–92). Albany, NY: SUNY Press.

———. (1996). *The enigma of health*. Stanford, CA: Stanford University Press.

———. (1997). Reflections on my philosophical journey. In L. E. Hahn (Ed.) *The philosophy of Hans-Georg Gadamer* (pp. 3–63). Chicago: Open Court.

Gallagher, S. (1992). *Hermeneutics and education*. Albany, NY: SUNY Press.

Garrison, J. (1996). A Deweyan theory of democratic listening. *Educational Theory, 46*(4): 429–51.

Geertz, C. (1973). *The interpretation of cultures*. New York: Basic Books.

———. (1980). Blurred genres: The refiguration of social thought. *American Scholar, 49*: 165–79.

Gergen, K. (1988). If persons are texts. In S. B. Messer, L. A. Sass, and R. L. Woolfolk (Eds.) *Hermeneutics and psychological theory* (pp. 28–51). New Brunswick, NJ: Rutgers University Press.

Giddens, A. (1984). *The constitution of society*. Cambridge: Polity Press.

———. (1990). *The consequences of modernity*. Cambridge: Polity Press.

———. (1991). *Modernity and self-identity*. Cambridge: Polity Press.

———. (1993). *New rules of sociological method* (2nd ed). Stanford, CA: Stanford University Press.

Goetz, J. P., and LeCompte, M. D. (1984). *Ethnography and qualitative design in educational research*. New York: Academic Press.

Goodman, N., and Elgin, C. (1988). *Reconceptions in philosophy and other arts and sciences*. Indianapolis, IN: Hackett.

Gordon, S. (1991). *The history and philosophy of social science*. London: Routledge.

Graf-Taylor, R. (1996). Philosophy of dialogue and feminist psychology. In M. Friedman (Ed.) *Martin Buber and the human sciences* (pp. 327–34). Albany, NY: State University of New York Press.

Greene, J. C., and Caracelli, V. J. (Eds.). (1997). *Advances in mixed-method evaluation: The challenges and benefits of integrating diverse paradigms. Vol. 74: New Directions for Evaluation.* San Francisco: Jossey-Bass.

Grondin, J. (1994). *Introduction to philosophical hermeneutics.* New Haven, CT: Yale University Press.

———. (1995). *Sources of hermeneutics.* Albany, NY: State University of New York Press.

Guba, E. G., and Lincoln, Y. S. (1989). *Fourth generation evaluation.* Newbury Park, CA: Sage.

Guignon, C. (1991). Pragmatism or hermeneutics: Epistemology after foundationalism. In D. R. Hiley, J. F. Bohman, and R. Shusterman (Eds.) *The interpretive turn* (pp. 81–101). Ithaca, NY: Cornell University Press.

Gustavsen, B. (1992). *Dialogue and development.* Maastricht, The Netherlands: Van Gorcum.

Habermas, J. (1973). *Theory and practice* (J. Viertel, Trans.) Boston: Beacon Press.

———. (1984). *The theory of communicative action: Vol. 1. Reason and the rationalization of society.* (T. McCarthy, Trans.) Boston, MA: Beacon Press.

———. (1988). *On the logic of the social sciences* (S. W. Nicholsen and J. A. Strak, Trans.) Cambridge, MA: MIT Press.

Hammersley, M. (1992). *What's wrong with ethnography?* London: Routledge.

Hanson, F. A. (1993). *Testing testing: The social consequences of the examined life.* Berkeley, CA: University of California Press.

Harding, S. (1992). After the neutrality ideal: Science, politics, and 'strong' objectivity. *Social Research, 59*(3): 567–87.

———. (1991). *Whose science? Whose knowledge?* Ithaca, NY: Cornell University Press.

Harvey, D. (1989). *The condition of postmodernity.* Oxford: Blackwell.

Henry, G. T., and Julnes, G. (1998). Values and realist evaluation. In G. T. Henry, G. Julnes, and M. M. Mark (Eds.) *Realist evaluation: Emerging theory in support of practice. Vol. 78: New Directions for Evaluation* (pp. 53–71). San Francisco: Jossey-Bass.

Hiley, D. R., Bohman, J. F., and Shusterman, R. (Eds.). (1991). *The interpretive turn.* Ithaca, NY: Cornell University Press.

Hollis, M. (1994). *The philosophy of social science.* Cambridge: Cambridge University Press.

Holt, M. (1987). *Judgment, planning and educational change.* London: Harper and Row, Ltd.

House, E. R. (1983). How we think about evaluation. In E.R. House (Ed.) *Philosophy of evaluation. Vol. 19: New Directions for Program Evaluation* (pp. 5–26). San Francisco: Jossey-Bass.

———. (1991). Evaluation and social justice: Where are we? In M. W. McLaughlin and D. C. Phillips (Eds.) *Evaluation and education: 90ᵗʰ Yearbook of the National Society for the Study of Education, Part II* (pp. 233–47). Chicago: University of Chicago Press.

———. (1993). *Professional evaluation*. Newbury Park, CA: Sage.

———. (1994). Integrating the quantitative and the qualitative. In C. S. Reichardt and S. F. Rallis (Eds.) *The qualitative-quantitative debate: New perspectives. Vol. 61: New Directions for Program Evaluation* (pp. 13–22). San Francisco: Jossey-Bass.

———. (1995). Putting things together coherently: Logic and justice. In D. M. Fournier (Ed.) *Reasoning in evaluation: Inferential links and leaps. Vol. 68: New Directions for Evaluation* (pp. 33–48). San Francisco: Jossey-Bass.

House, E. R., and Howe, K. R. (1999). *Values in evaluation and social research*. Thousand Oaks, CA: Sage.

Howe, K. R., and Eisenhart, M. (1990). Standards for qualitative (and quantitative) research: A prolegomenon. *Educational Researcher*, 19(4): 2–9.

Jacob, M. C. (1992). Science and politics in the late twentieth century. *Social Research*, 59(3): 487–503.

Jodalen, H., and Vetlesen, A. J. (1997). *Closeness: An ethics*. Oslo: Scandinavian University Press.

Joint Committee on Standards for Educational Evaluation. (1981). *Standards for the evaluation of educational programs, projects, and materials*. New York: McGraw-Hill.

———. (1994). *Program evaluation standards* (2ⁿᵈ ed.) Thousand Oaks, CA: Sage.

Jonsen, A. R., and Toulmin, S. (1988). *The abuse of casuistry*. Berkeley: University of California Press.

Kaplan, A. (1964). *The conduct of inquiry*. San Francisco: Chandler.

Karlsson, O. (1996). A critical dialogue in evaluation: How can interaction between evaluation and politics be tackled? *Evaluation*, 2: 405–16.

———. (1998). Socratic dialogue in the Swedish political context. In T. A. Schwandt (Ed.) *Scandinavian perspectives on the evaluator's role in informing social policy. Vol. 77: New Directions for Evaluation* (pp. 21–38). San Francisco: Jossey-Bass.

Kerdeman, D. (1998). Hermeneutics and education: Understanding, control, and agency. *Educational Theory* 48(2): 241–66.

Kirk, J., and Miller, M. (1986). *Reliability and validity in qualitative research*. Newbury Park, CA: Sage.

Krathwohl, D. (1993). *Methods of educational and social research*. New York: Longman.

Kvale, S. (1995). The social construction of validity. *Qualitative Inquiry*, 1(1): 19–40.

Lasch, C. (1991). *The true and only heaven*. New York: W. W. Norton.

LeCompte, M. D., and Preissle, J. P. (1993). *Ethnography and qualitative design in educational research* (2ⁿᵈ ed.). New York: Academic Press.

Lincoln, Y. S. (1991). The arts and sciences of program evaluation. *Evaluation Practice, 12*(1), 1–7.

———. (1995). Emerging criteria for quality in qualitative or interpretive research. *Qualitative Inquiry 1*(3): 275–89.

Lincoln, Y. S., and Guba, E. G. (1985). *Naturalistic inquiry.* Newbury Park, CA: Sage.

Lindbloom, C. E. (1990). *Inquiry and change.* New Haven: Yale University.

Lowi, T. J. (December 11, 1991). The pernicious effects of economics on American political science, *The Chronicle of Higher Education, 38*(16): 131–32.

Mabry, L. (Ed.). (1997). *Evaluation and the postmodern dilemma. Advances in program evaluation.* Greenwich, CT: JAI Press.

MacIntyre, A. (1981). *After virtue.* Notre Dame, IN: University of Notre Dame Press.

———. (1984). *After virtue* (2nd ed). Notre Dame, IN: University of Notre Dame Press.

Mallioux, S. (1990). Interpretation. In F. Lentricchia and T. McLaughlin (Eds.) *Critical terms for literary study* (pp. 121–34). Chicago: University of Chicago Press.

Marcus, G. E., and Cushman, D. (1982). Ethnographies as texts. *Annual Review Of Anthropology, 11:* 25–69.

May, W. F. (1992). The beleaguered rulers: The public obligation of the professional. *Kennedy Institute of Ethics Journal, 2*(1): 25–41.

McCarthy, T. (1987). Introduction. In J. Habermas, *The philosophical discourse of modernity* (F. G. Lawrence, Trans.) Cambridge, MA: MIT press.

McEwan, H. (1995). Narrative understanding in the study of teaching. In H. McEwan and K. Egan (Eds.) *Narrative in teaching, learning, and research* (pp. 166–83). New York: Teachers College Press.

Mertens, D. (1995). Identifying and respecting differences among participants in evaluation studies. In W. R. Shadish, D. L. Newman, M. A. Scheirer, and C. Wye, (Eds.) *Guiding principles for evaluators. Vol. 66: New Directions for Program Evaluation,* (pp. 91–97). San Francisco: Jossey-Bass.

Merton, R. (1973). *The sociology of science: Theoretical and empirical investigations.* Chicago: University of Chicago Press.

Michelfelder, D. P., and Palmer, R. E. (Eds.). (1989). *Dialogue and deconstruction: The Gadamer-Derrida encounter.* Albany, NY: SUNY Press.

Miles, M. B. and Huberman, A. M. (1984). *Analyzing qualitative data: A source book for new methods.* Newbury Park, CA: Sage.

Miller, R. B. (1996). *Casuistry and modern ethics: A poetics of practical reasoning.* Chicago: University of Chicago Press.

Molander, B. (1990). Socratic dialogue: On dialogue and discussion in the formation of knowledge. In B. Göranzon and M. Florin (Eds.) *Artificial intelligence, culture and language: On education and work* (pp. 229–43). London: Springer-Verlag.

Moody-Adams, M. M. (1997). *Fieldwork in familiar places: Morality, culture, and philosophy*. Cambridge, MA: Harvard University Press.

Morgan, G. (1983). *Beyond method*. Newbury Park, CA: Sage.

Nagel, T. (1981). *The view from nowhere*. Oxford, England: Oxford University Press.

Newman, D., and Brown, R. (1996). *Applied ethics for program evaluation*. Newbury Park, CA: Sage.

Noddings, N. (1984). *Caring: A feminine approach to ethics and moral education*. Berkeley: University of California Press.

———. (1996). On community. *Educational Theory*. 46(3): 245–67.

Nussbaum, M. C. (1990). *Love's knowledge: Essays on philosophy and literature*. New York: Oxford University Press.

———. (1997). *Cultivating humanity: A classical defense of reform in liberal education*. Cambridge, MA: Harvard University Press.

Oliver, M. (1992). Changing the social relations of research production? *Disability, Handicap, and Society*, 7(2): 101–14.

Outhwaite, W. (1975). *Understanding social life: The method called Verstehen*. London: George Allen and Unwin.

Pålshaugen, Ø. (1994). *A Norwegian programme of action research for participative democracy*. Oslo, Norway: Arbeidsforskningsinstituttet [Work Research Institute].

Patton, M. Q. (1997). *Utilization-focused evaluation* (3rd ed.). Thousand Oaks, CA: Sage.

Pellegrino, E., and Thomasma, D. C. (1993). *The virtues in medical practice*. Oxford: Oxford University Press.

Pendlebury, S. (1995). Reason and story in wise practice. In H. McEwan and K. Egan (Eds.) *Narrative in teaching, learning and research* (pp. 50–65). New York: Teachers College Press.

Phillips, D. C. (1987). *Philosophy, science, and social inquiry*. New York: Pergamon Press.

———. (1993). Gone with the wind? Evidence, rigor and warrants in educational research. Papers of the Philosophy of Education Society of Great Britain, April 16–18, pp. 9–11.

———. (2001). *The expanded social scientist's bestiary*. Boulder, CO: Rowman and Littlefield.

Pollitt, C. (1995). Justification by works or faith? Evaluating the new public management. *Evaluation*, 1(2): 133–54.

Porter, T. M. (1995). *Trust in numbers: The pursuit of objectivity in science and public life*. Princeton, NJ: Princeton University Press.

Power, M. (1997). *The audit society: Rituals of verification*. Oxford, England: Oxford University press.

Prawat, R. S. (1993). The value of ideas: Problems versus possibilities in learning. *Educational Researcher*, 22(6): 5–16.

Proctor, R. N. (1991). *Value-free science? Purity and power in modern knowledge*. Cambridge, MA: Harvard University Press.

Rabinow, P., and Sullivan, W. J. (Eds.). (1979). *Interpretive social science*. Berkeley: University of California Press.

———. (1987). *Interpretive social science: A second look*. Berkeley: University of California Press.

Rawls, J. (1971). *A theory of justice*. Cambridge, MA: Belknap.

Reichardt, C. S., and Rallis, S. F. (Eds.). (1994). *The quantitative-qualitative debate: New perspectives. Vol. 61: New Directions for Program Evaluation*. San Francisco: Jossey-Bass.

Rein, M. (1983). *From policy to practice*. London: Macmillan.

Richardson, V. (1990). At-risk programs: Evaluation as critical inquiry. In K. A. Sirotnik (Ed.) *Evaluation and social justice: Issues in public education. Vol. 45: New Directions for Program Evaluation* (pp. 61–75). San Francisco: Jossey-Bass.

Ricoeur, P. (1981). The model of the text: Meaningful action considered as text. In J. B. Thompson (Ed. and Trans.) *Hermeneutics and the human sciences* (pp. 197–221). Cambridge: Cambridge University Press.

Risser, J. (1997). *Hermeneutics and voice of the other: Re-reading Gadamer's philosophical hermeneutics*. Albany, NY: SUNY Press.

Root, M. (1993). *Philosophy of social science*. Oxford: Blackwell.

Rorty, R. (1979). *Philosophy and the mirror of nature*. Princeton: Princeton University Press.

———. (1982). *Consequences of pragmatism*. Minneapolis, MN: University of Minnesota Press.

———. (1983). Method and morality. In N. Haan, R. N. Bellah, P. Rabinow, and W. M. Sullivan (Eds.) *Social science as moral inquiry* (pp. 155–76). New York: Columbia University Press.

———. (1985). Solidarity or objectivity? In J. Rajchman and C. West (Eds.) *Post-analytic philosophy* (pp. 3–19). New York: Columbia University Press.

———. (1989). *Contingency, irony, and solidarity*. Cambridge: Cambridge University Press.

Ross, D. (1991). *The origins of American social science*. Cambridge: Cambridge University Press.

Rossi, P. H. (1994). The war between the quals and quants: Is a lasting peace possible? In C. S. Reichardt and S. F. Rallis (Eds.) *The quantitative-qualitative debate: New perspectives. Vol. 61: New Directions for Program Evaluation* (pp. 23–36). San Francisco: Jossey-Bass.

Rossi, P. H., and Freeman, H. E. (1989). *Evaluation: A systematic approach* (4th ed.).Newbury Park, CA: Sage Publications.

———. (1993). *Evaluation: A systematic approach* (5th ed.) Newbury Park, CA: Sage.

Roth, P. A. (1987). *Meaning and method in the social sciences: A case for methodological pluralism*. Ithaca, NY: Cornell University Press.

Ryan, K. E., and DeStefano, L., (Eds.). (2000). *Evaluation as a democratic process: Promoting inclusion, dialogue, and deliberation. Vol. 85: New Directions for Evaluation.* San Francisco: Jossey-Bass.

Sarbin, T. (1986). The narrative act as root metaphor for psychology. In T. R. Sarbin, (Ed.) *Narrative psychology: The storied nature of human conduct.* New York: Praeger.

Schön, D. (1983). *The reflective practitioner.* New York: Basic Books.

Schwandt, T. A. (1989). Recapturing moral discourse in evaluation. *Educational Researcher, 18*(8): 11–16, 34.

———. (2000). Three epistemological stances for qualitative inquiry: Interpretivism, hermeneutics, and constructionism. In N. K. Denzin, and Y. S. Lincoln (Ed.) *Handbook of qualitative research* (2nd ed.) (pp. 189–213). Thousand Oaks, CA: Sage.

———. (2001a). *Dictionary of qualitative inquiry* (2nd ed.) Thousand Oaks, CA: Sage.

———. (2001b). Responsiveness and everyday life. In J. C. Greene and T. A. Abma (Eds.) *Responsive evaluation: Roots and wings. Vol. 92: New Directions for Evaluation* (pp. 73–88). San Francisco: Jossey-Bass.

Scriven, M. (1980). *The logic of evaluation.* Inverness, CA: Edge Press.

———. (1983). Evaluation ideologies. In G. F. Madaus, M. Scriven, and D. L. Stufflebeam (Eds.) *Evaluation models* (pp. 229–60). Boston: Kluwer-Nijhoff.

———. (1991). *Evaluation thesaurus* (4th ed.). Newbury Park, CA: Sage.

———. (1993). *Hard-won lessons in program evaluation. Vol. 58: New Directions for Program Evaluation.* San Francisco: Jossey-Bass.

———. (1994). Types of theory in evaluation. *Theories of Evaluation* (Newsletter of the American Evaluation Association Topical Interest Group on Theories of Evaluation), 2: 1–4.

———. (1995). The logic of evaluation and evaluation practice. In D. M. Fournier (Ed.) *Reasoning in evaluation: Inferential links and leaps. Vol. 68: New Directions for Evaluation* (pp. 49–70). San Francisco: Jossey-Bass.

———. (1997). Truth and objectivity in evaluation. In E. Chelmisky and W. R. Shadish (Eds.) *Evaluation for the 21st century* (pp. 477–500). Thousand Oaks, CA: Sage.

Sechrest, L. (1992). Roots: Back to our first generation. *Evaluation Practice, 13*(1): 1–7.

Sechrest, L., Babcock, J, and Smith, B. (1993). An invitation to methodological pluralism. *Evaluation Practice, 14*(3): 227–35.

Seller, A. (1988). Realism versus relativism: Towards a politically adequate epistemology. In M. Griffiths, and A. Whitford (Eds.) *Feminist perspectives in philosophy* (pp. 169–86). Bloomington, IN: Indiana University Press.

Shadish, W. R. (March, 1996). Descriptive values and social justice. *Evaluation Theories* (Newsletter of the American Evaluation Association Topical Interest Group In Evaluation Theory), 4(1): 1–5.

———. (1994). Need-based evaluation theory: What do you need to know to do good evaluation? *Evaluation Practice, 15*(3): 347–58.

Shadish, W. R., Cook, T. D., and Leviton, L. (1991). *Foundations of program evaluation: Theories of practice*. Newbury Park, CA: Sage.

Shadish, W. R., Newman, D. L., Scheirer, M.A., and Wye, C. (Eds.). (1995). *Guiding principles for evaluators. Vol. 66: New Directions for Program Evaluation*. San Francisco: Jossey-Bass.

Shotter, J. (1993). *Conversational realities: Constructing life through language*. Thousand Oaks, CA: Sage.

Shulha, L. M., and Cousins, J.B. (1997). Evaluation use: Theory, research, and practice since 1986. *Evaluation Practice, 18*(3): 195–208.

Sievers, B. (1983). Believing in social science: The ethics and epistemology of public opinion research. In N. Haan, R. N. Bellah, P. Rabinow, and W. M. Sullivan (Eds.) *Social science as moral inquiry* (pp. 320–42). New York: Columbia University Press.

Simons, H. (1987). *Getting to know schools in a democracy*. London: Falmer Press.

Sirotnik, K. A. (Ed.). (1990). *Evaluation and social justice: Issues in public education. Vol. 45: New Directions for Program Evaluation*. San Francisco: Jossey-Bass.

Sirotnik, K. A., and Oakes, J. (1990). Evaluation as critical inquiry: School improvement as a case in point. In K. A. Sirotnik (Ed.) *Evaluation and social justice: Issues in public education. Vol. 45: New Directions for Program Evaluation* (pp. 37–59). San Francisco: Jossey-Bass.

Smaling, A. (1995). Open-mindedness, open-heartedness and dialogical openness: The dialectics of openings and closures. In I. Maso, P. Atkinson, S. Delamont, and J. C. Verhoeven (Eds.) *Openness in research: The tension between self and other* (pp. 38–60) Assen: Van Gordum.

Smart, B. (1996). Postmodern social theory. In B. S. Turner (Ed.) *The Blackwell companion to social theory* (pp. 396–428). Oxford: Blackwell.

Smith, D. E. (1990a). *The conceptual practices of power*. Boston: Northeastern University Press.

———. (1990b). *Texts, facts, and femininity: Exploring the relations of ruling*. London: Routledge.

Smith, J. K. (1993). *After the demise of empiricism*. Norwood, NJ: Ablex.

Smith, M. L. (1994). Qualitative plus/versus quantitative: The last word. In C. S. Reichardt, and S. F. Rallis (Eds.) *The quantitative-qualitative debate: New perspectives. Vol. 61: New Directions for Program Evaluation* (pp. 37–44). San Francisco: Jossey-Bass.

Smith, N. H. (1997). *Strong hermeneutics: Contingency and moral identity*. London: Routledge.

Sokolowski, R. (1997). Gadamer's theory of hermeneutics. In L. E. Hahn (Ed.) *The philosophy of Hans-Georg Gadamer* (pp. 223–34). Chicago: Open Court.

Stake, R. E. (1986). *Quieting reform*. Urbana, IL: University of Illinois Press.

———. (1991). Retrospective on the countenance of evaluation. In M. W. McLaughlin, and D. C. Phillips (Eds.) *Evaluation and Education: 90ᵗʰ Yearbook of the National Society for the Study of Education, Part II* (pp. 67–88). Chicago: University of Chicago Press.

————. (1997). Advocacy in evaluation: A necessary evil? In E. Chelimsky, and W. R. Shadish (Eds.) *Evaluation for the 21ˢᵗ century* (pp. 470–76). Thousand Oaks, CA: Sage.

Stake, R. E., and Trumble, D. J. (1982). Naturalistic generalization. *Review Journal of Philosophy and Social Science*, 7(1–2), 1–12.

Starr, P. (1982). *The social transformation of American medicine.* New York: Basic Books.

Stout, J. (1988). *Ethics after babel.* Boston: Beacon Press.

Strathern, M. (Ed.). (2000). *Audit cultures.* London: Routledge.

Straw, S. B., and Sadowy, P. (1990). Dynamics of communication: Transmission, translation and interaction in reading comprehension. In D. Bogdan and S. B. Straw (Eds.) *Beyond communication: Reading comprehension and criticism* (pp. 21–47). Portsmouth, England: Boynton/Cook.

Stufflebeam, D. L. (1994). Empowerment evaluation, objectivist evaluation, and evaluation standards: Where the future of evaluation should not go and where it needs to go. *Evaluation Practice*, 15(3): 321–38.

————. (2001). *Evaluation models. Vol. 89: New Directions for Evaluation.* San Francisco: Jossey-Bass.

Sullivan, W. M. (1983). Beyond policy science: The social sciences as moral sciences. In N. Haan, R. N. Bellah, P. Rabinow, and W. M. Sullivan (Eds.) *Social science as moral inquiry* (pp. 297–319). New York: Columbia University Press.

————. (1986). *Reconstructing public philosophy.* Berkeley: University of California Press.

Tarnas, R. (1991). *The passion of the western mind.* New York: Ballantine Books.

Taylor, C. (1985). *Philosophy and the human sciences: Philosophical papers. Vol. 2.* Cambridge: Cambridge University Press.

————. (1987). Overcoming epistemology. In K. Baynes, J. Bohman, and T. McCarthy (Eds.) *After philosophy: End or transformation?* (pp. 464–88). Cambridge, MA: MIT Press.

————. (1988). Wittgenstein, empiricism, and the question of the 'inner': Commentary on Kenneth Gergen. In S. B. Messer, L. A. Sass, and R. L. Woolfolk (Eds.) *Hermeneutics and psychological theory*, (pp. 52–58) New Brunswick, NJ: Rutgers University Press.

————. (1989). *Sources of the self: The making of the modern identity.* Cambridge: Cambridge University Press.

————. (1991a). The dialogical self. In D. R. Hiley, J. F. Bohman, and R. Shusterman (Eds.) *The interpretive turn* (pp. 304–14). Ithaca, NY: Cornell University Press.

————. (1991b). *The ethics of authenticity.* Cambridge, MA: Harvard University Press.

————. (1995). *Philosophical arguments.* Cambridge, MA: Harvard University Press.

Toulmin, S. (1958). *The uses of argument.* Cambridge: Cambridge University Press.

———. (1988). The recovery of practical philosophy. *The American Scholar,* 57(3): 345–58.

———. (1990). *Cosmopolis: The hidden agenda of modernity.* New York: Free Press.

Vetlesen, A. J. (1997). Introducing an ethics of proximity. In H. Jodalen, and A. J. Vetlesen (Eds.) *Closeness: An ethics* (pp. 1–19). Oslo: Scandinavian University Press.

Walker, M. U. (1992). Moral understandings: Alternative 'epistemology' for a feminist ethics. In E. B. Cole, and S. Coultrap-Mcquin (Eds.) *Explorations in feminist ethics* (pp. 165–175). Bloomington, IN: Indiana University Press.

Walton, D. N. (1989). *Informal logic.* Cambridge: Cambridge University Press.

Walzer, M. J. (1987). *Interpretation and social criticism.* Cambridge: Harvard University Press.

———. (1988). *The company of critics.* New York: Basic Books.

Weber, M. (1963). 'Objectivity' in social science and social policy. In M. Natanson (Ed.) *Philosophy of the social sciences.* New York: Random House.

Weiss, C. H. (1973). Where politics and evaluation research meet, *Evaluation* 1(3): 37–45.

———. (1977). Research for policy's sake: The enlightenment function of social research. *Policy Analysis, 3:* 531–45.

———. (1983). Ideology, interest, and information: The basis of policy decisions In D. Callahan, and B. Jennings (Eds.) *Ethics, social sciences, and policy analysis* (pp. 213–45). New York: Plenum.

———. (1987). The circuitry of enlightenment. *Knowledge: Creation, Diffusion, Utilization, 8:* 274–81.

———. (1998). Have we learned anything new about the use of evaluation? *American Journal of Evaluation, 19*(1): 21–33.

Winter, R. (1987). *Action research and the nature of social inquiry: Professional innovation and educational work.* Aldershot, England: Gower.

Wolin, S. (1972). Political theory as a vocation. In M. Fleisher (Ed.) *Machiavelli and the nature of political thought* (pp. 23–75). New York: Antheneum.

Yin, R. K. (1994a). *Case study research: Design and methods* (2nd ed.) Newbury Park, CA: Sage.

———. (1994b). Evaluation: A singular craft. In C. S. Reichardt, and S.F. Rallis (Eds.) *The quantitative-qualitative debate: New perspectives. Vol. 61: New Directions for Program Evaluation* (pp. 71–84). San Francisco: Jossey-Bass.

Young, R. (1990). *A critical theory of education.* New York: Teachers College Press.

Index

Studies in the Postmodern Theory of Education

General Editors
Joe L. Kincheloe & Shirley R. Steinberg

Counterpoints publishes the most compelling and imaginative books being written in education today. Grounded on the theoretical advances in criticalism, feminism, and postmodernism in the last two decades of the twentieth century, Counterpoints engages the meaning of these innovations in various forms of educational expression. Committed to the proposition that theoretical literature should be accessible to a variety of audiences, the series insists that its authors avoid esoteric and jargonistic languages that transform educational scholarship into an elite discourse for the initiated. Scholarly work matters only to the degree it affects consciousness and practice at multiple sites. Counterpoints' editorial policy is based on these principles and the ability of scholars to break new ground, to open new conversations, to go where educators have never gone before.

For additional information about this series or for the submission of manuscripts, please contact:

> Joe L. Kincheloe & Shirley R. Steinberg
> c/o Peter Lang Publishing, Inc.
> 275 Seventh Avenue, 28th floor
> New York, New York 10001

To order other books in this series, please contact our Customer Service Department:

> (800) 770-LANG (within the U.S.)
> (212) 647-7706 (outside the U.S.)
> (212) 647-7707 FAX

Or browse online by series:

> www.peterlangusa.com